The Political Science Student Writer's Manual

Sixth Edition

Gregory M. Scott
Stephen M. Garrison

University of Central Oklahoma

PEARSON
Prentice
Hall

Upper Saddle River, New Jersey 07458

Library of Congress Cataloging-in-Publication Data

Scott, Gregory M.
    The political science student writer's manual/Gregory M. Scott, Stephen M. Garrison.—6th ed.
      p. cm.
    Includes bibliographical references and indexes.
    ISBN-13: 978-0-13-602945-8 (alk. paper)
    ISBN-10: 0-13-602945-0 (alk. paper)
    1. Political science—Authorship—Handbooks, manuals, etc. 2. Political science—Research—Handbooks, manuals, etc. 3. Academic writing—Handbooks, manuals, etc. 4. Report writing—Handbooks, manuals, etc. I. Garrison, Stephen M. II. Title.
    JA86.S39 2007
    808'.06632—dc22

                                 2007045279

Executive Editor: Dickson Musslewhite
Associate Editor: Rob DeGeorge
Editorial Assistant: Synamin Ballatt
Director of Marketing: Brandy Dawson
Senior Marketing Manager: Kate Mitchell
Marketing Assistant: Jennifer Lang
Production Manager: Wanda Rockwell
Creative Director: Jayne Conte
Cover Design: Jonathan Boylan
Full-Service Project Management/Composition: Karpagam Jagadeesan/GGS Book Services
Printer/Binder: R.R. Donnelly/Harrisonburg

Credits and acknowledgments borrowed from other sources and reproduced, with permission, in this textbook appear on appropriate page within text.

Pearson Education LTD.
Pearson Education Australia PTY, Limited
Pearson Education Singapore, Pte. Ltd
Pearson Education North Asia Ltd
Pearson Education, Canada, Ltd
Pearson Educación de Mexico, S.A. de C.V.
Pearson Education–Japan
Pearson Education Malaysia, Pte. Ltd

10 9 8 7 6 5 4 3 2

ISBN-13: 978-0-13-602945-8
ISBN-10:   0-13-602945-0

Contents

PART TWO   A Handbook of Style for Political Science

PART THREE Conducting Research in Political Science

PART FOUR   Critical Thinking and Acting in Politics

To the Student

We have designed this book to help you do two things: (1) improve your writing and (2) learn political science. Part One provides you with an introduction to the rich history of the thoughtful study of politics and some descriptions of some of the ways political scientists study government and politics today.

Part Two addresses fundamental concerns of all writers, exploring the reasons why we write, describing the writing process itself, and examining those elements of grammar, style, and punctuation that cause the most confusion among writers in general. A vital concern throughout this part, and the rest of the book as well, is the three-way interrelationship among writer, topic, and audience. Our discussion of this relationship aims at building your self-confidence as you clarify your writing objectives.

Writing is not a magical process beyond the control of most people. It is instead a series of interconnected skills that any writer can improve with practice, and the end result of this practice is power. Chapters 5 and 6 of this manual treat the act of writing not as an empty exercise undertaken only to produce a grade but as a powerful learning tool and the primary medium by which political scientists accomplish their goals. Chapter 7 explains the importance of formatting your writing properly and supplies you with format models for title pages, tables of contents, and so on. Chapter 8 explains how to cite sources and how to use source material ethically.

The chapters in Part Three of the book offer you general help in formulating and researching political science writing projects. Parts Three, Four, and Five provide structures writing assignments that will give you practice in using the materials provided in Part Two. We have based these assignments on the types of work political scientists actually do, both as academic professionals and as contributing citizens in local and in national political communities. The assignments will test your ability to think critically and come up with and express ideas that will improve all our lives.

Greg Scott
Steve Garrison

To the Teacher

This book helps you deal with three problems commonly faced by teachers of political science:

- Students increasingly need *specific directions* to produce a good paper.
- Political scientists, as always, want to *teach political science, not English.*
- Students do not yet understand fully how—and why—to avoid *plagiarism.*

Students often need substantial specific direction to produce a good paper. How many times have you assigned papers in your political science classes and found yourself teaching the basics of writing—not only in terms of content but form and grammar as well? This text, which may either accompany the primary text you assign in any class or stand on its own, allows you to assign one of the types of papers described in Parts Three, Four, and Five with the knowledge that virtually everything the student needs to know, from grammar to sources of information to reference style, is in this one volume.

Part One provides your students with an introduction to political science that will help them understand what the discipline in which they are participating is all about and offer them some ideas about how they may go about studying the topic they have chosen.

Part Two helps you to spend more time teaching political science and less time teaching English. It includes (1) a concise guide to writing well, (2) a summary of the most troublesome English grammar rules, (3) proper political science college paper formats, and (4) extensive instruction and examples on how to cite sources according to specifications published by the American Political Science Association (APSA).

Also, this book may well be your best insurance against plagiarism, for two reasons. First, Chapter 8, Section 2, provides a detailed, practical explanation of what plagiarism is and how to avoid it. Second, the paper assignments in Parts Three, Four, and Five of this manual provide very specific directions that make it much more difficult for students simply to appropriate uncredited material, even from the Internet, where, as you know, it is becoming easier for students to download relevant material and then modify it (insufficiently) for their own purposes.

In addition, this sixth edition is the *most substantial revision* of *The Political Science Student Writer's Manual* yet undertaken. Among the scores of changes throughout the volume, you will find the following:

A *totally new* Part One, including:

Chapter 1   The Creative Study of Politics
Chapter 2   Four Millenniums of Thinking About Politics
Chapter 3   Current Approaches to Studying Politics
Chapter 4   Some Quantitative Methods in Political Science

A *totally new* Chapter 17:

Chapter 17   Comparing Governments

Newly revised and presented Chapters 15 and 16:

Chapter 15   Elementary Policy Analysis: Position Papers
Chapter 16   Descriptive and Analytical Research Papers

And, *substantially revised* Chapters 10 and 11:

Chapter 10   Library Information Resources
Chapter 11   Internet Information Resources

We'd like to thank the following reviewers for their helpful comments and suggestions: Druscilla L. Scribner, University of Wisconsin at Oshkosh; and Jim Zaffiro, Central College.

We hope you find that the sixth edition helps you in your efforts to teach political science. We wish you the best in your endeavors, and we welcome your comments.

Greg Scott
Steve Garrison

CHAPTER
1

THE CREATIVE STUDY OF POLITICS

1.1 POLITICS AND POLITICAL SCIENCE

What do you already know about political science? You know it is an academic discipline, something taught in college, and something you are beginning to study. Something you may not yet know is that political science affects your daily life, directly and indirectly, in countless ways. Your freedom to select the school you want to attend, your confidence in the quality of canned tuna that you buy, the amount that is taken from your paycheck every week, all these aspects of your life and many more are determined by presidents, members of Congress, justices, and hundreds of other government officials. Many of these people gained their knowledge of politics and government directly from political science. Consider, for example, that America's founding fathers were avid students of some of history's greatest political analysts, whom we shall discuss later, and constructed a constitution based upon what they had learned from their studies. Consider further that attorneys are represented more than any other profession not only in the leadership of court system but also in national and state legislatures. What did these attorneys, as undergraduate students, major in, more than any other college major? The answer is political science. Even most of those who did not major in political science have had courses in politics and government in high school or college.

Whether it is being taught in a college classroom, formulated in a position paper, or practiced in a professional conference, political science is always a search for enlightenment. It is the energy, work, and product of a worldwide community of scholars, teachers, practitioners, researchers, and consultants engaged in a quest for understanding and answers. It is a living academic movement with deep divisions, debts to other disciplines, controversies, aspirations, and opportunities and challenges, tied together by a common purpose: the desire to understand politics. Political scientists today draw upon a distinguished heritage of four millenniums of thoughtful observation of politics, and they invite you to participate with them in one of humanity's most stimulating intellectual adventures.

The Dynamics of Politics

What has your own experience told you about the political aspects of life? We seem to know politics when we see it, but we often find it hard to define. Some things appear to be very political, and others not at all. What quality makes some things political and others not? Consider the following:

- President Bush's State of the Union Address
- a letter from Senator Governor Mitt Romney to the citizens of Massachusetts
- the 2008 platform of the Republican Party
- a political cartoon by Doonesbury
- a campaign speech by John McCain
- an editorial in the *New York Times*

The items above are obviously political. We readily understand that they are for the purpose of expressing or furthering one person's or a group of people's views or interests. Now examine the following list:

- *anonymously* donating to the American Lung Association
- reading a bedtime story to a child
- giving blood to the Red Cross
- refinishing an old table
- dancing in the rain
- cooking fettucine

Although there may possibly be something political about the items on the list above, we do not normally think about them as being political. These activities do not involve people who are attempting to further their own political interests. There are many aspects of life that are not political. Look at this list:

- a teacher's attempt to get you to learn
- your attempt to influence a teacher to get a better grade
- an argument with your brother or sister over who gets to drive the car, with an appeal to your parents
- a sermon
- a conversation at a cocktail party
- a speech at a meeting of the Rotary Club

What is it that makes each of these situations at least potentially political? What quality do they all share? To answer these questions, it is necessary to understand the fundamental nature of politics.

Politics: A Definition

Politics has been defined by many people in many different ways. According to some of the more popular definitions, politics is

- the science of who gets what, when, and how (Harold Lasswell, *Politics: Who Gets What, When, How, 1936*)
- the authoritative allocation of values (David Easton, *The Political System, 1953*)

- the activity by which differing interests within a given unit of rule are conciliated by giving them a share in power in proportion to their importance to . . . the whole community (Bernard Crick, *In Defense of Politics, 1962*)
- the processes by which human efforts toward attaining social goals are steered and coordinated (Karl Deutsch, *The Nerves of Government: Models of Political Communication and Control, 1963*)
- the process of making government policies (Austin Ranney, *Governing: An Introduction to Political Science, 1990*)
- the art of looking for trouble, finding it everywhere, diagnosing it incorrectly, and applying the wrong remedies (Groucho Marx)

In spite of the differences among these definitions, however, several qualities are common to them all:

- Politics is *relational*, that is, it has to do with relationships among people or groups of people.
- Politics concerns *interests and power*. The signature of political activity is the attempt on someone's part to further one's own interest, increase one's own power, or to reduce the influence of someone else.
- Politics is *dynamic*. This means that politics is not a snapshot of an event or a place in time, nor is it a collection of snapshots. It is a process or an activity that is perpetually in motion, constantly changing, continually expressing, transforming, and conforming to the people, trends, and events through which it operates.

The immediate connotation of the word "politics" is usually negative. We normally see politicians as manipulators who do things for people in order to get something in return from them. The fact is, however, politics is an absolute necessity to our lives. Think about it. As human beings, we find ourselves in a world where we have many physical and emotional needs and desires but insufficient resources to meet all of them. In such a situation, we have, perhaps, three basic alternatives for getting our needs met. We can

1. deny our needs in favor of the needs of others
2. attempt to take what we need by force, or
3. attempt to communicate our needs to others, to resolve need conflicts through nonviolent processes, often in procedures established to promote participation and fairness

The first alternative is *altruism*. When we act altruistically we abandon politics by declining to further our own self-interest, giving preference instead to the needs of others. We are all altruistic to a certain extent, but consistent altruism surpasses our normal desires and capabilities. Mother Theresa, for example, spent most of her life caring for sick and dying people in conditions that posed a threat to her health, but most of us are not willing to follow her example, at least for any extended period of time.

The second alternative, taking what we need by force, is *coercion*. Like the first course of action, it also ultimately abdicates politics. In a superficial sense, force is the quintessential political act because its intent is furthering one's self-interest. On the other hand, an act of force destroys relationships and exchanges normal political channels—communication, bargaining, manipulation, and compromise—for physical compulsion.

The third course of action described above is what we usually mean by the term *politics*: a method of mediation that meets our needs and does not lead to such undesirable consequences as war or neglect of the self. Perhaps politics may therefore be best understood as a quality of the interactions that spring directly from our attempts to meet our own needs without coercion. Viewed in this way, politics occupies the center of a spectrum whose polarities are coercion and altruism:

altruism   politics   coercion

The Eternal Paradox

Two basic emotional needs figure prominently in politics because they are fundamental aspects of human interaction in society: the need for *community* (or unity) and the need for *individuality*. We emerge from the womb with a sense, even if not understood intellectually, of being separate, cut off from others. Studies have shown that infants who are not held or given human interaction in the days following birth may actually die of emotional deprivation. As the years go by, we try to overcome this sense of separation in a number of ways, including bonding with our mothers and family, making friends, and getting married. We also seek acceptance in larger communities. We join a church, a sorority, a bowling league or the Kiwanis Club, a political party, or we experience community when we share a sense of national pride or make a contribution to a candidate who articulates our views.

While we seek community with others in some or all of these ways, we simultaneously exhibit an opposing impulse: individuality. To feel unique, to desire recognition as a special human being unlike any other individual, is as deep a human need as the desire for unity and community. Much of the energy we devote to our careers is motivated by a need for recognition of our personal talents and contributions.

The behavior that often results from simultaneously responding to these two opposing drives (community and individuality) sometimes appears odd and contradictory, perhaps most noticeably during adolescence. Teenagers conform desperately to norms set by their peers. Having the right brand of clothing, the right style of shoes, and the right group of friends becomes vitally important to students in junior high and high school. At the same time, however, adolescents express their individuality continuously by breaking rules or norms set by the adult world and by demonstrating in many large and small ways their independence from their parents.

It is not an exaggeration to say that the primary task of the founding fathers in writing the Constitution of the United States was to construct a government system that simultaneously maximizes opportunities for both individuality and community. In fact, the entire history of politics is largely the story of how communities and nations resolved the inherent conflict between the universal needs for community and individuality. Consider a few examples.

- Ancient Athenians built an empire and history's first democracy at least partly upon a strong loyalty, a bonded unity, to their city. When asked to identify themselves, they did not hesitate to respond "We are Athenians." This sense of loyalty to the polis ironically allowed Athenians to express their personal individual views strongly within the citizens' assembly.
- Citizens of Rome proclaimed innate natural rights of citizens to equal treatment before the law (individuality), while seeking to bring the world together under the Roman Empire (community).
- American patriots adopted a constitution to bind the states together in a document that established majority rule (community) in a new society while insisting upon a bill of rights (individuality).
- In virtually every case it decides, the U.S. Supreme Court is called upon to consider the interests of individual citizens (individuality) in comparison to the interests of the society as a whole (community).

Governments deal in many ways with the tension between the competing needs for community and individuality, attempting to satisfy both. Congress struggles every year with the rights of businesses to operate free from government interference and with the need of the public to be assured of product quality and safety. The president, in times of war and national emergency, must balance the lives of individual members of the armed services against the need of the country to be secure from terrorism or assaults against our national interest. Politics is in large part the story of how people resolve such conflicts as these. When politicians attempt to strike a balance between the individuals and the community, they are attempting to bring order to society. Perhaps, then, it is most appropriate to say that

Politics is ordering societal relations.

Politics is often a chaotic clash of interests and values, striving for acceptance or dominance. In other words, people in politics strive toward constructing an order conducive to the goals they seek. Political action aims at order at all levels, including the micro- (small groups such as family members), the medial- (larger groups like community associations), and the macrolevel (states, provinces, and nations). This means that politics is a way in which we meet our emotional needs for unity and individuality, as well as our physical needs.

Having established a definition of politics, it is relatively easy for us to define *government*, the arena in which politics is most visible, and therefore most intensively studied. Government is a forum and authoritative structure for making, interpreting, and enforcing the rules through which politics operates in society. Government is the laws, institutions, and processes that set the rules and create the mechanisms through which human relations are publicly carried out. Governments make laws about the limits of marriage, proper conduct in family life, business relations, use of the physical environment, national defense, and other matters. In its most basic sense, it is the set of rules and institutions that establish the order within which politics is conducted in society. In most simple terms, then,

Government is ordering politics.

The Focus of Political Science

It is important to understand that *politics* and *political science* are not exactly the same things. While politics operates in all levels of life (family, community, and government), political science as a discipline focuses mostly upon the more complex levels of political interaction, and especially upon governments and activities related to them. While economists direct their attention to money and finance and sociologists are primarily interested in other aspects of social life such as the family life and cultural norms, political scientists analyze *public* relationships. The phenomena of most interest to political scientists have to do with activities of people in their communities and their private activities as they affect governments.

Three Activities of Political Science

Political science, the quest for knowledge about politics, is conducted through *three basic activities*:

- *investigation:* finding the facts
- *interpretation:* discerning patterns in the facts
- *application:* putting the patterns to use

Investigation means finding the facts. For example, to investigate the attitudes of voters in Ohio, a survey might be designed that would identify characteristics of people who vote in Ohio primary elections.

Interpretation means discerning patterns in the facts, and the processes that cause, control, or effect these patterns. For example, interpreting the results of an investigation into the attitudes of Ohio voters might lead us to the following conclusion: "voting in primaries in Ohio increases as voter knowledge of economic issues increases."

Application means putting the knowledge gained through investigation and interpretation to use. By applying the information gained in our example, we might establish a program designed to educate Ohio voters about economic issues and begin a study to determine the effects of the program upon voting behavior.

The methods political science uses to conduct these three activities are discussed in detail in Chapter 4 of this book, "Some Quantitative Methods in Political Science." It is only relatively recently that all three of these activities have gained acceptance as components of political science. For centuries, people have debated which of the three activities ought to be properly included within the discipline, and the debate is not entirely over, as we shall see in later chapters of this book. The table below illustrates some of the ways in which political scientists perform them.

	INVESTIGATION	INTERPRETATION	APPLICATION
Definition →	*Finding the facts*	*Discerning patterns in the facts, and the processes that cause, control or affect these patterns*	*Putting the knowledge gained through investigation and interpretation to use*
Example 1: Political participation →	A survey designed to identify characteristics of people who vote in primary elections in Ohio	Analysis of the survey data; drawing conclusions such as "voting in primaries in Ohio increases as education on economic issues increases"	A program designed to educate Ohio voters about economic issues, accompanied by a study to determine the effects of the program upon voting behavior
Example 2: Public administration →	A study which identifies both personnel procedures and administrative problems in the Department of Defense	An examination of the relationship between personnel procedures and administrative problems, which concludes that some personnel policies are causing problems	A revision of personnel policies accompanied by a study to determine if the revisions actually solve administrative problems
Example 3: International relations →	A study which identifies the amount, value, and types of economic interaction between Japan and the United States	An estimation of the relative benefits of economic interdependence to Japan and the United States, which concludes that Japan benefits more than the United States	Recommendations for altering trade agreements between Japan and the United States, followed by an assessment of the results of changes caused by altering the trade agreements

1.2 POLITICAL SCIENCE AS CREATIVITY

In *The Courage to Create* psychologist Rollo May (1975, 71–72) describes the relation between science and creativity:

> Scientists themselves, particularly the physicists, have told us that the creativity of a science is bound up with the freedom of human beings to create in the free, pure sense. In modern physics it is very clear that the discoveries that later become utilized for our technological gains are generally made in the first place because a physicist lets his imagination go and discovers something

simply for the joy of discovery. . . . I am proposing that . . . creativity . . . is not only important for art and poetry and music; but is essential in the long run also for our science.

Creativity is the heart of political science, as it is of all science. Creativity is the essential common element and primary driving force in all three major activities of the discipline. Investigation is the attempt to gain new knowledge, and to gain knowledge in new ways. Interpretation is the attempt to make sense out of the knowledge that is gained, to derive meaning from it. Application is the attempt to apply new understandings to the problems and opportunities of our lives.

This notion of the importance of creativity in political science is so important and so complex that it is worth exploring a little further. If we continue to view political science as a creative, dynamic process, one that actively helps people to establish an understanding of the way their world works, we can make an analogy between the world of the political scientists and the world of the artists. When an artist paints a tree, the painting creates an interpretive image of the tree, a representation of the tree as perceived by the artist. In the same way, political science creates interpretive images of the phenomena of politics as perceived by the political scientists. The goal, for both artists and political scientists, is the same: to make us *see*, to help us *understand*.

Speaking of the great French Impressionist painter Paul Cezanne, Rollo May (1975, 77–78) provides a clear explanation of the process of creative representation:

> Cezanne sees a tree. He sees it in a way no one else has ever seen it. He experiences, as he no doubt would have said, "being grasped by the tree." The arching grandeur of the tree, the mothering spread, the delicate balance as the tree grips the earth—all these and many more characteristics of the tree are absorbed into his perception and are felt throughout his nervous structure. These are part of the vision he experiences. This vision involves an omission of some aspects of the scene and a greater emphasis on other aspects and the ensuing rearrangement of the whole; but it is more than the sum of all these. Primarily it is a vision that is now not the tree, but Tree; the concrete tree Cezanne looked at is formed into the essence of tree. However original and unrepeatable his vision is, it is still a vision of all trees triggered by his encounter with this particular one.
>
> The painting that issues out of this encounter between a human being, Cezanne, and an objective reality, the tree, is literally new, unique, and original. Something is born, comes into being, something that did not exist before—which is as good a definition of creativity as we can get. Thereafter, everyone who looks at the painting with intensity of awareness and lets it speak to him or her will see the tree with the unique powerful movement, the intimacy between the tree and the landscape, and the architectural beauty which literally did not exist in our relation with trees until Cezanne experienced and painted them. I can say without exaggeration that I never really *saw* a tree until I had seen and absorbed Cezanne's paintings of them.

Political science does for our understanding of politics what Cezanne's representation of a tree does for our perception of trees. As thousands of readers can attest, the following works, all written by incisive, keenly observant political scientists, will help you to *see*, as if for the first time, the meanings behind the most fundamental of political concepts. You may not yet have read any of these works, but if you continue your exploration of political science, you will. And you have a marvelous adventure in store for you.

ONCE YOU READ . . .	YOU WILL UNDERSTAND . . .	. . . AS YOU NEVER HAVE BEFORE
Plato's *Allegory of the Cave*	democracy	
Machiavelli's *The Prince*	political strategy	
David Easton's *The Structure of Political Systems*	the interrelationships of political phenomena	
Richard Flathman's *The Philosophy and Politics of Freedom*	freedom	
James MacGregor *Burns' Leadership*	political leadership	
Gabriel Almond's *The Civic Culture*	political socialization	

When you do political science, and do it well, you participate in this drama of creativity.

This book cannot tell you exactly how to be creative. You must try it yourself, and persevere until you succeed. There is available, however, some information on the traits and characteristics of creative people that you may find helpful. Psychologists have studied creativity intensively, and John Dacey has summarized the findings of many of their studies. Dacey finds agreement in the scientific literature that eight personal qualities are strongly associated with creativity:

- tolerance of ambiguity
- stimulus freedom
- functional freedom
- flexibility
- risk taking
- preference for disorder
- delay of gratification
- androgyny

Tolerance of ambiguity is, according to the literature, the most important characteristic of creative people. An ambiguous situation is one in which there are no clear indications about how to respond, no rules or guidelines for conduct. Imagine, for example, that you are middle aged, newly divorced, and about to go out on your first date in twenty years. Again, perhaps you are visiting a religious shrine in Japan, and you have no knowledge of the practices and customs of the religion, but you do not wish to offend anyone. People who can tolerate ambiguity do not refrain from entering into situations in which they do not know the rules. They do not attempt to escape, but rather become inquisitive and attempt to find their own ways of dealing with the situations.

Stimulus freedom has to do with following rules. According to Dacey, "When the stated rules of a situation interfere with the creative ideas of people who have stimulus freedom, those people are likely to bend the rules to their needs. More important, they do not assume that rules exist when the situation is ambiguous" (1989, 22). Creative people have a way of doing what intuitively makes sense, rather than attempting to follow the rules. Thomas Jefferson, for example, broke the rules of previous diplomatic understandings when he arranged for the Louisiana Purchase.

Functional freedom concerns learning how to make things work in new ways. As our experiences in life teach us how things work, we begin to think that the patterns we observe are unchangeable, and we become "functionally fixed," which is the opposite of being functionally free. Functionally free people can find new uses for things. For functionally free people, garden implements become sculptures, and armies undertake humanitarian missions.

Flexibility is the ability to see an entire situation, not just parts of it. People without flexibility seize one aspect of a problem and take it as far as they can go while ignoring many other possibilities. It is therefore the ability to change your focus to new aspects of a situation. If you are observing political candidates speech, for example, do you focus only upon their words, or do you also note their body language, their dress, their mannerisms, their tone, and other things?

Risk taking is a trait shared by creative people, who tend to take moderate risks more consistently than people who are not creative. Less creative people are more prone to take only minimal risks, or to take risks wherein the chance of failure is excessively high. Moderate risk taking, as Dacey notes, correlates highly with a tolerance for ambiguity (1989, 30). People who seek political office, for example, risk time and effort, not knowing many of the factors that will eventually determine the results of the election.

It seems strange that people who are creative have a *preference for disorder*, but in fact disorder presents opportunities for creating order, and this is the challenge that creative people gladly accept. Complexity in relationships and asymmetry in design make for different and, therefore, intriguing matters with which the creative mind can grapple.

The ability to delay gratification is what enables some people to work quietly and carefully for years on something they consider to be important, without any reward in the meantime. Dacey notes that Thomas Edison had to conduct 2,004 laborious experiments before he found the right filament for a light bulb.

Androgyny is the final item on Dacey's list. It means that creative people, either men or women, have a combination of what have been conventionally known as masculine and feminine traits. They may be assertive (masculine) and sensitive (feminine), for example, in their attitudes, likes, and dislikes. Men who tend to be extremely masculine in their attitudes and women who tend to be extremely feminine are not likely to be as creative as those who have characteristics of both genders. Thinking about the characteristics of creative people may help you to become more creative as you pursue the study of politics, and do other things in your life.

The Creative Approach: Thinking like Einstein

At one point early in his career, Albert Einstein (1879–1955) became fascinated with tea leaves. For several days he sat, hour after hour, watching tea leaves fall to the bottom of a tea cup. Einstein would stir the cup and watch the tea leaves fall over and over again, enchanted by the simplicity of the motion he observed. Furthermore, when he commuted to work on a train he sat motionless for hours, concentrating all his thought on the image of telegraph poles going past the window. Fixing his gaze on tea leaves falling to the bottom of a cup and telegraph lines whizzing past a train window, Einstein began to see both motion and time in a whole new way, a way which eventually revolutionized scientific concepts of time, motion, and matter. Einstein is by no means the only great scientist or thinker to have made important discoveries after painstaking observation of what seems common and obvious. Jean Piaget (1896–1980), for example, one of the twentieth-century's greatest psychologists, wrote some of the most important works in the field of developmental psychology after spending weeks watching children play in a playground, and observing their behavior.

Great discoveries often have small and ordinary beginnings. A succession of careful, seemingly insignificant observations may lead to a new vision of political life. Einstein and Piaget drew much of their inspiration from

- intense, prolonged, repeated observation of the most elementary phenomena
- systematic examination and analysis of what they observed
- creative thinking about the results of their observations

The author of this book asks you to consider that the great future discoveries of political science may well be made in exactly this manner. The history of political science, like the history of any science, is normally written as the story of the great advances, the great discoveries. Most people think of great scientific discoveries being made by geniuses who grasp complexities far beyond the capabilities of people of average intelligence, and there is certainly truth in this. Some of the greatest scientific discoveries, however, have been made not only by attempting to assemble complex patterns but also by clearly perceiving the ordinary, the simple, and the obvious. In fact, we are all able, in a very important respect, to think like Albert Einstein. As a student of political science, you may find that your most meaningful discoveries come from intense, prolonged observation of simple things; from carefully discovering, sorting, and examining the political phenomena you encounter. *To think like Einstein, oddly enough, is to be fascinated with the most fundamental aspects of life, to examine them closely and systematically, and to think creatively about them.*

This book is written to help you to "think like Einstein." It provides the introductory materials necessary for you to begin to become a political scientist.

Its chapters provide what may seem to be a bewildering array of topics to study. Its discussions of research methods introduce you to the basic means of conducting investigations into the world of politics. It challenges you to supply the single most important ingredient in the process of making discoveries about politics: creativity.

Creativity for Understanding, or Creativity for Change?

As you begin to study politics, you must be aware that there are two schools of thought regarding the uses to which political science should be put. Some political scientists claim that political science should only describe and interpret reality in a strictly objective manner. Others believe that such objectivity is neither possible nor desirable, and that the greatest potential benefit of political science is its potential for changing society. The controversy that engendered these viewpoints will be explained in detail in Chapter 6 of this book. At this point, however, let us look at option two: the potential of political science, as an expression of creativity, to change society. Rollo May (1975, 71–73) captures the potential of political insights in the form of poetry to change political systems:

> The creativity of the spirit does and must threaten the structure and presuppositions of our national, orderly society and way of life . . . Just as the poet is a menace to conformity, he is also a constant threat to political dictators. He is always on the verge of blowing up the assembly line of political power. We have had powerful and poignant demonstrations of this in Soviet Russia. Itappeared chiefly in the prosecution and purge of artists and writers under Stalin, who was pathologically anxious when faced with the threat that the creative unconscious posed to his political system. Indeed, some students believe that the . . . situation in [Soviet] Russia shows an ongoing struggle between rationality and what we have been calling "free creativity."

Changes brought about by the release of creativity may be chaotic yet peaceful, as in the collapse of the Soviet Union or violent as in the French and Russian revolutions. Creativity expressed in new political ideas may constructively transform the course of history. Beliefs are powerful. The history of political science is the history of how politics has been studied. Because some students of politics, like Karl Marx, have founded vastly influential intellectual movements, the history of political science is also in part the history of beliefs that have changed the world. Beliefs have legitimized slavery and freed the slaves, instigated the holocaust and inspired liberation of India, and reinforced the Holy Roman Empire and spurred the civil rights movement.

Political science is not only the discovery of facts about politics but also the process of creatively using those facts. James Madison studied political science and creatively applied the lessons he learned from Roman statesman Cicero (106–43 BCE), English philosopher John Locke (1632–1704), and French political and legal historian Charles Secondat, Baron de Montesquieu (1689–1755), to build a constitution that has lasted more than 200 years. Martin Luther King (1929–1968) studied Mohandas Gandhi's (1869–1948) liberation movement in

India and creatively applied the lessons he learned to lead the American civil rights movement.

We live in a world of a dialectic of belief and action. This means that people who define politics change the course of the world, and the change in the world, in turn, defines politics anew. Examine the following examples:

- In 506 BCE, Cleisthenes believed that personal action of citizens makes a difference in politics, and with this belief he founded the world's first democracy.
- In 1787, James Madison, Thomas Jefferson, and others accepting Montesquieu's idea that the legislative, executive, and judicial powers of government should be placed in separate offices held by separate people founded what has become one of the world's oldest continuous democracies.
- In 1848, Karl Marx believed that class struggle is the most important motive in political life, and his philosophy became the driving force behind a worldwide communist movement.

Creative ideas that accurately describe some aspects of political existence can revolutionize life.

The Creative Attitude

You may believe that the proper role of political science is only to discover the facts and that to interpret the facts involves the application of values beyond the range of science. On the other hand, you may believe that the very purpose of political science is to change society. The author of the book, you are reading, is not interested in supporting either point of view, but rather wishes to suggest that both viewpoints are accepted (and debated) today within the discipline of political science as a whole. In any case, however you interpret the role and work of political science, do it with passion! Theodore Lowi (1993, 394), a former president of the American Political Science Association (APSA), spoke with vision and wisdom when he said:

> [A]mong the sins of omission of modern political science, the greatest of all has been the omission of passion. There are no qualifications for member-ship in the APSA, but if I had the power to establish such standards they would be something like this: one must love politics, one must love a good constitution, one must take joy in exploring the relation between the two, and one must be prepared to lose some domestic and even some foreign pol-icy battles to keep alive a positive relation between the two. I do not speak for the passion of ideology, though I don't count it out. I speak for the pleasure of finding a pattern, the inspiration of a well-rounded argument, the satisfac-tion in having made a good guess about what makes democracy work, and a good stab at improving the prospect of rationality in human behavior. . . . This is not an opportunity to play philosopher king. It is an opportunity to meet our own intellectual needs while serving the public interest. And we need not worry how to speak truth to power. It is enough to speak truth to ourselves.

As you begin your adventure in political science, to take up Professor Lowi's challenge. The men and women who, in the second half of the twentieth century, transformed the study of politics from a fledgling offshoot of history and economics into a substantial and powerful influence in academics and public life are now fading away. A new generation will do political science for the first half of the twenty-first century, a generation that will continue to devote themselves to traditional tasks but will do so in creative ways with new results.

What kind of attitude will you need in order to participate in the creation of the next generation's contribution to political science? You will need an attitude that starts in the classroom with a desire to participate earnestly and actively. You will need an attitude that carries your research in the library and amidst the turmoil of actual politics with dignity, perseverance, honesty, and a passion for accuracy. And, if you are to make a significant contribution to the study of politics, which some of you will do, you will need to learn to develop and apply your ability to think creatively. For this reason, the remainder of this introductory chapter is devoted not to politics, but to a brief discussion of creative thinking and to suggested exercises that will help you begin to think more creatively and to apply your creativity to politics.

Grasping the Future of Political Science

This book will introduce you to the history of past controversies and the status of some present challenges to political science. Although political science, as the study of politics, is now four millenniums old, the answers to the following questions are still investigated and debated—and, perhaps, always will be:

- What are our strengths and limitations as human beings?
- What factors govern political behavior?
- How can we maintain diversity and community?
- How can we maintain group discipline and still encourage creativity?
- What role does/should the state play in history?
- What shall be done about poverty and the creation of wealth?
- What is the meaning of equality and inequality?
- What are the causes of violence and extremism?
- What can be done about violence/extremism?
- What is efficiency in government?
- What is effectiveness in government?
- What have we learned about the nature of politics?
- Who are we as political beings? What are our capabilities and limitations?
- What sources of information can we depend upon?
- What common values can we adopt?
- How can we make better government policy?
- How can we make a better government policymaking process?

As political scientists we accept the search for answers to these questions and many more. As creative political scientists we know no bounds in asking questions about politics. As responsible political scientists we are bounded in our investigations by integrity, ethics, respect, openness, sincerity, faith in ourselves, and respect both for our own limitations and for the perspectives of others.

In 1925, APSA President Charles Merriam (1993, 129–146) had these words to say about the importance of political science, words as meaningful today as they were more than seventy years ago:

> Social science and political science are urgently needed for the next great stage in the advancement of the human race. As custodians of the political science of our time, the responsibility rests upon us to exhaust every effort to bring the study of government in its various stages to the highest possible degree of perfection, to exhaust every effort to obtain effective knowledge of political forces, to bring to bear every resource of science and prudence at our command.

CHAPTER
2

FOUR MILLENNIUMS OF THINKING ABOUT POLITICS

2.1 POLITICAL SCIENCE AS THE CONTINUING CREATIVE SEARCH FOR TRUTH

Whatever else it might be, political science is a creative expression of our attempts to understand how we relate to one another in communities larger than the family, in other words, tribes, counties, states, nations, and international organizations. An examination of the history of political science reveals much about how people have answered the questions that continually arise when they relate to one another within their own communities and with other societies in the world.

If we define political science as thoughtful consideration of politics, then political science began at least as early as 2000 BCE, as recorded in the Old Testament and other ancient writings. The history of political science has been detailed in numerous volumes, and classifications of periods have appeared from time to time. Each of these classifications interprets political history in a unique way. For example, the leading political scientist of the 1920s, Charles Merriam (1993, 137), classified four eras of political science, according to the predominant method of inquiry which scholars used in each period:

1. The a priori and deductive method down to 1850
2. The historical and comparative method, 1850–1900
3. The tendency toward observation , survey, measurement, 1900–present
4. The beginnings of the psychological treatment of politics

We introduce Merriam's classification to provide a contrasting example to the one developed by David Easton. Probably the most well known recent such classification system, Easton's (1993, 292) analysis divides the history of political science into four stages:

- *formal*, which emphasized the study of laws and constitutions
- *traditional*, which focused on informal political processes, political parties, pressure groups
- *behavioral*, which described and collected information about political processes

- *postbehavioral*, which, as a reaction to behavioralism, has not yet achieved a central focus

Easton's categories are insightful and serve to illustrate trends in the development of political science in the United States for the last two centuries. They do not, however, comprehend the long and complex history of political science. In particular, they do not adequately reflect three characteristics of the discipline. First, contemporary political science is the product of centuries of development which cannot be reflected adequately in a framework that addresses only more recent periods. A typology that is comprehensive in chronological scope is therefore needed. Second, the discipline today addresses the same essential questions that it addressed millenniums ago, if in a different manner, and a typology that is comprehensive in conceptual scope would be more descriptive of the discipline as a whole. Finally, although American political science generates the largest share of published works today, political scientists around the world have contributed in many ways to the discipline. A new set of categories is needed, therefore, which is comprehensive not only in chronological and conceptual scope but in geographic scope as well. This new set of categories will help us see more clearly the whole history of the discipline, which will in turn enable us to think more creatively about the discipline and to identify its significant moments.

In order to begin to construct this new and more comprehensive set of categories, let us look back across the history of the discipline. We find that the careful and systematic study of politics has progressed through seven great eras, each defined by two characteristics, (1) the objectives of the people who studied politics, and (2) the methods they employed to meet their objective. A summary of the seven eras is presented in the following table:

ERA	TIME SPAN	NAME OF THE ERA	THE OBJECTIVE OF OBSERVERS OF POLITICS	THE PREDOMINANT METHOD OF OBSERVERS OF POLITICS
1	To 2000 BCE	Myth	Unity	Denial of politics
2	2000 BCE to 400 BCE	Politics	Individuality	Participation in politics
3	400 BCE to 400 CE	Philosophy	Good government	Logic and observation of politics
4	400 to 1500	Theology	Godly government	Revelation and reason about politics
5	1500 to 1900	History	Consensual government	Rational analysis of political experience
6	1900 to 1970	Science	Facts	Observing political behavior
7	1970 to present	Eclecticism	Disciplinary identity	Creative synthesis methods and data

The seven eras have been given the following names: Myth, Politics, Philosophy, Theology, History, Science, and Eclecticism. Placed on a time line continuum, the seven eras appear like this:

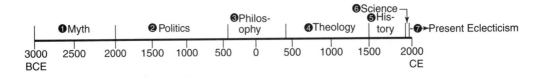

2.2   THE ERA OF MYTH (TO 2000 BCE)

Archaeologists and anthropologists have discovered evidence for the proposition that there was once a time before politics, when a consciousness politics, at least as we know it today, did not exist. At this early moment in history, human consciousness did not perceive social interactions as being political in the way we do today. We call this period the era of myth because people lived according to myths, narratives wherein gods were constantly expressing the creative forces of the universe. We use the term "myth" here in its classical sense rather than in its contemporary meaning. Today a myth is a fictional story, something that is not true. In a classical sense, however, a myth is the opposite: it is complete or ultimate truth. In this sense, myth is a story that expresses our perception of an ultimate truth that is beyond our limited human capacity to understand fully.

Mircea Eliades' classic anthropological study *Myth of the Eternal Return or Cosmos and History* (1971) explains that primitive people had a consciousness of the world around them that is much different from ours today. In this consciousness, life seemed to be "eternally returning" in cycles of day–night–day and summer–spring–winter–fall, instead of progressing from one point to another. Ancient religious practices, living patterns, and art have revealed patterns of consciousness that deny or reject fundamental facets of political life as we know them:

- the existence of human beings as autonomous individuals
- a sense of time and of history
- a sense of the difference between good and evil

According to Eliade, "The chief difference between the man of the archaic and traditional societies and the man of the modern societies, with their strong imprint of Judeo-Christianity, lies in the fact that the former feels himself indissolubly connected with the Cosmos and the cosmic rhythms, whereas the latter insists that he is connected only with History" (Eliade 1971, iii). When primitive people, for example, emerged from their caves in the morning, they experienced themselves as an undifferentiated part of the cosmos as it unfolded around them. They were, along with the rocks, the trees, the river, the sun, and the stars, an inseparable part of the continuing flow of life and death. According to Eliade, it would not have occurred to our primitive people to think of themselves as individual human beings, distinct from the motion and processes of life. They had no concept of time or of history, for life appeared as an unending series of cycles, and therefore night turned to day and back to night; winter, summer, spring, and fall followed winter, summer, spring, and fall; and all life flowed and cycled in an uninterrupted rhythm.

As Eliade explains, what is "real" to us today was not meaningful to primitive people, for whom there were two planes of existence, (1) a higher, transcendent, "sacred" realm of existence in which the gods are in the perpetual process of creating the world, and (2) a lower realm, the "profane" world, which was made up of only the ordinary acts of existence that had not been sanctified by ritual. Only the first, the higher realm constituted what was, for primitive people, truly real. Dances and feasts, for example, were religious ritual activities that sanctified hunting, birth, death, and other important aspects of life. As Eliade explains (1971, 3–27):

> Evidently, for the archaic mentality, reality manifests itself as force, effectiveness, and duration. Hence the outstanding reality is the sacred; for only the sacred *is* in an absolute fashion, acts effectively, creates things and makes them endure. . . . If we observe the general behavior of archaic man, we are struck by the following fact: neither the objects of the external world nor human acts, properly speaking, have any autonomous intrinsic value. Objects acquire a value, and in so doing become real, because they participate, after one fashion or another, in a reality that transcends them . . . We might say that the archaic world knows nothing of "profane" activities: every act has a definite meaning—hunting, fishing, agriculture; games, conflicts, sexuality—in some way participates in the sacred. . . . [T]he only profane activities are those which have no mythical meaning, that is, which lack exemplary models.

The real world, then, for primitive people, was the world of the sacred, which they entered psychologically and spiritually by performing rituals. Every time they performed a ritual, they recreated one of the original acts of the gods by which the universe was created. Primitive people were, therefore, continually engaged, as they performed their daily rituals, in participating in the original creative acts of the universe. Eliade observes that "[I]n the particulars of his conscious behavior, the 'primitive,' the archaic man, acknowledges no act which has not been previously posited and lived by someone else, some other being who was not a man. What he does has been done before. His life is a ceaseless repetition of gestures initiated by other." (Eliade 1971, 4).

Since their true reality consisted in recreating original acts of the gods, primitive people did not perceive the passage of time as we do today. "Through repetition of the cosmogonic act, concrete time, in which the construction takes place, is projected into mythical time, *in illo tempore* when the foundation of the world occurred" (Eliade 1971, 20). In this primitive consciousness, people saw the sun, the moon, artifacts, and animals as deities. The creation of the universe was the center of their religious concern. The only acts that had meaning were the original creative acts which brought the universe into being. The gods' creation of the universe was a continuous process with no beginning and no end. Primitive people could participate in the process of creation through religious ceremonies, which reenacted the creative acts of the gods.

Because, for primitive people, reality consisted of being one with the universe, and because the only meaningful acts were those that repeated the cosmological creations of the gods, there was no conception of good and evil, no idea of morality. Trees, animals, the acts of the gods, or other people were neither good nor evil. They simply existed. Primitive people, in this respect, are like newborn infants are today. In their first months of life, infants have no conception of good or bad. They see, hear, think, respond, and explore, but they have no idea that things are good or bad until those concepts are taught to them.

When a consciousness of politics first began to appear to primitive people, it was perceived as a threat to their existence. To act politically, that is, to assert rights or attempt to claim power, was to be an individual, isolated from God and the warmth of life in the unified community, and operating in the realm of profane existence was unfamiliar and frightening. Primitive people, therefore, rejected politics in two primary ways. The first was to continue to seek unity through religion. Priesthoods developed to lead people in religious ceremonies that celebrated the creative acts of the gods, and many of these rituals continue today. Christian celebrations of the birth of Christ at Christmas and the resurrection of Christ at Easter, for example, are contemporary parallels to these rituals.

The second method of rejecting politics was and continues to be organizational hierarchy. Hierarchy is a method of arranging an organization in a strict configuration of leadership so that there is a definite chain of command in which every participant has a defined place. In a hierarchy, workers report to a supervisor, supervisors report to managers, managers report to executives, and executives report to a chief executive. Politics has to do with making decisions, with the struggle with others to help make the decisions that affect the life of the community; to the extent that everyone in a hierarchy obeys the orders of the person above him or her, politics is eliminated. No hierarchical organization can eliminate politics completely, of course, but hierarchy reduces the free flow of political action, and in extreme cases, such as military operations in time of war, politics may be largely eliminated from daily life.

In comparison even with corporate life today, ancient organizations were strongly hierarchical. Emperors and kings ruled with divine sanction and with authority of life and death over their subjects. The greatest part of daily politics was eliminated.

2.3   THE ERA OF POLITICS (2000–400 BCE)

We call this period the era of politics not because it was more political than other eras, but because it was the era in which a consciousness of the nature, power, value, and dangers of politics, as we know them today at all levels of life (family, community, nation, and world), was conceived.

During the previous period, the period of myth, people rejected the personal responsibility that comes through free and open politics and attempted to eradicate politics in society both through religious ceremony, which tied politics to their primitive consciousness, and through organizational hierarchy. The era of mythical consciousness came to an end in various places in the world at different times, but our most clearly recorded early examples are from Israel and Greece.

A consciousness of politics, as we understand it, first appeared as people developed an awareness of morality, of personal responsibility for good and evil. One of its earliest symbolic expressions of this dawning awareness was recorded by the ancient Hebrews in the *Book of Genesis.* The Garden of Eden was a world without good or evil. Adam and Eve were at peace with God, and the animal world knew no competition and strife. Then the world of peace with God was shattered. Adam and Eve ate the forbidden fruit, the fruit of the tree of the *knowledge of good and evil.* Symbolically, the knowledge of good and evil is the central dilemma of humanity. If we have no knowledge of good and evil, we cannot be held accountable for our actions. Because Adam and Eve received the knowledge of good and evil, they were then responsible for the morality of their actions. Their moral eyes were open. Their struggle began when they came to know good from evil but were not always capable of doing good. And so their children, Cain and Abel, fully possessed of human consciousness, struggled for power and for recognition from God, and politics was conceived. The story of Adam, Eve, Cain, and Abel tells symbolically how the transformation from nonpolitical consciousness to political consciousness took place.

Old Testament stories about the patriarchs (Abraham, Isaac, Jacob, and Joseph) are full of political intrigue. In the story of Joseph, for example, Jacob's favorite son is sold into slavery by his jealous brothers and thrown into prison, only to eventually become, by interpreting dreams for the pharaoh, administrator of the Egyptian empire. Several generations later, the descendants of the Hebrews whom Joseph brought to Egypt become so powerful that the Egyptians, reacting from fear, enslave them and make them build the pyramids. Hearing the people cry out for freedom, God calls Moses to lead them out of Egypt to the promised land.

In his book *Exodus and Revolution* (1985), political scientist Michael Walzer explores the political implications of the biblical story of the Exodus. For Walzer (1985, 12–13), *Exodus,* perhaps the most famous and often repeated political liberation story of all time, marks the end of the mythical consciousness of cyclical time and the beginning of the modern concept of linear or historical time.

> A political history with a strong linearity, a strong forward movement, the Exodus gives permanent shape to Jewish conceptions of time, and it serves as a model, ultimately, for non-Jewish conceptions too. We can think of it as the crucial alternative to all mythic notions of eternal recurrence—and hence to those cyclical understandings of political change from which our word "revolution" derives. The idea of eternal recurrence connects the social to the

natural world and gives to political life the simple closure of a circle: birth, maturity, death, and rebirth. The same story is enacted again and again; men and women and the timely deeds of men and women alike lose their singularity; one represents another in a system of correspondences that extends upward, hierarchically, into the mythic realm of nature and nature's gods. Biblical narrative generally, Exodus more particularly, breaks in the most decisive way with this kind of cosmological story-telling. In Exodus, historical events occur only once, and they take on their significance from a system of backward- and forward-looking interconnections, not from the hierarchical correspondences of myth.

In the book of *Exodus,* the Hebrew God demands that the Hebrews reject the myth and rituals of primitive consciousness and look to a God who helped them create singular, nonrepeatable events that have become chapters of a history of a progressive time in which the same creative events are not repeated over and over. The God of the Hebrews also demands that the people take moral responsibility for their actions, to realize that their true humanity was fulfilled in being moral actors in an ongoing history that had a beginning and an end. Inasmuch as the Hebrews were now to accept the challenge of making their own history and to communally help decide their fates, the Hebrews were called by God to accept the challenge of politics: to treat one other morally while consciously accepting their individual and collective responsibilities for building a society that would reflect the will of God in a new land. In *The Myth of the Eternal Return,* Mircea Eliade (1971, 104), agreeing with Walzer, says of the God of *Exodus*:

> This God of the Jewish people is no longer an Oriental Divinity, creator of archetypal gestures, but a personality who ceaselessly intervenes in history, who reveals his will through events. . . . It may be said with truth that the Hebrews were the first to discover the meaning of history as the epiphany of God, and this conception, as we should expect, was taken up and amplified by Christianity.

Political consciousness in Israel developed, therefore, through a religious tradition in which individuals and the community as a whole were responsible to God for making moral choices. In Greece, consciousness of a political way of life had arrived by the time of the Homeric epics. Written probably around 1000 BCE, the *Odyssey* and the *Iliad* tell tales of the great Greek heroes of the Trojan War. In the following centuries, Greeks viewed these poetic renderings of heroism as expressing essential qualities of life, and together they constituted a sort of Greek historical bible, a new myth by which to live. In the *Odyssey,* Odysseus has a series of adventures in which he encounters multiheaded creatures, a Cyclops, and other supernatural beings. Constantly in the background are the "fates," which shape important aspects of the story, but which are entirely beyond human control. The Greeks of the Homeric era viewed life in the same way. Supernatural forces, the gods, the forces of nature, were believed to shape human life in important ways. The moral message of Homer's stories is that guidance from the gods was necessary for success in life.

The implications of the Homeric perspective on life are profound. To the extent that external forces control our lives, politics is irrelevant, for all our political efforts may come to nothing. Homer's characters are not entirely directed by fate, however, and the beginnings of political consciousness appear particularly in an emerging new view of hierarchy. There is an ongoing academic debate about the strength of hierarchy and the extent of democracy in the Greek army as it is portrayed in the Homeric poems. One side of the argument, which is propounded later by the fifth-century BCE philosopher Socrates, holds that military life in Homer's epics is authoritarian. When his rule is challenged by someone under his command, Odysseus says, in Book II of the *Iliad*, "Surely not all of us Achaians can be kings here. Lordship for many is no good thing. Let there be one ruler, one king, to whom the son of devious king Kronos gives the scepter and the right of judgment to watch over his people." (Illiad 2: 204–6). But one proponent of the opposing interpretation, the idea that the Greek military exhibited definite democratic features, is American journalist I. F. Stone, who writes in *The Trial of Socrates* (1988, 34–35):

> When Odysseus has finally prevailed on everyone else to sit down at the assembly, only Thersites refuses to be silent. Despite Homer's invidious description of Thersites as a man of disorderly speech, he speaks here not only boldly, but succinctly and to the point. Odysseus replies with violence. In front of the whole assembly, he beats Thersites until he bleeds, humiliating him and threatening that if Thersites ever again dares "take the name of kings in your mouth," Odysseus will strip him naked before the assembly and send him "wailing to the swift ships."

In reply to Stone it may be noted, of course, that to be beaten bloody by a king is not exactly a sign of a vital democracy. Stone responds (1988, 21) to this point, however, by noting other features of Greek army organization:

> Agamemnon was not the absolute king the Socratics idealized. Instead, the Greek host before Troy already exhibited in embryo the features common to the polis and modern parliamentary and presidential systems. Agamemnon was the presiding officer. He was advised by a council of elders made up of aristocratic landowners and warriors. Below this council, there was a general assembly of the warriors. So the Iliad shows us not absolute kingship but a government of three branches, an Executive, a Senate, and an assembly of the "Commons."

Although the debate concerning the democratic features of Greek life around 1000 BCE may never be conclusively resolved, there is little doubt that a variety of conditions and trends in the following 500 years led to the establishment of democracy in Athens in the century after 508 BCE. The first of these trends was that Greece, which had been ruled by Crete and other empires previous to this time, was left for long periods without interference from outside empires. A series of city states (polis) emerged, each developing a strong sense of independence. The typical Greek polis had a free market economy, few government agencies to interfere with trade, and a military based primarily on an independent militia consisting of citizens. The farmers of Athens, who became the backbone of the citizen class, were sufficiently wealthy to own their own shield and lance. Known as hoplites, these militia men fought fiercely in wars and then returned immediately to their farms and families. Developing a sense of self-sufficiency within the unity of the polis, the hoplites attempted to gain from the oligarchic (wealthy, aristocratic) families a greater voice in making decisions in government.

Scientific discovery also fanned the emergent flames of democracy in Greece. Several influential philosopher-scientists came to Greece from Ionia, which is presently the nation of Turkey, and other areas of the Mediterranean. Thales of Miletus became known as the first scientific philosopher. Accurately predicting an eclipse on May 25, 585 BCE, he introduced to the Greek world the idea that Homer did not adequately describe reality. For Thales (640–546 BCE), these were natural phenomena rather than the activities of the gods, which explained events in the world. Accurate measurement and calculation were important for Thales, and he calculated the circumference of the world. Looking for the essential components of existence, Thales said the ground of the universe is water, which is fluid and changes into many forms.

A number of other sixth- and fifth-century BCE scientists, also asking many of the same questions Thales had raised, came up with different answers. Anaximander (611–547) said that the fire in the physical universe and the fire of life in the human soul are of the same essential substance and that the energy represented by fire is the basic element of existence. Anaximenes proposed that air, which can be visible as clouds or invisible, was the fundamental substance. Democritus provided an important concept for science when he developed atomic theory, claiming that atoms are those particles which are not divisible; have motion, extension, and mass; and are infinitely small.

The result of all these investigations was that the universe began to look less and less like the product of the actions of the gods and more and more like the result of the interaction of natural elements. This perception had theological and political consequences. Zenophenes, for example, who became known as the first major skeptic, reached the conclusion that we anthropomorphize our deities. In other words, we create gods in our minds who resemble human beings. Zenophanes claimed that there is only one god, and this god was essentially unlike man. Protagoras (500–430 BCE) rejected a theocentric view of the universe and declared that "man is the measure of all things."

These discoveries may appear inconsequential today, but at the time they were made, their political implications were revolutionary. If "man is the measure of all things," if people are in control of at least the social if not the physical environment, then they may have a sense of political efficacy. Efficacy is the belief that one's actions do actually make a difference. Voting studies in the United States and elsewhere have demonstrated that groups that have a high sense of political efficacy, in other words, groups that believe that their activities and votes count, are much more active in politics and have a much greater effect on the political system than those who believe their efficacy is limited. The Athenian hoplites began to believe that they could have a major and effective role in the governmental decisions that affected them. If they, not the gods, were the measure of all things, they were individually important. So in 508–507 BCE, when the Athenian aristocrat Cleisthenes offered the hoplites a strong role in government in return for their support, the hoplites were ready to accept.

From 508 to 507 BCE, Cleisthenes instituted a number of reforms, which completed some developments already in progress. One of these was to give substantial power to a popular assembly. Any Athenian citizen could attend the assembly, and it was often crowded with as many as 6,000 citizens. Athens' poets and playwrights enjoyed freedom of speech similar to that of modern day political cartoonists, and the typical Greek democrat, always open to spoof and ridicule, is caricatured by Aristophanes (1969, 9–10) in his play *The Acharnians*. In the following sequence, a citizen waiting for the assembly to convene complains about the leadership:

> There's a stated meeting of the Assembly called for dawn, and here's the Pnyx [the forum in which the assembly was held]—completely empty! Everybody's down at the Agora [the marketplace], gabbing, cackling, running away from the Masters-at-arms. Nobody's going to rope them into their civic duty. No, sir! The Executive Board hasn't come! Oh, it will, shoving and jostling—you know how—streaming down in a bunch to get the first bench; but they don't give a damn for peace and how to get it. Oh, Athens, Athens! So I come to the Assembly—as usual, first—and sit. But what's to do when you're all alone? Well, I sigh, I yawn, I stretch, sometimes I fart. I try to think of things to do. I write, I pluck out my hairs, I balance my books. I fix my eyes upon my fields and lust for peace. I loathe the stingy, greedy city. I long for my own ungrudging countryside, my generous village. . . . Good-bye to that! So here I am. By god, I'm ready, to boo, to interrupt, to heckle every speaker who dares to say a word on any subject but peace. Well, look! Here's the Executive Board— and it's noon. Didn't I tell you? Just what I was saying; every last one of them pushing to sit up front.

The reforms of Cleisthenes were both broad and deep. In addition to the popular assembly of all the citizens, a council of 500 was established as a permanent legislative body, which could debate and formulate policy. Cleisthenes accomplished a major political reform when, overlooking the potentially divisive tribal groups that formed Athens, he established a system of ten new tribes, not defined by the old geographic boundaries, but constituting new political units, each of which contained elements from the countryside and the city. By this reorganization, Cleisthenes was able to break down traditional political antagonisms and form a new sense of unity in which citizenship in the polis of Athens was the most important factor. In the Athenian process, members of the council of 500 were chosen not by election, but by lot, 50 from each tribe, for one-year terms so that every citizen had the opportunity to share leadership at some time in his life. Ten archons, or administrative rulers, and ten strategos, or generals, were also chosen. In addition, the heliaea became the centerpiece of the judicial system. It consisted of 6,000 jurors from whom juries of 51–1,501 were chosen.

Pericles (495–429 BCE), Cleisthenes' nephew, who became Athens' leader in the mid-fifth century, expanded democratic reforms and led Athens to the height of its wealth and power. Among the interesting procedures developed in classical Athens was ostracism, which means to banish. Ostracism comes from the word ostraka, which refers to shards of pottery on which could be scratched the names of people to be ostracized. When an ostracism was called, citizens would gather and write on an ostrakon the name of a person whom they wanted to ostracize. If at least 6,000 ostraka were cast, the person whose name most frequently appeared upon them was sent out of Athens for a period of ten years. The ostracized person could retain property but could not come to Athens or participate in its politics. Today, this procedure sounds almost barbaric, but at the time, ostracism was a solid step forward from the normal method of changing political regimes in the ancient world, which was violent revolution. Under ostracism a leader could be voted out of town so that an opposition group could install its leaders without problems caused by the former leadership, and the former leader retained his life. Ostracism is therefore an innovation in nonviolent regime change.

In some ways, such as the fact that citizens took turns holding office, Athens was the most democratic government to ever exist in history. In other ways, however, the democracy was very limited. Citizenship was restricted to males born to citizen parents. Not only women but also large numbers of resident aliens and slaves were excluded from any effective political participation. Citizens, in fact, made up less than 20 percent of the people of Athens.

2.4   THE ERA OF PHILOSOPHY (400 BCE–400 CE)

Enjoying his democratic freedom of speech in fifth-century BCE Athens was Socrates (c. 469 or 480–399 BCE), a balding philosophic gadfly whose influence, along with his student Plato's (427–347 BCE), upon the history of philosophy is difficult to overestimate. Socrates is democracy's greatest philosophic enemy (since Plato wrote the dialogues in which Socrates is the speaker, it is difficult to tell whose views are being recorded, so we shall treat the two philosophers as if they are the same author). Socrates (Plato) believed that democracy violated all principles of reason. He compared the Greek democrats to residents of a cave, chained to a wall, allowed to see only the shadows cast on the opposite wall by marionettes manipulated by politicians. He believed that democratic freedom was merely an illusion. Greek democrats believed that in their assembly they could openly debate the great issues of the day and that they, as citizens, had the capacity to make intelligent decisions on the basis of the struggle of competing ideas voiced in public. Socrates scoffed at this notion, arguing that the citizens were merely deluding themselves, deceived by great orators into thinking they were making decisions whereas in reality they were merely manipulated into thinking what those in power wanted them to think.

Socrates proposed that the value of life was the human ability to seek and find the truth. Plato records in *The Republic* that Socrates was fond of saying "the unexamined life is not worth living." Truth could be found not through democratic discussion, but through a method known as the Socratic dialectic. The dialectic is a process of asking questions and testing the answers. Someone, for example, would propose a question to Socrates, such as, "Does not the worst evil for a state arise from anything that tends to rend it asunder and destroy its unity, while nothing does it more good than whatever tends to bind it together and make it one?" Socrates will then test this statement through a process of deductive logic in which statements are measured against their conformance to general principles. If a statement appears to be true, Socrates might exclaim, "That is true!" Then, as other speakers add subsequent statements, a philosophy develops. The participants in this dialogue reject statements that appear to be false, in a process similar to the reasoning that occurs in mathematics. Socrates' knowledge of and affinity for geometry and similar forms of mathematical reasoning are evident in his remarks.

Socrates asserted that a higher realm, beyond the physically perceptible aspects of daily life, exists in which "forms," perfect representations of physical objects, may be found. In other words, in the world of the forms there are forms of chairs, trees, animals, and people. A form of a person is a perfect person, more real than people on earth. It is almost as if forms are ideas in the mind of God, who then creates earthly men, women, trees, and animals, which are imperfect imitations of the forms. The function of philosophy, for Plato, is to develop wisdom, and the purpose of wisdom is the use of reason to perceive the forms. Only those in society who are the most intelligent, and who have been suitably educated, are able to perceive the forms, the perfect manifestations of all things. Since there is a form for everything that exists, there is a form for government. Since only a few select people can perceive the form for government and therefore know best how to rule, these gifted people should be made philosopher-kings. Plato's most famous dialogue, *The Republic*, contains Socrates' dialectical quest to define both justice and the best form of government, one which will result in a just society.

For Socrates and Plato, the best government is one that reflects the natural capacities and inclinations of humanity. People are composed of body, mind, and spirit (a spirited or courageous nature). Those ruled by their bodies seek first sensual satisfaction. Those ruled by their minds seek the height of reason, and these, a small minority, should obviously rule the others. Those ruled by their spiritedness seek military conquest. For Socrates, according to *The Republic*, everyone had a proper role to fulfill in society, and only those who were qualified, by virtue of their intelligence and leadership skills, could rule. When the proper people ruled, society experienced justice.

In a world where everyone knows his or her place and one person or a few make the decisions for all the rest, politics ceases to exist, and this is precisely what Plato intends. Rejecting the politics of Greek democracy of his day, Plato attempts to revive the conditions of the myth, the mental framework of primitive man, to build a more modern society. With an absolute hierarchy and a belief in forms—which take the place of the gods in a more sophisticated mind—Plato accomplishes an astounding feat: he translates the powerful primal needs of primitive psychology, which remain with us today as manifestations of the subconscious mind, into a rational mental framework acceptable to the modern world. For this accomplishment, Plato is read with intense interest almost two and a half millenniums after his death. As Mircea Eliade has noted in *The Myth of the Eternal Return,* "Plato could be regarded as the outstanding philosopher of primitive mentality" that is, as the thinker who succeeded in giving philosophic currency and validity to the modes of life and behavior of archaic humanity (Eliade 1971, 34).

Aristotle was a student of Plato, but the differences perhaps more than the similarities between the approaches of the younger philosopher and his mentor have fascinated students for centuries. In a lecture on Aristotle, Barnard College's political science professor Dennis Dalton points out how wonderfully the Renaissance painter Raphael captures the dispute between Plato and Aristotle in his famous painting *School of Athens.*

In the center of this painting, Plato extends an index finger toward the heavens, indicating that truth and wisdom are to be found in the world of the forms. Aristotle, to the contrary, extends his hand outward directly from his waist, indicating that truth is found not in the heavenly world of the forms but in the observation of physical reality in this world and comes through living life in moderation. For Aristotle, Plato was guilty of going to extremes. In attempting to imitate the ideal world of the forms, Plato's philosophy led to the sanctioning of what seemed at the time to be outrageous concepts, such as communal property for the military class, and even political equality for women.

While Plato had based his concept of human reasoning on mathematics, Aristotle (384–322 BCE), a physician and the son of a physician, based his philosophy on the natural sciences and observation of nature. He developed the system of classification of living organisms into phylums, genuses, and species that is still used in the science of biology, and as we can see in this excerpt from his *The Politics* (1290b), he used the same methods to investigate government.

> If we aimed at a classification of the different kinds of animals, we should begin by enumerating the parts, or organs, which are necessary to every animal. These include, for example, some of the sensory organs: they also include the organs for getting and digesting food. . . . [T]hey further include the organs of locomotion. . . . States too, as we have repeatedly noticed, are composed not of one but of many parts. One of these parts is the group of persons concerned with the production of food. . . . A second . . . is . . . occupied in the various arts and crafts. . . . A third part is what may be termed the marketing class; it includes all those who are occupied in buying and selling. . . . A fourth part is the serf class composed of agricultural laborers; and a fifth element is the defense force.

Rather than looking at the power of deductive reasoning to find the ideal form of government, Aristotle turned to inductive reasoning, beginning with observation. Recording features of some 350 Greek governments, both historical and contemporary, Aristotle sought to discover how existing forms of governments worked and how their structures related to their strengths and weaknesses. Aristotle employed the same methods that he used in his investigation of biological organisms, classing governments into two types, each having three manifestations. Aristotle observed that there are (1) good governments, those that rule in the interests of all the classes of people in society, and (2) bad governments, those that rule in the interests of the ruling class only. Further, both good and bad governments may be composed of (a) one person, (b) a few people, or (c) a majority, the poor masses of society. Good governments ruled by one he called monarchies, good governments of a few were aristocracies, and good governments of the many he called polities or constitutional governments. Bad governments ruled by one were tyrannies, bad governments of the few were oligarchies, and bad governments ruled by the many were democracies. Why did Aristotle consider democracy to be a bad form of government? He perceived democracies as governments run by the masses of the poor, who ruled in their own interests only. Polities, however, which were ruled by the majority and considered the interests of all classes, were rare, but could be the best form of government. As he says in the *Politics*, "We have now to consider what is the best constitution and the best way of life for the *majority* of states and men. . . . It is clear from our argument, first, that the best form of political society is one where power is vested in the middle class" (Aristotle 1295a). For Aristotle, the middle class was composed of those who had neither too much nor too little. Versed in the ways of moderation, they were best suited to govern the society as a whole.

Continuing to carefully classify his observations, Aristotle investigated many matters pertaining to political theory, including the causes of revolution:

> The principle and general cause of mind which disposes men towards change is the cause of which we have just spoken. There are some who stir up sedition because their minds are filled by a passion for equality, which arises from their thinking that they have the worst bargain in spite of being the equals of those who have got the advantage. There are others who do it because their minds are filled with a passion for inequality (i.e. superiority), which arises from their conceiving that they get no advantage over others (but only an equal amount, or even a smaller amount) although they are really more than equal to others. (Either of these passions may have some justification; and either may be without any.) Thus inferiors become revolutionaries in order to be equals, and equals in order to be superiors (Aristotle 1302a).

Although we have confined our discussion to Western thinkers to this point, it is important to note that much was happening in the Eastern countries throughout the history of political thought as well. An interesting example is Mencius (372–289 BCE), second only to Confucius in his philosophical leadership of Confucianism. Mencius is concerned to establish the principle, which also became the cornerstone of Western political thought in the Middle Ages, that the state is the product of divine inspiration. When asked who gave the Chinese empire to the emperor, Mencius answered, "Heaven gave it to him" (Bary 1966, 110). Reasoning much as Aristotle had about the origin of the state, Mencius asserted: "Men are in the habit of speaking of the world, the state. As a matter of fact, the foundation of the world lies in the state, the foundation of the state lies in the family, and the foundation of the family lies in the individual" (Bary 1966, 110). Mencius advocated humane government and presaged Jesus' emphasis on service to humanity when he declared that in the affairs of the state, "the people rank the highest, the spirits of land and grain come next, and the ruler counts the least" (Bary 1966, 110).

The era of philosophy began as an attempt by Plato to eradicate democratic politics, if not all features of political life. Ironically, politics flourished throughout the era, finding eloquent theorists such as Cicero during the period of the Roman Republics and then coming under attack again during the time of the Roman empires.

2.5   THE ERA OF THEOLOGY (400–1500)

In the fourth era of the development of political science, Western civilization, in all its aspects, reflected the social, philosophical, moral, and often the political dominance of the Roman Catholic Church. This period was marked by momentous theological struggles in which the Church leaders attempted to come to terms with both the spirituality of their faith and the hard realities of the world of practical politics.

From the beginning of the Middle Ages, the Catholic Church decisively rejected the apolitical and antipolitical implications and lessons of the teachings of Jesus Christ in favor of a philosophy, implied in the Old Testament and in the New Testament writings of the apostle Paul, which embraced political power. Because the theology of the Catholic Church dominated the study of politics in the Middle Ages in Europe, it is necessary to understand the Church's perspective on politics. To do this, we must first examine the teachings of Jesus as presented in the four Gospels and the way these teachings were understood by the early church.

Early in his ministry, according to the Gospel of Luke, Jesus announced that his primary mission was to announce the kingdom of God (or kingdom of heaven):

> And he came to Nazareth, where he had been brought up; and he went to the synagogue, as his custom was, on the Sabbath day. And he stood up to read; and there was given to him the book of the prophet Isaiah. He opened the book and found the place where it was written,
>
> > "The spirit of the Lord is upon me to preach good news to the poor.
> > He has sent me to proclaim release to the captives
> > and recovering of sight to the blind,
> > to set at liberty those who are oppressed,
> > to proclaim the acceptable year of the Lord."
>
> And he closed the book, and gave it back to the attendant, and sat down; and the eyes of all in the synagogue were fixed on him. And he began to say to them, "Today this scripture has been fulfilled in your hearing." (NIV Luke 4:16–22)

Most of the teachings of Jesus, as they are recorded in the Gospels, are in the form of parables, which are about the qualities of the kingdom of God. In his actions, in his parables, and in his teachings, Jesus decisively announces that the kingdom of God is not of this world; it is not a political kingdom. At the end of his forty days in the wilderness, Jesus decisively rejects the "political temptation" to rule the political kingdoms of the world:

> And the devil took him up, and showed him all the kingdoms of the world in a moment of time, and said to him, "To you I will give all this authority and their glory; for it has been delivered to me, and I give it to whom I will. If you, then, shall worship me, it shall all be yours." And Jesus answered him, "It is written 'You shall worship the Lord your God and him only shall you serve.'" (NIV Luke 4:5–8)

Thereafter Jesus purposely refutes any suggestion that he was attempting to seek political power. If the kingdom of heaven is not political, then what is it? According to Jesus' parables, one participates in the kingdom of heaven when one acts like the good Samaritan, when one gives his or her wealth to the poor, when one forgives debts, when one claims the lowest seat at the banquet table, when one washes another's feet, and when one seeks humble service to others rather than honor. The kingdom of God, then, is everything that political kingdoms are not. The kingdom of heaven is not the struggle for power; it is the absence of the struggle for power. The kingdom of heaven is not jostling for privilege and the protection of one's interests; it is, in fact, a spiritual state in which one is indifferent to political power and its privileges. When the Pharisees approached Christ, attempting to trap him into either supporting tax payments to the Roman Empire (which the Jewish people abhorred) or rebelling against Roman authority, and thereby becoming a political figure, Jesus said "Render unto Caesar that which is Caesar's," indicating that a coin bearing Caesar's image is of no special consequence to the kingdom of heaven, which recognizes neither wealth nor poverty as merit, but is concerned with things which the power of money does not represent. When one renders unto God that which is God's, one gives up one's political ambition, for what is owed to God is to love him with all one's heart, soul, and mind. There is little room left for accumulating political power when one is dedicated to God.

This interpretation of the Gospels, which presents Jesus as a figure who cut though politics because he denied the eternal importance of politics, was prevalent in the early church during the first four centuries of the Christian era. Most Christians in these centuries declined to initiate rebellions, for they did not aim to seize political power. On many occasions, however, they refused to carry out acts of the Roman state which they believed contrary to the kingdom of God. They refused to worship Caesar or to recognize any god but their own. For this lack of allegiance to the Roman state they were often persecuted. Christians were not purposefully rebellious because rebellion was also a political act, and they were normally obedient to the Roman regime, when it required things of them that did not conflict with their worship of God. The strongest biblical injunction to obey the laws of the state is found in Romans 13, verses 1–7: "All souls must place themselves in submission to the governing authorities. For there is no authority except by God" (Romans 13:1). Paul apparently did not intend this command to imply absolute obedience for two obvious reasons. First, he ends this passage with an admonition: "Pay back to everyone that which is owed: to one (owed) taxes, the taxes, to the one (owed) duty, the duty, to the one (owed) respect, the respect to the one (owed) honor, the honor" (Romans 13:7). The implications of this statement are that loyalty to the state is limited to that which is owed and that the state is not owed loyalty which conflicts with the will of God.

But while Paul insists that followers of Jesus fulfill certain civic duties, he strongly implies that the emperor is *not* owed worship, which is reserved for God; nor is the centurion owed obedience when he demands that a Christian stop believing or preaching the gospel. In fact, Paul, Peter, and other apostles spent much time in jail, where they were often placed for disobedience and where they wrote some of their most famous letters; and all of the apostles but John reportedly were killed at the hands of those who were acting for the governing authorities. One of the most famous stories of the death of martyrs is that of the burning at the stake of Polycarp, an aging but courageous gentleman of Smyrna:

> And when the governor insisted, saying, "Take the oath, and I will let you go; revile Christ," Polycarp said,
>
> "For eighty-six years I have been his slave, and he has done me no wrong; how can I blaspheme my king who has saved me? . . .
>
> When he (the governor) still insisted, and said, "Swear by the fortune of Caesar,"
>
> "If you imagine that I will swear by the fortune of Caesar, as you say, and pretend not to know who I am, let me tell you plainly, I am a Christian. And if you want to learn the doctrine of Christianity, set a day and hear me."
>
> The governor said, "Convince the people."
>
> Polycarp said, "I thought you worth reasoning with; for we have been taught to pay suitable honor to governments and authorities, appointed by God, if it does us no harm; but as for these others, I do not think they are worth defending myself before them" (Goodspeed 1950, 250–251).

The kingdom of God, therefore, as seen by most of its early adherents, was not political, and the new religion was therefore apolitical or overtly antipolitical. Tertullian, a leading theologian of the first three centuries of Christianity, summed up his belief in the apolitical nature of the kingdom of God by asking, "What indeed has Athens to do with Jerusalem?" a question which contrasts Athens, the symbol of politics, with Jerusalem, the holy city.

But herein lies a paradox. The existence in society of an antipolitical religion had serious political implications. Society was concerned that people whose first loyalty was to God, people who refused to take up the sword and instead followed Christ's admonitions to nonviolence, might be unreliable citizens, especially in times of emergency or war, when their loyalty and help were needed by their fellow citizens.

In the year 325 CE an unexpected event occurred. The Roman emperor Constantine converted to Christianity. Whereas previously Christians had been officially persecuted, now they found themselves enjoying the official endorsement of the Roman Empire. They began to believe that perhaps, now that the Empire was officially Christian, the long-awaited return of Christ would unfold before their eyes. But their enthusiasm was short lived. In 410 CE, Alaric and the Goths conquered Rome, and Roman Christians, who had been reluctant to fight in any political cause, were blamed for the disaster. It was said that they were not good citizens because they gave allegiance first to their God and only secondly, if at all, to the state.

The very vitality of the Catholic Church itself seemed at stake. The Church, with its tradition of pacifism and indifference to politics, had no apparent basis upon which to respond to this threat. At this critical point a Catholic Bishop in the town of Hippo in North Africa wrote a work that was to reject the antipolitical teachings of Jesus and permanently revolutionize and politicize the church. Shortly after the fall of the empire, Augustine published the *City of God*, in which he divided human experience into two cities, the city of God and the city of this world. According to Augustine, two cities have been formed by two loves: "love of self, even to the contempt of God; the heavenly by the love of God, even to the contempt of self." The city of God was the spiritual realm where the virtues of Jesus were practiced. Only Christians, selected by God through his grace, were citizens of this realm. Only Christians could know the joy of the love of God. Everyone else, excluded from the kingdom of God for reasons known only to God, were citizens only of this world, where the bitter conflicts of politics were fought. The critical point of Augustine's theology is that Christians, though they are citizens of the city of God, are also citizens of the kingdoms of this world. They are placed in this world by God to interact in it. As citizens of this world they are good and loyal subjects of the governments whose protection they enjoy. As such, they must fight to defend their earthly kingdoms when it is just to do so. Augustine then develops a doctrine of a just war. Rejecting Christ's admonition to his disciples to reject violent conflict, Augustine asserts that wars may be justly waged by Christians under several specific conditions, including self-protection, the correcting of wrongs, and the establishment of peace.

The Catholic Church warmly received Augustine's doctrine, because through it the Church gained a rationale for exercising political power. In the minds of many people, however, the Church paid a high price for this power, gaining the kingdom of the world, the kingdom of politics, but losing the kingdom of God. Although there are individuals throughout the history of the Church who practiced the apolitical faith of Christ, the Church establishment followed Augustine's doctrine and pursued political power.

For the next 1,000 years, the Church increased its financial and political power. At a time when land was the primary source of wealth, the Church was the largest land owner in Europe. The year 1000 was important, for many Christians believed references in the *Book of Revelation* suggesting that Jesus would return at the time of the millennium (1,000 years). When he did not return, and when feudal wars and plagues added to their desperation, many began to question their faith and the Church. "Millenarian" movements, which claimed the coming of the millennium signaled the return of Christ, spread across Europe, taking many forms but sharing some common themes. They would often begin, for example, when someone emerging from the contemplation in a wilderness claimed to be the resurrected Christ or John the Baptist or another prophet with a mission from God. The millenarian prophets would march from town to town, gaining bands of followers as they preached a coming transformation of the world. Some of these prophets and their followers became flagellants, who would themselves bloody in public, repenting of their sins before God and crying out for his mercy. Others turned their anger outward, killing village priests whom they thought, in their resentment at the wealth and power of the Church, to be agents of Satan. The millenarians also robbed and burned Jewish settlements, killing many along the way. The millenarian prophets justified their actions by claiming to have received direct revelation from God.

Alarmed by these developments, the Church nevertheless could not reject revelation as a source of morality. To counter the depredations of the millenarians, the Church fathers claimed that reason was also the voice of God and that mob violence violated the bounds of reason. Thomas Aquinas, one of the scholars helping to start Europe's great universities, provided a rationale by which the Church could integrate reason into its doctrine of revelation. In his *Summa Theologica*, Aquinas argued that the ability to reason is a gift from God for human use to understand his purpose. Revelation, whether in the form of scripture or voiced announcements of God's appointed speakers in the Church, is completely compatible with reason. Aquinas thereby maintained the Church's claim to revelation while allowing it to develop a reasoned philosophy that helped consolidate the Church's power.

Aquinas's philosophic method is of great importance. He was a leading figure in the scholastic movement, which in the thirteenth century discovered for Christianity the manuscripts of Aristotle that Islamic scholars had known for years. Aquinas combined Aristotle's scientific-dialectical method of reasoning with Christ's revelation of the kingdom of heaven. Aristotle believed that human beings are inherently political and that developing their political talents was the essence of social behavior. In combining Aristotle's politics with the New Testament, Aquinas integrated into the Church's theology a rationale for Christians to be highly political and, at the same time, obedient to the authority of government. In the following passage from the *Summa Theologica*, Aquinas presents his rationale for monarchy. His argument sounds very much like Aristotle, and his political goal, which is unanimity and peace, is directly inspired by Jesus, the "Prince of Peace."

> The aim of any ruler should be directed toward securing the welfare of that which he undertakes to rule. . . . Now the welfare and safety of a multitude formed into a society lies in the preservation of unity, which is called peace. If this is removed, the benefit of social life is lost and, moreover, the multitude in its disagreement becomes a burden to itself. The chief concern of the ruler of a multitude, therefore, is to procure the unity of peace. . . . Now it is manifest that what is itself one can more efficaciously bring about unity than several—just as the most efficacious cause of heat is that which is by nature hot. Therefore the rule of one man is more useful than the rule of many. . . . This is also evident from experience. For provinces or cities which are not ruled by one person are torn with dissensions and tossed about without peace. (Aquinas)

Because the Church represents a higher realm (spirituality), reasoned Aquinas, the Church should be able to at least strongly advise secular leaders upon important temporal political questions, if not actually settle them.

2.6   THE ERA OF HISTORY (1500–1900)

History without political science has no fruit;
Political science without history has no root.

—SIR JOHN ROBERT SEELEY (1896)

In 1858, upon assuming the first chair in political science at an American university, Francis Lieber had this to say about the importance of history to political science (1993, 23):

> Political science treats of man in his most important earthly phase; the state is the institution which has to protect or check all his endeavors, and, in turn, reflects them. It is natural, therefore, that a thorough course of this branch should become, in a great measure, a delineation of the history of civilization, with all the undulations of humanity. . . . Need I add that the student, having passed through these fields and having viewed these regions, will be the better prepared for the grave purposes for which this country destines him, and as a partner in the great commonwealth of self-government? If not, then strike these sciences from your catalog.

We designate the fifth era of political science (1500–1900) as the era of history because the primary method of understanding politics throughout this period was to learn lessons from history and then attempt to apply them to politics. Further, the goal of most serious students of politics during this period was not the study of politics for its own sake but, rather, the study of politics for a purpose: applying the lessons of history to achieve better government. Many of the most important works of the period were philosophical in approach and focused on legal issues, but these discussions were almost always tested by the lessons of history. For the most important thinkers of this period, the type of government sought is consensual government, that is, government in which the people who are ruled agree to the extent, limits, and character of the power given to the authorities.

This era begins with the person often credited with ushering in modernity, Nicolo Machiavelli (1469–1527). "Modernity" is the period marked by the end of the Church's domination of thoughts and institutions that defined the Middle Ages, and the beginning of the time when secular or nonreligious thoughts and institutions became preeminent. Machiavelli's work *The Prince* (1513) is a classic of modern political realism. Machiavelli, a senior government official in Florence, Italy, who had lost his position when the Medicis came to power wrote *The Prince* for Lorenzo de Medici in hopes of gaining the ruler's favor and being reinstated in his previous position. Rejecting the works of Thomas Aquinas and the scholastic movement, which speak only about government as it *should* be, *The Prince* talks about government as it *is*. Machiavelli advises Lorenzo to rule with calculating shrewdness, to appear to be the champion of virtues such as honesty and fairness, but to never draw back from being deceitful and ruthless when it is necessary. Machiavelli provides many lessons from history to support his advice, such as the following one about an Italian Machiavelli admired, the Duke of Milan (1979, 99–100):

> After the Duke had taken Romagna and had found it governed by powerless lords who had been more anxious to plunder their subjects than to govern them, and had given them reason for disunity rather than unity, so that the entire province was full of thefts, fights, and of every other kind of insolence, he decided that if he wanted to make it peaceful and obedient to the ruler's law it would be necessary to give it good government. Therefore, he put Messer Remirro de Orco, a cruel and able man, in command there and gave him complete authority. This man, in little time, made the province peaceful and united, and in doing this he had made for himself a great reputation. Afterward, the Duke decided that such excessive authority was no longer required, for he was afraid that it might become despised; and he set up in the middle of the province a civil court with a very distinguished president, wherein each city had its own counselor. And because he realized that the rigorous measure of the past had generated a certain amount of hatred, he wanted to show, in order to purge men's minds and to win them to his side completely, that if any form of cruelty had arisen, it did not originate from him but from the harsh nature of his minister. And having come upon the opportunity to do this, one morning at Cesena he had Messer Remirro placed on the piazza in two pieces with a block of wood and a bloody sword beside him. The ferocity of such a spectacle left those people satisfied and amazed at the same time.

In the midst of the English Civil War of the 1640s, yet another prominent political scholar arose. Thomas Hobbes wrote *Leviathan* as a systematic examination of the origin of government and the proper approach to rule. Written midst a violent conflict in which life indeed seemed "solitary, poore, nasty, brutish and short," Hobbes proposed that maintaining order in society was the primary role of government. Contrary to theologians who had assumed that government is ordained and established by God, Hobbes said that government comes not from God but from men. Human beings, in their natural condition before they become civilized, which Hobbes called a state of nature, are characteristically in conflict with one another. They come together and form a government in order to protect themselves from violence. Hobbes proposed that citizens should enter into what he termed a social contract with a leviathan, a powerful ruler who would provide security in return for their pledge of allegiance and assignment of the right to rule. For Hobbes, as with Machiavelli, human history, not the action of God, provides the framework for understanding politics.

Half a century after Hobbes published *Leviathan*, John Locke further developed Hobbes' concept of the social contract. For Locke, government was established by the consent of the people it rules in order to secure "life, liberty, and property." Writing during the nonviolent English revolution of 1688, Locke had much more faith than Hobbes did that people could secure a wide range of rights, especially those that allowed them to prosper economically. Locke argued that a social contract is no longer valid if broken by the ruler and that, once the ruler violates his people's trust, they have the right of revolution—a concept that had a substantial influence on Thomas Jefferson and the signatories to the American Declaration of Independence. Locke's approach to the study of politics, like that of Hobbes before him, was to draw lessons from history and construct a philosophy of government based upon the consent of the people.

Karl Marx, the founding father of communism, is discussed in more detail in Chapter 4 of this book. It is important to note here, however, that Marx proclaimed that he was the first, Machiavelli, Hobbes, and Locke notwithstanding, to base his analysis of politics not upon deductive philosophy but upon observation of what was actually going on in history. Marx reported that he had perceived the major trend of history, a dialectical movement of change propelled by class conflict in which the proletariat (the working class) would eventually overthrow the bourgeoisie (the middle class) just as the bourgeoisie had overthrown the feudal aristocracy centuries earlier. Marx's most lasting contribution to the development of political science is his emphasis on class conflict as the fundamental cause of political events.

An examination of many other theorists such as Edmund Burke, John Stuart Mill, and Friedrich Nietzsche, who have made important contributions to our understanding of politics is included under a variety of appropriate headings in the upcoming chapters of this book. Before proceeding with our discussion of them, however, we shall complete our overview of the history of the development of the study of politics by turning to a discussion of the teaching of politics in American universities in the years leading to recognition of political science as a discipline.

According to Anna Haddow's *Political Science in American Colleges and Universities: 1636–1900* (1969), a remarkable study of the early history of the discipline, "Ethicks" and "Politicks" were discussed in Harvard classes as early as 1642. Politics was a topic of discussion in history classes throughout the colonial period, and one of the earliest texts was Grotius' *De Jure Belli et Pacis*, published in 1625, "in which," so Grotius claims, "are explain'd the Laws and Claims of Nature and Nations, and the Principal Points that relate either to Publick Government, or the Conduct of Private Life." The writings of French political theorist Jean Jacques Rousseau were assigned in classes at the College of William & Mary in 1798 and not long after that, Locke and Hobbes were being read there, and, as Haddow notes, "The College of William and Mary claims the distinction of having actually established the first American professorship of law, as a result of the changes instituted by Governor Jefferson and President Madison in 1779." (Haddow 1969, 87). Masters theses at Harvard from 1770 to 1791 included the following titles (Haddow 1969, 107):

- Is the federal system the best fitted, above all other human institutions, for fighting a royal tyrant?
- Does a democratic form of government contribute more than any other to preserve the liberty of the people?

- Is it more necessary in a republic than in any other form of government that young men should be instructed in political science?
- Is public virtue the best security of republican liberty?
- Is a government despotic in which the people have no check on the legislative power?

The first chair of history and political science at an American university was awarded to Francis Lieber at Columbia University in May 1857. In 1876, Johns Hopkins became the first university to establish a political science department. In 1880, a graduate school of political science began to enroll students at Columbia University, and when the University of Chicago opened in 1892 the Department of Political Science was one of its original twenty-three departments. Finally, in 1903, the APSA was established at the Annual Meeting of the American Historical Association at Tulane University. From the earliest conception, the role of political science at American universities was not only to advance the knowledge of politics but also to equip students to be good citizens and to resolve the many difficult issues that politics entail. As Francis Lieber put it in 1858,

> One of the means to insure liberty—that difficult problem in history . . . —is the earnest bringing up of the young in the path of political truth and justice, the necessity of which is increased by the reflection that in our period of large cities man has to solve, for the first time in history, the problem of making a high degree of general and individual liberty compatible with populous cities (Lieber 1881, 26–27).

Haddow (1969, 249–251) notes that some of the most popular political science textbooks of the nineteenth century included:

THE FEDERALIST PAPERS

Alexis de Tocqueville's *Democracy in America* (1935)
Theodore Dwight Woolsey's *Political Science* (1878)
Woodrow Wilson's *The State* (1889)
John W. Burgess' *Political Science and Comparative Constitutional Law* (1890)
Woodrow Wilson's *The State: Elements of Historical and Practical Politics* (1911)
Woodrow Wilson's, *Congressional Government* (1885)
James Bryce's, *The American Commonwealth* (1912)
Frank J. Goodnow's *Politics and Administration* (1900)

The first major political science journals appeared during this period. The *Political Science Quarterly* was established at Columbia University in 1886; the University of Pennsylvania began publishing the *Annals of the American Academy of Political and Social Science* in 1890. The *American Political Science Review* began publication in 1906. By the turn of the twentieth century, several departments were issuing doctoral degrees, and today they number 117.

2.7   THE ERA OF SCIENCE
(1900–1970)

By the turn of the century, the goal of many leading political scientists in the country was to establish political science as an independent, scientifically acceptable discipline within the social sciences. Through inductive, accurate observation of political behavior, they ushered in the discipline's sixth era: the era of science. Their first task was to gain a new perspective on politics and political movements. Their second task was to break away from confinement to the methods of their parent discipline, history, and to seek a new place among the others disciplines from which they had borrowed much: philosophy, law, and economics.

Gaining a new perspective on politics entailed seeing things differently from both European political scientists and American politicians. Some of the most interesting commentaries on American politics and political scientists have been written by Europeans. Political science students today normally become familiar with Alexis de Tocqueville's *Democracy in America* (1835), for example, at some time in their undergraduate studies. In courses in American Political Thought they are often introduced to James Bryce's *The American Commonwealth* (1912). Following in the tradition established by Tocqueville and Bryce, in his book *The American Science of Politics* (1960) British political analyst Bernard Crick points out that the development of political science at the beginning of the twentieth century was in part a response to the progressive agrarian, labor, and educational reform movements that characterized the era. Crick notes how the reform movements of American politics constituted a development that was fundamentally different from the ideological and doctrinal struggles of Europe. Whereas the European movements sought to create collective national identities under strong dictatorial communist regimes, American progressives directed their energies to an ideal of individualism. Even so, says Crick (1960, 188), American political scientists, reacting to the reforms, began to see the political process differently from the ways in which the leaders of the movements viewed them: "Progressive reformers might still try to hold fast to the ultra-individualism of direct democracy, but the new political scientists began to see politics as a contest for marginal privilege by a great many pressure groups, mostly regional and economic rather than primarily ideological and doctrinal."

Because American political scientists were beginning to see politics differently from both Europeans and the leaders of the reform movements, American political science began to develop a unique character. As Farr and Seidleman note in their thorough history of the discipline, turn-of-the-century political scientists did share with reformers a desire to have the knowledge they gained become "an instrument for change in society" (Farr and Seidelman 1993, 107–112).

In the first decade of this century, political scientists spent much of their energies in comparing the histories of civic and cultural institutions, a method of studying politics which became known as "formalism." They believed themselves to be focusing upon the same general phenomena that were studied by historians and economists, but from a different perspective, which was described by W. W. Willoughby in 1903. Willoughby noted that the discipline at that time was composed of three studies: (1) political theory or philosophy, (2) public law, and (3) forms and functions of government and administration (Willoughby 1993, 60). All three of these areas of study were grounded in the methods of historians. In fact, the APSA had its origins in the American Historical Association, many of whose members taught political history and political science courses. The founding of the APSA occurred at a joint meeting of the American Historical Association and the American Economic Association on December 30, 1903. At this meeting, Frank J. Goodnow, professor of administrative Law at Columbia University, was elected president . The first vice presidents were Woodrow Wilson (later President of the United States), Paul S. Reinsch, and Simeon E. Baldwin.

By 1908, however, a reaction against formalism began to brew. Arthur Bentley, one of the leaders of the "revolt against formalism," proposed that the proper focus of the discipline is upon the political process, that is, the competition for power and influence among interest groups. From the founding of APSA to the end of World War I, two notable developments within the discipline took place.

The first trend of the World War I period was a direct result of the war itself. Championed most notably by Woodrow Wilson, a movement for world peace started that became known as political idealism. World War I was far more gruesome and deadly than any previous war in history. For the first time, submarines roamed unseen beneath the seas, sinking passenger, freight, and military vessels. Tanks appeared on the battlefield, and the force of artillery became far more effective and deadly. The technology of the machine gun far exceeded the intelligence of the general officers of armies on both sides, who sent their soldiers in wave after wave up over the tops of the trenches into the face of machine-gun fire for no effective purpose. Political idealists such as Woodrow Wilson believed that the technology of war was advancing so quickly that soon there would be weapons capable of destroying the entire human race. They were correct in their predictions, for it was only twenty-seven years after the signing of the treaty of Versailles, ending World War I, that the first atomic bombs were dropped on Hiroshima and Nagasaki, effectively marking the end of World War II.

The idealists reasoned that if war would shortly be so destructive as to end humanity altogether, an alternative to war must be found. The League of Nations was Wilson's answer. Wilson hoped that a community of national leaders, led by the Western democracies, could come together to resolve disputes peacefully and enforce a ban on war. Wilson's hopes, of course, were not to be realized. Wilson failed to gain the Senate's approval for U.S. participation, and the League that was established was far less effective than it would have been with strong American support. By the late 1930s, Germany, Italy, and Spain had installed Nazi or Fascist regimes, and the Soviet Union's communist government was well entrenched and carrying out a campaign of terror against its own citizens. One effect of these events upon the discipline of political science was to cast doubt, in the minds of American political scientists, on the heretofore unassailable notion of the permanence of democracy. Under the weight of these disappointments, political idealism faded, and by the mid 1950s the American realist movement, which believed in a strong military and active intervention in world affairs, had secured its domination of international political thought.

The second notable development after World War I was a quest for the basis for a scientific method of political study. Overshadowed by the events surrounding the war, the quietly developing strategies of political scientists blossomed in the 1920s in a series of activities.

Three national conferences on the Scientific Study of Politics were held in the early 1920s. Research into political attitudes began to reveal that, when it came to politics, the average citizen was neither very rational nor well informed. Political attitudes became the primary focus of research, and as political science began producing information of interest to practical politics, political scientists began to have a more active role in government. Charles Merriam, for example, the most prominent political scientist of the 1920s, became an advisor to President Roosevelt. An early leader of what became known as the behavioralist movement, Merriam taught many of the twentieth-century's leading political scientists during his tenure at the University of Chicago.

In an article entitled "Recent Advances in Political Methods," published for the *American Political Science Review* (APSR 1923, 17: 274–95) in 1923, Merriam noted several trends in political science at that time:

- a shift from philosophical a priori or deductive reasoning to pragmatism
- generation of scientific studies in criminology
- a continuation of historical inquiry into the development of political institutions
- comparative descriptions of political institutions
- increased observation and description of the actual processes of government
- increased use of surveys as an instrument of data collection
- new interest in the political applications of psychology

For many political scientists, the period of 1920–1950 was a struggle to determine what political *science* was all about, to develop a consensus on a concept of the science of politics and a set of methods such as had been achieved in other social sciences, especially economics. It was a task that called for imagination, energy, and a certain boldness of thought—qualities that, unfortunately, seemed in short supply in the country's universities during the middle years of the century. In *The Bias of American Political Science* (1940), Benjamin E. Lippincott described the reluctance among conservative faculty members, who felt vulnerable from a lack of financial independence, to bring forth new ideas. Lippincott also complained that far too little of the knowledge gained in the study of economics was being integrated into the study of political science. A third problem with the discipline, as Lippincott (1993) explained, was that an extreme adherence to empiricism had led to a dearth of theory:

> In view of our conception of the scientific method, it is hardly surprising that political science has restricted its scope so largely to the study of law,

organization, structure, and machinery of government. Most political scientists have been exponents in some degree or other of empiricism, and empiricism leads to a concentration on these aspects. Empiricism worships two doctrines: first, that if you collect all the relevant facts and classify them, they will speak for themselves (i.e., laws or principles will emerge somehow automatically); second, that preconceived theories or ideas about the facts are not only unnecessary but positively dangerous. . . . Hostility to theory has meant that political scientists would describe our legal and political arrangements rather than explain them. ... The truth is the empiricist is a victim of the illusion of objectivity, which must prevent him from being a thoroughgoing scientist ... The political scientist, to speak in more general terms, is guilty of two sins: a sin against reason and imagination, and a sin against courage. His sin against reason and imagination explains his failure to search beyond empiricism to a more creative scientific method, it explains his failure to widen the scope of his inquiries, and it explains his failure to transcend his middle-class assumptions. His sin against courage explains his easy acceptance of an autocratic system of government in his own bailiwick, although such government is contrary to the best thought of his science.

Criticisms such as this led to the birth of a new movement in political science called behavioralism. From 1950 to 1970, political science was dominated by the debate between the behavioralists and the traditionalists. Leading traditionalists, who preferred the historical, philosophical, and institutional approaches of previous generations, will be discussed in detail in Chapter 7 and therefore will not be discussed here.

Leading behavioralist David Easton notes in *Political Science in the United States: Past and Present* (1991) that *behavioralism* should not be confused with *behaviorism*: "Political science has never been behavioristic, even during the height of its behavioralistic phase. Behaviorism refers to a theory in psychology about human behavior and has its origins in the work of J.B. Watson" (Easton 1991, 278).

Describing the behavioral movement in which he had played an important role, Easton identifies several characteristics of behavioralism that make it distinct from earlier developments in the history of political science. Behavioralism believes, according to Easton (1991, 278–79) , that "discoverable uniformities in human behavior" can be "confirmed by empirical tests," including "quantification whenever possible," and which are "value-free or value-neutral" and place "emphasis on pure theory as against applied research."

In 1961, prominent behavioralist and Yale political scientist Robert Dahl, in an article entitled "The Behavioral Approach in Political Science: Epitaph for a Monument to a Successful Protest," noted the success of the behavioralist revolution in political science and outlined some of the causes for its rise. Among these were the efforts of Charles Merriam, the influx of European scholars in the 1930s, the practical experiences of scholars who worked in government positions in World War II, the Social Science Research Council, the survey as a research tool, and philanthropic foundations (Dahl 1961).

2.8   THE ERA OF ECLECTICISM
(1970 TO PRESENT)

"A new political science for a world itself quite new"
—TOCQUEVILLE, *DEMOCRACY IN AMERICA* (1835)

In the 1960s, political science entered an era that Easton (1991, 61) has called the postbehavioral era:

> What I have called the postbehavioral revolution—a name generally used for this next phase—began during the 1960s and is still with us today. It represents a deep dissatisfaction with the results of behavioralism but has not led to the abandonment of scientific method in political science. The postbehavioral movement, in its broadest meaning, represented the awakening of the modern world to the dangers of rapid and unregulated industrialization, ethnic and sexual discrimination, worldwide poverty, and nuclear war.

Although David Easton has called the present period in the development of political science the postbehavioral era, the time has come to give this era a new name. Political science is now in the process of attempting to define its own identity, to understand its place and role in the world. The label "postbehavioral" does not describe the character of the present era, except to say that it falls chronologically after the behavioral era. A more specific term, which aptly describes the character of the present stage of development of the discipline, can help political scientists better understand their challenges and opportunities for contributing to the broader human search for knowledge.

Anyone who studies the vast array of subjects being studied and methodologies employed within what is called political science will quickly see that the one term that most accurately describes the present state of the discipline is *eclectic*. This means that instead of having a single method and focus, political science is currently reaching out to virtually every branch of knowledge, borrowing ideas, combining concepts in new ways, and creating a study, which is fascinating in its variety and fantastic in its creative breadth. In the pages that follow in this book, which describe only a small and roughly representative sample of studies being conducted in the discipline, you will read many ideas that have originated in political science, but also many more that were first given expression in economics, history, psychology, education, business, biology, sociology, literature, physics, philosophy, law, and other disciplines.

Some political scientists are hesitant to adopt this term for fear it might imply a lack of internal cohesion and originality on the part of political scientists. But this hesitation must be overcome for two reasons. First, it is more honest to describe the discipline as it is than to avoid what at first may appear to be an unfavorable label. Second, and more important, eclecticism is a powerful approach to developing a discipline. Astronomers have told us that over the span of thousands of centuries galaxies expand and contract in regular cycles. Shrinking to small masses with incredible densities, they then explode in a myriad of new constellations.

Studies of the history of science show that academic disciplines also expand and contract in reasonably predictable cycles. As established methods or approaches (called "paradigms") become accepted, disciplines contract in the types of studies that are conducted. As paradigms fall apart, a flood of new ideas compete to build the new accepted method. For example, while historical formalism was the dominant mode of study of politics early in this century, it fell to scientific challenges in the 1920s. Behavioralists gained ascendancy in the 1950s, but by the 1990s a new profusion of approaches and concerns had emerged.

We are now in a period between paradigms, which is to say there is no dominant accepted method or approach, but many that are competing for attention. While this transitional period may appear to be a state of confusion, it is actually vibrant with creative potential. In fact, no period in the history of the study of politics has been more challenging or exciting.

Political science today hosts many specialties. In the United States, the field is organized by the APSA, which encompasses a number of regional and state associations that hold annual meetings at which papers are presented and discussions are held on a diverse range of topics. Below is a list of "sections," groups within the association organized to study a specific topic such as the American presidency or religion and politics. Looking at the list of sections you can get an idea of the diversity of topics studied within the discipline of political science.

Broadly speaking, the study of political science in the United States is divided into four major areas:

- Political theory and methodology
- American government, political behavior, public policy, and administration
- Comparative politics and area studies
- International relations

The 103rd Annual Meeting of the American Political Science Association, held in Chicago, Illinois, from August 31 to September 2, 2007, focused on the theme "Political Science and Beyond." with the purpose of "embrace[ing] the extraordinary potential of linking political scientists with researchers, teachers, and scholars from other disciplines." The meeting featured scores of sessions in which hundreds of papers were discussed by more than 6,500 members, exhibitors, and guests.

Panels at annual meetings are arranged in thirty-seven formal program sections, which are listed below to give you an idea of the range and breadth of contemporary political science:

APSA Organized Sections

1. Federalism and Intergovernmental Relations
2. Law and Courts
3. Legislative Studies
4. Public Policy
5. Political Organizations and Parties
6. Public Administration
7. Conflict Processes
8. Representation and Electoral Systems
9. Presidency Research

10. Political Methodology
11. Religion and Politics
13. Urban Politics
15. Science, Technology, and Environmental Politics
16. Women and Politics Research
17. Foundations of Political Theory
18. Information Technology and Politics
19. International Security and Arms Control
20. Comparative Politics
21. European Politics and Society
22. State Politics and Policy
23. Political Communication
24. Politics and History
25. Political Economy
26. New Political Science
27. Political Psychology
28. Political Science Education
29. Politics, Literature, and Film
30. Foreign Policy
31. Elections, Public Opinion, and Voting Behavior
32. Race, Ethnicity, and Politics
33. International History and Politics
34. Comparative Democratization
35. Human Rights
37. Qualitative Methods

In addition to the organized sections listed above, the following "Related Groups" met at the 103rd annual meeting to discuss their own favorite political topics:

African Politics Conference Group
Across Generations: Scholarship on Women and Gender
Aging Politics and Policy Group
American Enterprise Institute
American Public Philosophy Institute
Asian Pacific American Caucus
Association for Politics and the Life Sciences
Association for the Study of Nationalities
Association of Chinese Political Studies
Association of Israeli Studies
Association of Korean Political Studies in North America
British Politics Group
Campaign Finance Research Group
Canadian Politics Study Group
Center for the Study of Federalism
Center for the Study of the Constitution
Christians in Political Science

Committee for Political Sociology
Committee for the Analysis of Military Operations and Strategy
Committee on Health Politics
Committee on the Political Economy of the Good Society
Communitarian Network
Comparative Urban Politics
Conference Group on German Politics
Conference Group on Italian Politics and Society
Conference Group on Taiwan Studies
Conference Group on the Middle East
Conference Group on Theory, Policy, and Society
Ecological and Transformational Politics
Eric Voegelin Society
European Consortium for Political Research
French Politics Group
Global Forum of Chinese Political Scientists
Iberian Studies Group
Indigenous Studies Network
Institute for Constitutional Studies
International Political Science Association Research Committee #12
    (Biology and Politics)
International Political Science Association Research Council #36 (Power)
Japan Political Studies Group
Labor Project
Latin American Studies Association
Latino/a Caucus in Political Science
Law and Political Process Study Group
Lesbian, Gay, Bisexual, and Transgendered Caucus
McConnell Center for Political Leadership
Miller Center of Public Affairs
National Humanities Institute
Policy Studies Organization
Politica: Society for the Study of Medieval Political Thought
Political Studies Association of the United Kingdom
Project on American Constitutionalism
Publius: The Journal of Federalism
Society for Greek Political Thought
Society for Romanian Studies
Society of Catholic Social Scientists
The Cato Institute
The Churchill Centre
The Claremont Institute for the Study of Statesmanship and Political
    Philosophy
The Walter Bagehot Research Council on National Sovereignty
Women in International Security
Women's Caucus for Political Science

C H A P T E R

3

CURRENT APPROACHES TO STUDYING POLITICS

3.1 BASIC PROBLEMS AND CHALLENGES FOR THE *SCIENCE* OF POLITICS

We call the time in which we now live the era of eclecticism because beyond the idea that political science is the search for knowledge about politics, there is little profession-wide consensus on either method or subject matter. People calling themselves political scientists still *disagree* widely on two vital and basic questions:

- What is valid information (truth) concerning politics?
- How do we go about finding it?

These questions are known to philosophers as concerns of *epistemology* (the study of what can be known) and *metaphysics* (the study of how knowledge can be accumulated). The controversies that surround these two questions have appeared throughout the history of political science and continue today. Political science is by no means unique in this respect. Jonathan Hale has noted the lack of consistency in contemporary architecture, and many professions and disciplines are presently examining their most fundamental beliefs and approaches to finding the truth.

In order to understand the complexity of the problems involved in developing a political science hermeneutic, it is helpful to examine the strengths and weaknesses of the fundamental aspect of the process of acquiring knowledge in science: the inductive–deductive dialectic.

Political science, like all science, is dialectical. This means that there is a continuous evolving interaction among the attributes of the search for knowledge. Meaning flows from a chain of insights, passed back and forth from one part of the brain to another, from one insight to another, from one experiment to another, from one person to another, and from one discipline to another. In order to provide you with an idea of how the dialectical process applies to all aspects of the discipline, we shall illustrate dialectical process first from classical writing, then from logic and the conduct of scientific investigation today.

The most famous classical demonstration of dialectic as a method for discovering truth is found in the dialogues of Plato, written in the fourth century BCE, which we have discussed in previous chapters. In the dialogues, Socrates, Plato's mentor, seeks understanding through a process of questions and answers. A speaker (such as Socrates) asks a question, "What is justice?" Another person (such as Thrasymachus) answers, "The interest of the powerful." The first person then responds to the second person's answer, attempting to find a problem in the second person's logic. If the second person's statement is persuasive, the two go on to the next statement or stage in the discussion, attempting to build upon what they have agreed in order to gain more understanding. The dialectic is the process of evolution and change that occurs in the perception of truth held by the two speakers as the argument progresses. The back-and-forth action of the statements, objections, counter-objections, and confirmations eventually yield a conclusion about the subject at hand.

Socratic dialectic, like much traditional philosophy, is *deductive* in nature. This means that it begins with a *general* principle and then uses logic to deduce s*pecific* conclusions from the general premise. For example, Socrates states the general principle that reason is a higher capacity than courage or bodily strength, and from this principle he *deduces* that people who have the most highly developed intelligence should rule those who are bold and strong.

The first steps of any investigation in science, however, are normally *inductive*. This means that science studies specific phenomena and then induces general principles from what has been observed. Aristotle's study of governments, for example, was inductive. He studied about 350 individual Greek city-states and then developed a classification of governments and drew conclusions from his classification. From the observation of specific governments, then, Aristotle *induced* the properties of good governments and bad governments.

In all science, induction and deduction work together in a dialectical relationship to produce knowledge. Suppose that political scientists are trying to find the cause of voter apathy in local elections. They survey hundreds of *specific* registered voters across the country about their participation in *specific* local elections. The patterns they observe allow them to *induce* a certain general conclusion, such as "voters are more likely to vote in local elections when tax increases are at issue." Having induced this general principle, they may then examine a particular subsequent local election, such as an election for Mayor in Dallas, and *deduce* the proposition that if there is no tax increase on the ballot, voter turnout in the election will be relatively low. They can then test their deduction by determining if there is a tax increase on the ballot, and whether voter turnout is high or low.

A dialectical pattern is evident among the three major activities of political science: investigation, interpretation, and application. Investigation results in data. Data is interpreted. The interpretation leads both to further investigation and to application. Application leads to further interpretation and application.

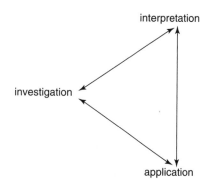

Although political scientists of all sorts employ the induction–deduction dialectic as a normal procedure for advancing our knowledge of politics, philosophers of science have found some important problems inherent in this procedure itself. The contributions of Thomas Kuhn and Karl Popper provide good examples.

Two points made by philosopher Karl Popper have stirred considerable controversy within the discipline. First, Popper argues that the structure of logic underpinning the process of induction is faulty. Induction proceeds on the belief that general principles can be found by examining individual phenomena and discovering patterns among them. Suppose that I observe, for example, a cow eating grass. I then observe several more cows eating grass. I find more and more cows and find that they all eat grass. I induce the general principle, "cows eat grass." I expect then to feel confident that I can thereafter deduce, upon encountering a new cow, that it will also eat grass. Popper points out that my conclusion is in error. Even if every cow I find does eat grass, there may be one somewhere that does not. In fact, no matter how many cows I find eating grass, there is still the possibility of finding one that does not. Inductively discovered principles, therefore, are not reliable for deduction. The whole process, followed daily by physical scientists and social scientists, is theoretically unreliable.

Popper points out a second problem with the way in which political science is normally conducted: observation is not value-free. Some political scientists had claimed that they observed only facts [statements about phenomena that can be supported by empirical (sensory) observations], instead of stating values (statements about the desirability or usefulness of a phenomena). In other words, facts concern what *exists*, and values concern what *should be*. Popper was fond of mocking scientists who, he believed, could achieve a value-free science by starting his college classes with a command to his students: "Observe!" They would sheepishly look around at one another wondering what it was they were supposed to observe. Popper's point is that when we observe we constantly make choices about what to observe and how to observe it, and that these choices unavoidably involve value choices. Science, therefore, is never value-free.

Thomas Kuhn pointed out another problem with one of the major assumptions of both traditional and behavioral political science. Scientists had long believed that scientific progress comes from collecting facts and testing theories. When new facts are discovered that contradict current theories, new theories are devised and tested. Kuhn noted, however, that although much progress is made in, precisely, this manner in day-to-day science, the truly great scientific breakthroughs come not from finding errors and making incremental progress, but from the creative ideas of geniuses who see basic relationships in an entirely new way. One good example comes from the theories of Ptolemy and Copernicus. Ptolemy believed that the sun and the planets revolve around the earth. Through many centuries, astronomers continued to believe this theory even though many of their observations did not seem to confirm it. Instead of coming up with new theories, they kept adding caveats to Ptolemy's theory. It was only when Copernicus made a giant leap to a whole new theory, the idea that the earth and the planets revolve around the sun, that science was truly able to progress. Kuhn's point is that, contrary to popular belief, merely adding more facts to the pile of knowledge does not necessarily result in scientific progress. Adding facts does, Kuhn maintains, further "normal science" in which important discoveries that aid our understanding are made. Popper and Kuhn together have helped demonstrate, therefore, both the strengths and the weaknesses of the dialectical process of the scientific method.

Before proceeding to look at some of today's leading approaches to the study of politics, it is worth noting that political science is still struggling with some epistemological difficulties that are now nearly a century old. In a 1925 article entitled "Recent Advances in Political Methods," Charles Merriam, a leader of then new scientific movement in political science, outlined four of the most important problems in attempting to study politics with the scientific method. The first problem was "the difficulty of isolating political phenomena sufficiently to determine precisely the causal relations between them." For example, to what extent do attitudes affect voting patterns? Is it possible to isolate the influence of certain attitudes from others, and from other factors in the environment, to determine the cause of a vote for a given candidate? The second problem, Merriam lists, is "the difficulty of separating the personality of the observer from the social situation of which he is a part." How, for example, can we frame survey questions so that they do not bias the respondent toward a particular answer? If we ask, for example, "Do you think the government is wasting too much money?" the way we have phrased the question may lead respondents to answer in the affirmative, which may not accurately express the respondents' actual belief.

A third problem was "the difficulty of obtaining the mechanism for accurate measurement of the phenomena of politics." How reliable, for example, are polls? Can we trust what people tell us is actually what they will do? How else can we get good, objective measurements of other influences upon politics, such as economics, ethnicity, and family relationship? Merriam's fourth problem, finally, was "the absence of what in natural science is called the controlled experiment." While we can test rats in a laboratory and hold constant the environment for a series of different stimuli, in the human political arena many factors change all at once. It is relatively difficult to conduct experiments under these complex conditions.

By 1996, some of the aspects of the problems Merriam mentioned have been resolved, as we shall see. Some of Merriam's concerns, however, remain.

The progress of the discipline toward solving these problems and the challenges that remain are the subject of this chapter and are discussed further in the remainder of this book.

3.2   GABRIEL ALMOND'S SCHOOLS AND SECTS OF POLITICAL SCIENCE

Contemporary political science today forms an intricate web of beliefs, approaches, methods, and philosophies. In order to understand how they are similar to and differ from one another, we must seek some ways to place them into intelligible categories. One of the more interesting and widely discussed categorizations of the divergent forces in political science is "Separate Tables: Schools and Sects in Political Science." Written by Stanford professor Gabriel Almond in 1988, this typology divides the discipline into four categories, two ideological (left and right) and two methodological (hard and soft). Although Almond's typology is twenty years old, the divisions it presents are still very much in evidence in the discipline today and are particularly helpful for providing students who are new to the discipline a broad perspective for orienting a wide variety of approaches and methods within the discipline as a whole.

Almond divides the discipline into four ideological–methodological groups: the "soft left," the "soft right," the "hard left," and the "hard right."

	Left	Right
Soft	Soft Left	Soft Right
Hard	Hard Left	Hard Right

"Soft" methodologies are descriptive and philosophical. They describe political movements, historically and philosophically analyze the attributes of political institutions. A biographical study of the Presidency of Jimmy Carter would be an example of a "soft" study. "Hard" methodologies are quantitative. They gather data that can be analyzed mathematically and statistically. Hard methodologies study directly observable behaviors such as voting and political campaigns. They use methods similar to those of economics and psychology.

Almond's methodological categories "hard" and "soft" parallel the long-standing division between behavioralists and traditionalists. Behavioralists are "hard" political scientists because they attempt to produce quantifiable (hard) data. Traditionalists employ methodologies called "soft" because their findings describe politics in qualitative, not mathematically expressed ways. Almond uses the term "right" to refer to approaches that focus on power and rational think-ing, and the term "left" to describe perspectives that concern social, economic, or political equality. Students should be aware that there are many groups in each of Almond's four categories, and this chapter provides only examples of each of them.

The Soft Right

Traditional Political Analysis

The first political science programs were traditionalist in content. They were heavily influenced by the German model, which emphasized history, economics, and law, and focused upon describing institutions of government and evaluating their effects upon the political process. The goal of the traditional approach is to improve government through understanding the way it works. Traditional stud-ies, therefore, describe government institutions, their constitutions and struc-tures, and then offer observations on the way the institutions serve the "public interest," and affect the values of freedom, equality, equity, justice, and order in society. Among the elements commonly found in political studies are:

- history
- biography, leadership, management, or personality
- institutions
- constitutions, law, and legislation
- issues
- philosophies, theories, methods, and concepts like freedom, justice, equality

The earliest examples of the traditional approach appear in the form of political histories such as Thucydides' *History of the Peloponnesian War*, which describes the war between Athens and Sparta in the fifth century BCE (Thucydides I.23). Thucydides lists the events of the war in detail, including the speeches given at major debates and celebrations, and concludes that "What made war inevitable was the growth of Athenian power and the fear which this caused in Sparta."

Roy Macridis, attempting to make the study of comparative politics more truly comparative, published an effective critique of the traditional approach to comparative politics in his 1955 book, *The Study of Comparative Politics*. Macridis found that the traditional approach, as it had been practiced in the field of com-parative politics to that time, was essentially noncomparative, descriptive, parochial, static, and monographic.

Macridis points out that supposedly comparative traditional studies only claimed to be comparative, but that even though they may present the constitu-tions, institutions, and political practices of several nations, they failed to con-struct criteria for comparison and then to apply these criteria to the countries studied. These studies, therefore, were essentially only descriptive, typically focus-ing on either the historical growth of specific institutions or the legal framework of a nation's power structure, including its constitution and laws. When Macridis claims that traditional studies are parochial, he means that most of them had focused on Western Europe and that relatively little had been done in studying the politics of the rest of the world. Since 1955 there have been many "area studies" of countries in all parts of the world, but some commentators claim that Western Europe is still overrepresented in studies of comparative government.

When Macridis says that traditional studies were "essentially static," he means that traditional studies had ceased to be innovative in their methodology and they continued to look again and again upon institutions from the same limited methodology:

> In general the traditional approach has ignored the dynamic factors that account for growth and change. It has concentrated on what we have called political anatomy. After the evolutionary premises of some of the original works in the nineteenth century were abandoned, students of political institutions apparently lost all interest in the formulation of other theories in the light of which change could be comparatively studied." (Macridis 1955, 11).

Macridis' final criticism of traditional studies in the field of comparative government is that "The most important studies of foreign systems, aside from basic texts, have taken the form of monographs that have concentrated on the study of the political institutions of one system or on the discussion of a particular institution in one system." For Macridis, and others engaged in the behavioral movement, to simply describe the institutions of other nations is not enough. The development of criteria to definitively compare a series of nations, or all nations, was needed. Political scientists such as Gabriel Almond and David Easton, whose contributions have been discussed in previous chapters, responded to Macridis' call with new methodological approaches such as systems analysis and structure-functionalism, which will be described later in this chapter. Before proceeding we shall examine two other individuals who have become very famous within the discipline of political science by using traditional methods, and who, responding to critics like Macridis, challenged the value-free emphasis of the behavioralist movement: Leo Strauss and Eric Voegelin.

Leo Strauss and Eric Voegelin

Standing above or perhaps beyond the rest on the "soft right" of political science is Leo Strauss. From his professorship at the University of Chicago, during the middle decades of the twentieth century, Strauss formed a school of thought that is unique in the discipline. It approaches politics so differently, in fact, that "Straussians" and other political scientists often find little upon which they can agree. In *Natural Right and History*, Strauss proclaims that modernism, relativism, and skepticism have poisoned Western culture. Modernism, to Strauss, is a trend in modern thinking which has given up the pursuit of truth. Claiming that all observations are valid only in relation to a particular place and time (relativism), modern science denies the existence of fixed, eternal truth, applicable at all times and all places (skepticism). But modern thought, Strauss believes, is wrong. Moral truths may in fact be found by clarification of the classical texts, especially those of Plato and Aristotle. These texts, carefully examined, reveal an objective moral order in which, by use of our reason, we may discern the existence of natural rights that ensure the protection and dignity of every human being. The essence of Strauss's method is to attempt to understand the texts of the ancients not in terms of our attitudes today, but in terms of the authors of the texts themselves. In *What Is Political Philosophy*, Strauss (1959, 68) declares that:

> [T]he seemingly infinite variety of ways in which a given teaching can be understood does not do away with the fact that the originator of the doctrine understood it in only one way, provided he was not confused. The indefinitely large variety of equally legitimate interpretations of a doctrine of the past is due to conscious or unconscious attempts to understand its author better than he did himself. But there is only one way of understanding him as he understood himself.

Modern approaches to politics, claims Strauss, mistakenly deny the existence of natural right, which, to Strauss, creates the foundation for relations in society. Natural right is a concept that derives from the natural order of the universe the principles of the innate dignity of human beings and their universal equality before the law. The rejection of natural rights by the modern world leads to nihilism, or the loss of all value. When political science gave up the search for objective truth, Strauss argues, it lost its value as a discipline. Condemning the "scientific" study of politics, Strauss announces that, "Generally speaking, one may wonder whether the new political science has brought to light anything of political importance which intelligent political practitioners with a deep knowledge of history, nay intelligent and educated journalists, to say nothing of the old political science at its best, did not know at least as well beforehand."

Eric Voegelin's *The New Science of Politics* (1952) also helped to revive the study of classical authors. Voegelin believed that representation is the central issue of politics. By this, Voegelin meant not merely the manner in which a member of the House of Representatives represents his or her constituents. More important, however, is the manner in which the values and interests of the members of society are represented in political processes and institutions. Voegelin called "gnostic," those modern political movements, like Nazism and Marxism, which mistakenly attempt to artificially resolve the long-standing problems of politics, and in so doing attempt to establish social patterns on earth in a manner that misrepresents human ability to live together. Gnosticism is the easy and wrong answer to the difficulties of life. Gnostic movements start when someone announces himself or herself as having the answer to life's political problems. This answer rejects the difficult way of faith, which calls upon people to rest in the beneficence of God. Gnostic movements attempt to "immanentize the eschaton." The eschaton is the final fulfillment of meaning in history. In Christianity it is described in the *Book of Revelation*, wherein Christ returns to free the earth of evil and establish a permanent kingdom of peace. To immanentize the eschaton is to try to bring final salvation from life's problems, however they may be conceived, to earth here and now. For Voegelin, Karl Marx immanentized the eschaton by proclaiming that the communist movement would one day bring an order of peace in which politics would be so minimal that the government would "wither away." Adolf Hitler's conception of the Third Reich could also be an example of a vision of an immanentized eschaton in which the Aryan race subjugated or eliminated all other people, who were viewed as being inferior. The problem with gnostic visions is that they often, as in the cases of Hitler and Stalin, lead to tragic results, including the deaths of millions of innocent people. Ironically, the result of Gnosticism is the destruction of the very goals it is trying to achieve because Gnosticism, so full of spiritual symbols, kills the vitality of spiritual life:

> The death of the spirit is the price of progress. Nietzsche revealed this mystery of the Western apocalypse when he announced that God was dead and that He had been murdered. This Gnostic murder is constantly committed by the men who sacrifice God to civilization. The more fervently all human energies are thrown into the great enterprise of salvation through world-immanent action, the farther the human beings who engage in this enterprise move away from the life of the spirit. And since the life of the spirit is the source of order in man and society, the very success of a gnostic civilization is the cause of its decline. (Voegelin 1952, 131)

Studies of the State

Strauss and Voegelin fall into Almond's category "soft right" because their research methods are traditional in that they examine the perennial questions of history and philosophy, and the conclusions of their research are conservative, that is, they point toward the reawakening of long-held values. Traditionalist methods are also evident in other schools of thought that may also be classified as "soft right." Believing that behavioral methods such as systems analysis and structural–functional analysis reduce political societies to so many parts that it is difficult to understand the unity of political systems, some specialists in comparative studies have recently given new attention to the state as a unit of analysis, and in so doing have to a large extent revived the traditional approach. Although many analytical concepts are used in conducting them, the new studies of the state continue the legacy of the traditionalist approach by focusing upon the state as the central entity in politics and government. More than just a government, they assert, the state is a cohesive set of systems that determine political life. The state is not merely an institution that responds to other forces in society but is a creative and vital source of important initiatives. These theorists believe that studying the substantially autonomous elites (groups that hold political or economic power that direct states, such as corporate executives or military leaders) will lead to explanations of domestic and international political events. In "Putting States in Their Place: State Systems and State Theory," Lancaster University (United Kingdom) political scientist Bob Jessup identifies "six crucial factors about the state or state system" that are most often examined by "state-centered theorists":

- geo-political position
- military
- internal powers

- external powers
- state managers
- pathologies

The *geo-political position* of a state is the status which a state holds in the hierarchy of nations because of the relative importance of its location. A state's geo-political position changes from time to time in history. Venice, Italy, for example, developed great wealth by taking advantage of being in a central location for trade in the Mediterranean in the late Middle Ages. Venice lost its geo-political importance, however, when other great European trading cities developed at the end of the Middles Ages. Holland, Spain, Portugal, France, the United Kingdom, and the Untied States came to power in turn, using the geo-political advantages of their locations to develop military and commercial empires. Geo-political power changes from one century to the next. Panama's importance to world trade is always significant because the Panama Canal shortens the ocean voyage from the Atlantic to the Pacific, but is less so at the end of the twentieth century than it was at the end of the nineteenth because forms of freight movement other than ocean shipping are now more available. American decisions to intervene in Kuwait's invasion by Iraq, but not in Serbian attacks in Bosnia, are largely a result, for example, of the fact that the oil resources and strategic location of Kuwait in the Middle East make it of much greater concern than Bosnia to the United States.

The *role of the military* is of central importance in the daily affairs of most countries. In the United States, even after the end of the Cold War, defense appropriations continue to account for a significant part of the national budget. Even Switzerland, which has a long tradition of neutrality in the wars in Europe, requires its male citizens to participate in military preparedness activities at times throughout their adult lives. The role of the military is especially important in Middle Eastern countries where wars have erupted frequently in the twentieth century. Political scientists study the *direct* influences of the military upon the state, such as military leaders in civilian positions and the potential for a military coup, and *indirect* influences, such as the prestige of military careers or the potential for human rights violations by members of military units.

The *direct internal powers* of the state are the executive, legislative, and judicial powers that help organize society. The state may use the direct force of military or police. During the civil rights demonstrations and antiwar protests of the 1960s, the national guard was called upon by presidents and governors to quell demonstrations that led to violence. The state may also call upon quietly existing but substantial *indirect* internal powers such as a sense of obligation on the part of the people to obey laws, pay taxes, and serve in the military. Political leaders use the media to strengthen these indirect sources of power.

The *external powers* of the state are those exercised in international relations, such as the use or threat of use of the armed forces, or economic sanctions, or the ability to give foreign aid. Its natural, human, and economic resources have given the United States an exceptional ability to employ military, diplomatic, and economic external powers since World War II, making the United States the world's most powerful nation for the last half of the twentieth century.

States are led by elite groups that state theorists call *state managers*. Not all state managers actually hold government positions. Some may be private individuals who are wealthy or widely popular. In some countries like Kuwait, a hereditary aristocracy manages state affairs. In others, such as Iran, religious leaders have extraordinary influence. In Japan, the executives of major corporations have substantial influence on government policy. Political scientists who study state managers are interested in the state's decision-making process, how elites gain their positions of influence, and how they relate to one another to form a power structure that guides the society as a whole.

The *pathologies* of state systems, which are the aspects or elements of the system that do not work well, reveal much about the distribution of power in society. In any state, some elements of the system seem to work better than others, and the relative efficiency of units changes over time. In the United States, for example, citizens were more impressed with public secondary schools in the 1950s, except for those attending segregated schools, than they are in the 1990s. Some state systems are infested with so much corruption that they are susceptible to continuous regime changes through elections or revolutions. State analysts attempt to identify the factors that lead to increases in both stability and instability.

The Soft Left

Feminism

In Gabriel Almond's construct, feminism would be also found among the perspectives of the soft left. In an article entitled "Feminism and Politics," Diana Coole describes two waves of feminism in modernity. The first wave is a movement to assert women's political rights, which has continued since it first appeared in the seventeenth century. The second wave is an intellectual movement that represents a unique perspective on politics; it is more radical than the first wave and seeks a transformation of Western culture. As Coole points out, "Feminism is, then, both an intellectual perspective and a social movement; its theories and its practice are interwoven." Feminism has gained much support for its theories from psychoanalytical thought. According to Coole (1990, 30), women are universally given primary responsibility for the care of children, and so women profoundly affect their children in both positive and negative ways:

> The girl who is like her mother and is strongly identified with her, gains a secure sense of her sexual identity but a weak sense of her own autonomy and ego-boundaries, owing to the difficulty of separation. The boy, on the other hand, is always treated as different and must gain a sense of his sexual identity from the absent father; his masculinity is predicated on his being not-female. The result is a weak and abstract sense of masculinity but a stronger notion of self-identity. From these early differences we see subsequent gendered proclivities for different types of knowledge and being. Females evidence a capacity for empathetic relationships, for cooperation and caring; they feel at home in the world and relate strongly to their environment. Men, on the other hand, are more strongly attracted to modes of abstract thought which

reflect their own sense of separation from the world. They distrust subjectivity and favour rational, objective, impersonal forms of knowledge and association. They fear that which is associated with femininity and pursue projects of domination over it.

Perhaps one of the most important contributions of feminism as an intellectual movement is its assertion that ideas of what is masculine and what is feminine can change over time. Societies can become more masculine or feminine. Women may always bear children, but the implications of this fact for their role in politics is purely a matter of culture and is not physiologically determined. Femininity, therefore, is socially and not biologically acquired. Coole points out that some feminists have criticized value-neutral political analysis because it tends to support the status quo, which equates to male domination. She notes that feminism favors neither empiricism nor rationalism. Feminine thinking is more empathic, engaged, and open than masculine thinking, which is power based.

Feminists have a wide variety of views, from moderate positions, which want to broaden the range of opportunities for women, to radical perspectives which, according to Coole (1990, 27), see "patriarchy as the most pervasive feature of social life."

In addition to the controversies that radical feminist views have generated, feminists have made a profound and revolutionary contribution to the study of politics. Coole (1990, 32) defines this transformational contribution as the idea that "politics cannot be confined to the macro-levels of state processes; that politics is defined not by proximity to a particular *institution* but by a kind of relationship, namely one in which power and domination/subordination are present." This realization, that politics is not confined to governments but is ubiquitous in all personal relationships, broadens the scope of political science from a discipline that looks only at the workings of activities related to governments to a discipline that studies the political nature of all human relationships.

Coole notes further that feminist writers have challenged not only traditional views of the nature of politics but perspectives on scientific methodology as well. She explains that the scientific method incorporates masculine (rational) attitudes that may be used not only to discover facts about political life but to dominate political life as well. To the extent that political science is dominated by theories of power and the state, and both the state and the positions of power in the world are dominated by men, then the scientific method becomes a tool of patriarchy.

Feminists are not yet a leading influence within political science, but many in the discipline expect them to make a continually growing contribution. The recent trend toward more empirical political research in relation to women is, ironically, as Coole notes, helping to reinforce a masculine method that feminists reject.

Political Psychology

The potential applications of psychology to politics have only begun to be explored. The father of the discipline of psychology, Sigmund Freud, provided a dramatic response to other schools of political thought, especially Marxism, at the turn of the century. Karl Marx, following a course initiated by Jean Jacques Rousseau, had believed that human beings were naturally capable of living in peace and that class conflict in society was primarily the result of faulty institutions. Freud thoroughly and profoundly rejected Marx's view. Freud proposed that the human psyche is composed of the ego (rational consciousness), the superego (conscience, or the capacity of moral choice), and the id (subconscious desires). For Freud, the id, rather than the ego or the superego, is the controlling element. As human beings we may see ourselves as rational, moral creatures, but in actuality we serve our subconscious desires for sex, comfort, and power.

In *Civilization and Its Discontents* written on the eve of Hitler's reign of terror in Germany, Freud presented a pessimistic view of humanity's ability to reform itself in any fundamental way. He contrasted two human drives, one for love and community, and the other for death and destruction, and noted that these drives are perpetually in conflict with each other within individual human beings and that they recurrently express themselves in society in crime, violence, and war. Since Freud's monumental writings, the study of political psychology has made notable contributions to the discipline. We shall discuss a few of the most famous works briefly here, and note some recent developments in Chapter 15.

Immediately after World War II, revelation of the atrocities that had been committed in Nazi Germany and under Stalin's communism led to an intense interest in finding the root causes of mass violence. The *Authoritarian Personality* (1950), a famous study by a research team headed by Theodore Adorno developed a measurement, called the F scale, to determine the extent of authoritarian tendencies in an individual's personality. The scale measured the following attitudes:

1. *Conventionalism.* Rigid adherence to conventional, middle-class values.
2. *Authoritarian submission.* Submissive, uncritical attitude toward leaders.
3. *Authoritarian aggression.* Tendency to be on the lookout for, and to condemn, reject, and punish people who violate conventional values.
4. *Anti-intraception.* Opposition to the subjective, the imaginative, the tender-minded.
5. *Superstition and stereotypy.* The belief in mystical determinants of the individual's fate; the disposition to think in rigid categories.
6. *Power and "toughness."* Preoccupation with the dominance–submission, strong–weak, leader–follower dimension; identification with power figures; overemphasis upon the conventional attributes of the ego; exaggerated assertion of strength and toughness.
7. *Destructiveness and cynicism.* Generalized hostility, vilification of the human.
8. *Projectivity.* The disposition to believe that wild and dangerous things go on in the world; the projection outwards of unconscious emotional impulses.
9. *Sex.* Exaggerated concern with sexual "goings-on." (Adorno 1950, 157).

Adorno's research suggested that authoritarian personalities, which are found in all societies, were susceptible to mass movements and likely to support dictatorships. It pointed in a new direction for preventing the problems of Nazism and communism: finding ways to help authoritarian personalities become more at home in and less aggressive toward society.

Erich Fromm's *Escape from Freedom* explored and expanded some of the concepts addressed by Adorno. For Fromm, two primary human characteristics combine to produce authoritarian movements. The first is masochism, in which the individual has "feelings of inferiority, powerlessness, [and] individual insignificance" (Fromm 1960, 42). The second is sadism, which Fromm, ironically, finds in the same kind of personalities displaying masochism. According to Fromm, sadistic tendencies

> vary in strength, are more or less conscious, yet are never missing. We find three kinds of sadistic tendencies, more or less closely knit together. One is to make others dependent on oneself and to have absolute and unrestricted power over them. . . . Another consists of the impulse . . . to exploit them, to use them, to steal from them. . . . A third kind of sadistic tendency is the wish to make others suffer or to see them suffer. (1960, 143–44)

From these studies on authoritarian personality, political psychology has taken off in many directions. Robert Jervis, for example, wrote a fascinating study of the psychology of decision making in international relations. He found that one of the greatest problems that leaders face in foreign policy is their tendency to shape information that they receive into their own preconceived theories. Policymakers during the Vietnam War, for example, originally assumed that a timely, efficient, and nonnuclear victory over the guerrilla forces of North Vietnam was possible, and held that belief long after the evidence demonstrated otherwise.

The qualities of effective presidential leadership is a recurring topic in political psychology. Many commentators have discussed, for example, Richard Nixon's paranoia, Jimmy Carter's penchant for understanding the operations of government in minute detail, and Ronald Reagan's focus on ideological concepts and lack of interest in administration. James David Barber (1972) classified presidents into personality types, according to whether they were active or passive, positive or negative in pursuit of their goals. Active-positive presidents, for example, like Franklin Roosevelt, believe that the president should take a strong role in making policy and directing the course of the nation, and they enjoy their jobs. Passive-negative presidents, like Calvin Coolidge, see the presidency as an institution that should respond to the actions of Congress, and they seem to take little satisfaction in the daily duties of the presidency. Recent studies of the presidency incorporate psychological concepts to attempt to predict presidential actions based upon personality and management styles.

Critical Theory

Critical theory attempts to diagnose the problems in society in order to help find a cure. Karl Marx is given credit by some commentators for being the first critical theorist because he recognized that the alienation of labor was the basis of class conflict and described how that conflict was to be resolved. Marx's view was optimistic. He believed that the developing processes of interaction in society would bring forth the overthrow of the middle class by the laboring class, which would then institute a just and fair society. Marx is viewed by critical theorists as someone who subscribed to a theory of *social rationalization*, a process by which society appropriates nature to meet its needs, and builds social structures of authority and influence on the basis of who is best able to put to use nature's resources. Max Weber, an influential twentieth-century sociologist, also believed in social rationalization but was more pessimistic than Marx. Weber saw society degenerating into an ever more complex set of bureaucracies established supposedly to help people meet their ever-increasing needs. For Weber, then, social rationalization is a process by which society, as it develops from medieval to modern forms, instead of depending upon tradition to form its social arrangements, turns to reasoned principles and uses these principles to build structures of status and authority.

According to the critical theories of Theodore Adorno, Herbert Marcuse, and others of the "Frankfurt School," a group of scholars centered in Frankfurt, Germany, objectivity in political science is inappropriate. All students of politics, whether they admit it or not, are unavoidably involved in the struggle between the rich and the poor. Political science is impossible without ideological commitment. Theory and practice cannot be separated, nor can science and politics. Both theory and practice, further, can be explained only by economic analysis because economic conditions determine societal relations. The primacy of economics in political life defines, more than any other factor, the perspective of the left side of Almond's methodological spectrum. For the "hard left," as well as the "soft left," the class struggle between the wealthy and the poor is the ultimate basis of all political action.

A theorist who has gained substantial attention for further developing a concept of social rationalization is Jurgen Habermas. Habermas' *The Structural Transformation of the Public Sphere* (1962) argues that the public sphere has collapsed. In his commentary on Habermas entitled *Jurgen Habermas: Critic in the Public Sphere* Robert Holub explains that:

> The collapse occurs because of the intervention of the state into private affairs and the penetration of society into the state. Since the rise of the public sphere depended upon a clear separation between the private realm and public power, their mutual interpenetration inevitably destroys it. The role that the public sphere had played in the intellectual life of society is then assumed by other institutions that reproduce the image of a public sphere in a distorted guise. . . . As we progress into the twentieth century, the free exchange of ideas among equals becomes transformed into less democratic communicative forms, such as public relations. Party politics and the manipulation of the mass media lead to what Habermas calls a "refeudalization" of the public sphere, where representation and appearances outweigh rational debate. (1991, 6)

Habermas has set out to understand how capitalist societies have developed, and to understand their weaknesses and failures. He finds that, because of its process of social rationalization, capitalist society has established economic and administrative institutions that threaten the development of culture. He believes that instrumental rationality, which is a way of thinking that focuses on efficiently achieving goals, is superseded in importance by communicative rationality, which brings into public discussion not only the question of how to meet objectives but also the value to society of the objectives being met. Communicative rationality is conducive to mutual understanding and leads to forms of consensus that build stable and peaceful societies. Although Habermas is concerned first not to judge the values of modern societies, but to explore the evolution of communicative rationality within them, he is critical of modern capitalism, seeing its injustices and inequalities as problems for theorists to help solve.

The Hard Right

Rational Actor Theory and Decision-Making Analysis

Much analysis of public policy is conducted according to what is called the rational actor theory. Its precepts are found in the writings of the soft left, hard right, and soft right as well as the hard left. It is included in the section on the hard right because it is here, among hard right theorists, that it has been most highly developed. Rational actor theory assumes that people will normally act rationally, which means in particular that they will act to maximize what they perceive to be their own best interests.

A "contemporary classic" example of rational actor analysis, with a critique of the rational actor approach, is found in Graham Allison's *Essence of Decision: Explaining the Cuban Missile Crisis* (1971). The Cuban missile crisis marks the peak of the Cold War. On October 14, 1962, the United States discovered that Soviet strategic nuclear weapons had been placed in Cuba. The United States responded with a naval blockade of Cuba, challenging the entry of Soviet ships, and setting the stage for a possible nuclear war. The Soviet Union responded by withdrawing the missiles from Cuba, averting a nuclear confrontation.

The analyst of international relations who uses the rational actor model examines the history of an incident or series of interactions and attempts to explain why the events took place as they did by finding a rational pattern in them. In *Essence of Decision*, Allison applies the rational actor model and two alternative models (organizational process and governmental politics) to explain the crisis and then compares the strengths and weaknesses of the three models. Applying the rational actor model to the Cuban missile crisis, he identifies the options open to both the Americans and the Soviets, outlines the comparative costs and benefits of each possible action as each party saw them, and discovers in the pattern of events the reasoning process that each side used in making its decision. Allison notes that this approach seems quite reasonable. It assumes that most people will act in a rational manner most of the time, and that government policies are most often the result of rationally ordered decisions, made by the officials responsible for making them. But Allison uncovers a problem with the model. According to Allison, rational actor theorists:

- examine a situation
- identify what seem to be the logical choices for the actors in the situation
- examine the choices selected by the actors
- find a rationale for the choices the actors selected

The problem with this process, according to Allison, is that rational actor theorists keep looking for a rational explanation for an event until they find one. Their analysis has no way of taking into account whether their "rational" explanation had anything at all to do with what actually happened. Rational actor theorists, therefore, apply a synthetic answer for events after the fact, an answer that seems reasonable, but may in fact have had nothing to do with the actions being studied. In *The Cuban Missile Crisis* (1971), Allison gives an example of how this error was made by rational actor theorists Arnold Horelick and Myron rush, who had tried to answer the question, "Why did the Soviets place missiles in Cuba?"

> The most widely cited explanation of the Soviet emplacement of missiles in Cuba has been produced by Rand sovietologists, Arnold Horelick and Myron Rush. They conclude that "the introduction of strategic missiles into Cuba was motivated chiefly by the Soviet leaders' desire to overcome . . . the existing large margin of United States strategic superiority." How do they reach this conclusion: In Sherlock Holmes style, they magnify several salient characteristics of the action and use these features as criteria against which to test alternative hypotheses about Soviet objectives. (1971,11)

Allison then notes that University of Chicago political scientist Hans Morgenthau made the same mistake in his rational actor analysis of the causes of World War I:

> According to Hans Morgenthau, "The first World War had its origins exclusively in the fear of a disturbance of the European balance of power. In the pre-World War I period, the Triple Entente was a delicate counterweight to the Triple Alliance. If either bloc could have gained a decisive advantage in the Balkans, it would have achieved a decisive advantage in the balance of power. . . ." How is Morgenthau able to resolve this problem so confidently: By imposing on the data a "rational outline." (1971,11)

In order to determine if there are viable alternatives to the rational actor theory for explaining the Cuban missile crisis, Allison defines and applies two other approaches. The first is the organizational process model. The organizational process analyst views political events as the products of large organizations rather than as the choices of individual decision-makers. Analysts have shown, through a series of studies, that bureaucracies have sets of procedures that produce results different from what one would naturally expect from individual decision-makers. Organizations produce change incrementally, according to recognized procedures. When applied to specific situations, these procedures may have consequences that do not appear rational at all. One interesting question about the Cuban missile is, "Why did the Soviets place missiles in Cuba when they had previously been pursuing a policy of détente and much of their effort continued to be in the direction of détente?" For organization process analysts, the explanation, according to Allison, is simple. One part of the Soviet bureaucracy was pursuing détente while another part was attempting to increase Soviet influence in Cuba in order to enlarge the Soviet share of the balance of power. This explanation of Soviet behavior, according to Allison, is at least as good if not better than the explanation offered by the rational actor model.

Another alternative approach is the governmental politics model, in which "events in foreign affairs are understood . . . neither as choices nor as outputs . . . [but] as a *resultant* of various bargaining games among players in the national government." In the Departments of State, Defense, and Commerce, for example, competing interests attempt to influence decisions, and the policies finally announced are the result of compromises among these competing interests.

Allison provides an excellent metaphor to explain the differences among the three models he sets forth:

> Imagine a chess game in which the observer could see only a screen upon which moves in the game were projected, with no information about how the pieces came to be moved. Initially, most observers would assume . . . that an individual chess player was moving the pieces . . . But a pattern of moves can be imagined that would lead some observers . . . to consider a loose alliance of semi-independent organizations, each of which moved its set of pieces according to standard operating procedures. . . . [I]t is conceivable, furthermore, that a pattern of play might suggest [that] a number of distinct players, with distinct objectives but shared power over the pieces, could be determining the moves as the resultant of collegial bargaining. For example, the black rook's move might contribute to the loss of a black knight with no comparable gains for the black team, but with the black rook becoming the principle guardian of the palace on that side of the board. (1971, 7)

Allison's work has challenged political scientists to refine their methodologies, and many advances have been produced. Having introduced one of the leading concepts of *hard right* theorists, rational actor theory, we continue our discussion with a discussion of a hard right theory that has become, in the 1980s and 1990s, one of the most prominent methodologies in political science: public choice theory.

Public Choice Theory

At the forefront of the "hard right" is a group of studies known by three different names: "formal theory," "rational choice theory," and "public choice theory." Public choice theory follows techniques developed in economics. In public choice studies, voters are viewed as participants in a political marketplace. A founding father of the public choice school in political, James Buchanan explains that

> The critically important bridge between the behavior of persons who act in the marketplace and the behavior of persons who act in political process must be analyzed. The "theory of public choice" can be interpreted as the construction of such a bridge. The approach requires only the simple assumption that the same individuals act in both relationships. (1972a, 12)

Albert Weale describes public choice theory in more detail:

> Rational choice theory regards politics as a particular set of institutions forming a process for amalgamating individual preferences into a collective choice of policy or outcome. . . . There is no assumption in rational choice approaches

that these preferences are motivated entirely by selfish considerations. . . . There is an assumption, however, that whatever preferences persons have, they will want to maximize the chance of achieving their most favoured outcome, or, at least the outcome that seems most achievable in the circumstances in which they are placed. This maximizing assumption is crucial. . . . Instead of asking how, in practice, preferences are amalgamated or how ideally preferences ought to be amalgamated, it asks instead: under what conditions will preferences be amalgamated in a characteristic way? Two characteristics have been of particular concern to rational choice theorists. The first is that of stability. . . . [N]o individual in the system is able to change the outcome from the sum of individual choices, given that none of the other individuals is prepared to change their choices. . . . [The second,] optimality, is the principle that everyone is as well-off as they can be, in the sense that no one can be made better off without making someone else worse off. (1990, 196–97)

Public choice theorists assume that voters, like people who have money to spend in an economic marketplace, will act in a rational manner. This means that they, as a group (an aggregate), will make choices that tend to maximize gain, especially short-term gain. Public choice analysts assume that free market economic and political systems are alike in providing for the most efficient allocation of resources. Politicians, voters, and lobbyists strive for benefits in the form of executive, legislative, and judicial power.

The objective of public choice theory is to analyze the rational choices (votes, campaign contributions, etc.) of voters and their aggregate consequences. Buchanan provides just this kind of analysis in his study of problems in the British Health System. Buchanan finds that the British Health System is failing because more demands are placed on the system than it is prepared to meet. Buchanan argues that the problems plaguing the British Health System stem from the British people, who act simultaneously through the government and the private marketplace to have their health needs met. The British people, through their government, have set up the National Health Service to regulate the provision of health care services, and they have set limits to the extent and availability of those services. At the same time, as individuals, they demand more services than the National Health Service is capable of providing (Buchanan, 1972b , 33). Buchanan explains that

The individuals who are the demanders and those who are the suppliers are, of course, basically the same persons acting in two separate roles, and the facts themselves suggest the inconsistency. My central point is that this inconsistency does not in any way reflect irrationality on the part of individual decision-makers, but that it arises exclusively from the institutional setting for choice on the two sides of the account. (1972b, 28)

Buchanan proceeds to demonstrate how the National Health Service provides services at a low direct cost that drives up demand for services. Thus, the institutional arrangements made by the Nation Health Service create an artificial contradiction within the individual who acts in the public sphere, voting for representatives who will limit funds to the National Health Service, and who also acts in the private sphere, demanding more services than the NHS can provide.

Game Theory

Game theory is one of the approaches to understanding politics that has developed within the field of formal theory. Some people view politics as a game, and they correctly point to similarities between games and politics. Politics is a contest with rules, winners, losers, tactics, and strategies. It is perhaps analogous to poker. How you play the hand you hold is often more important than the hand itself, and winning depends upon your ability to assess what others are likely to do. Politics is not, however, like croquet, in the sense that croquet is played for fun without serious consequences, nor is it like professional football games, which have as their objective merely to entertain and prove who has the better team.

Game theorists attempt to represent the possibilities inherent in political action by constructing "games," which are scenarios that allow for the precise description of the choice of action that a political actor has in a particular situation. The prisoner's dilemma is a game strategy situation that mimics actual political situations. Making this comparison enables political scientists to better understand the costs, benefits, and options for political action in real life. The following description of the prisoner's dilemma was written by Peter Ordeshook in his book *Game Theory and Political Theory: an Introduction* (1986). The prisoner's dilemma presents two choices for each of two prisoners. One choice is more risky, assumes a lack of cooperation with the opposing side, and has a higher reward, while the second choice is less risky, is based upon a sense of cooperation, and has a lower reward. Many political choices seem to follow this pattern. The prisoner's dilemma according to Ordeshook follows this scenario:

> Suppose that two prisoners, who are factually guilty of a felony, are locked in separate cells by the district attorney [DA]. Contemplating their fates, they each perceive two strategies: (s1) stonewall the DA and admit nothing, and (s2) turn state's evidence and confess all. The DA, however, sees an opportunity to extract a confession if he keeps the prisoners from communicating with each other and if he implements the following incentives: Realizing that if neither prisoner confesses, a conviction on the felony is at best doubtful, he nevertheless promises to make life miserable with several lesser offenses and a 10-year sentence at one of the state's less luxurious incarceration facilities. With a confession, he can ensure a felony conviction, and if only one prisoner turns states evidence, then the DA promises him parole in eight years, while threatening the less cooperative felon with twenty years and no hope of parole. Of course, if both confess, then both are convicted and the DA regards himself as less bound by any promises made with respect to securing a confession (a confession is now a cheap commodity) and both felons receive 15-year sentences. (1986, 206–07)

The diagram below is Ordeshook's illustration of the possible outcomes if different choices are made by each of the prisoners. The numbers in the boxes represent the relative gains and losses that each player may expect under each combination of options. In the upper right box, for example, prisoner 1 does not confess, while prisoner 2 confesses. Prisoner 1 loses twenty years of his life to prison, while prisoner 2 loses only eight.

		Prisoner 2	
		S1 (don't confess)	S2 (confess)
Prisoner 1	S1	−10, −10	−20, −8
	S2	−8, −20	−15, −15

Game theory allows decision makers to categorize all of the possible outcomes of different decisions made within a particular situation. They thereby gain a clear comprehensive view of their options, allowing them to make better-informed decisions.

Political scientists borrowed game theory from economists, who used it to understand fluctuations in market conditions. Political scientists use game theory primarily to analyze decisions. Most decisions in politics are made with less than complete knowledge of how people in different interest groups, parties, or nations may respond. An example will help illustrate how game theory is conducted.

Suppose that a group of terrorists seize an airliner and threaten to blow up the plane and its 100 occupants if certain demands are not met. The terrorists demand that fifty specified "political prisoners" be released and that the terrorists themselves are guaranteed safe passage to a neutral country where they will be granted asylum. A government representative is assigned responsibility and authority for dealing with the terrorists. We shall simplify the situation, which may in fact involve many options, for the purpose of demonstrating game theory. The government shall have two basic choices: (1) to comply with the terrorist demands, or (2) refuse to comply with the demands. The terrorists have two choices: (1) kill the hostages, or (2) free the hostages. These choices are illustrated in the diagram below.

		terrorist options	
		Kill the hostages	free the hostages
government options	comply with demands	1 A −1	1 B 0
	refuse to comply with demands	0 C 0	0 D 1

The numbers in the boxes refer to the consequences of the decisions. The government's gains and losses are represented by numbers in the lower left corners of the boxes, and the terrorists' gains and losses are represented by numbers in the upper right corners. Look at the box labeled "B." The scenario portrayed in box B is that the government complies with the demand of the terrorists and the terrorists free the hostages. If this happens, the government will achieve an objective, which is to free the hostages, but only at the cost of complying with terrorist demands, which may encourage terrorists to attempt this type of action in the future. The government's gains and losses cancel each other out, and this result is represented by a "0" in the lower left hand corner of box B. The terrorists, in the box B scenario, achieve their primary objective, which is to free the political prisoners, and suffer no loss in freeing the hostages, so the terrorist's success is represented in box B by a "1." Looking at all boxes one at a time, the whole pattern of likely choices and consequences becomes clear.

Our example of a hypothetical dispute between the government and the terrorists is rather simple. Surprisingly, though, this is why game theory may be especially helpful in solving problems. Let us suppose that instead of two viable options, each side to the dispute has seven viable options, which might include, for the terrorists, such things as freeing some of the hostages. The game theory matrix would now have forty-nine boxes (7×7) instead of four (2×2). Many more combinations of results are now possible. Game theory helps analysts systematically think through all the possible combinations of decisions and the possible costs and consequences of those decisions.

Game theorists have identified three different types of games. A *zero-sum* game is one in which there is always a winner and a loser. If two people toss a coin to see who keeps the coin, the results will be heads or tails, one wins and one loses, the sum of the loss for one (-1) and the gain for the other (1) is zero. In a *zero-difference* game, the parties succeed or fail together. Suppose, for example, that Adam and Wyn are writing a report, due the next day, which has two sections, section A and section B. Both people are capable of writing both sections. To divide the work, they agree that in the evening Adam will write section A and Wyn will write section B. Adam, wanting some peace and quiet, decides to leave his house and go to his cottage at the lake, where there is no telephone. When he gets to the cottage he realizes that he cannot remember which section of the report he has agreed to write. Wyn, at her own home, has the same difficulty, and cannot remember which section to write. If they write different sections of the report, they will both "win" the game. If, however, they both write the same section of the report, the report will not be complete, and they will both lose the game.

A third type of game is an *inefficient* game. Suppose that Chris is baking cake and Molly is baking cookies. Chris owns an oven but does not have a mixer. Molly has a mixer but no oven. Chris knows he can mix the cake ingredients by hand, but would like to borrow Molly's mixer for just a half hour, and use the oven all the rest of the afternoon. Molly also needs the oven all afternoon, but will try to borrow Chris' and keep it for as long as she can, offering the mixer in trade. If Chris keeps the use of the oven all afternoon, he will lose the use of the mixer. If, however, he gives up the oven for a while, he is afraid he will have a hard time getting it back, because he knows how badly Molly wants to bake cookies. If the two can come to an agreement, they will both gain the use of both the oven and the mixer. This situation is an inefficient game because the lack of agreement between the two players will definitely result in an inefficient solution, that is, one in which neither gains or loses proportionately from the situation, but both will lose in some way if an agreement is not reached.

Systems Analysis

Systems analysis is the legacy of David Easton, who defines politics as the "authoritative allocation of values," and a system as "any set of variables regardless of the degree of interrelationship among them" (Easton 1966, 143–54). A political system, therefore, is a set of variables which together authoritatively allocate values. This means that any set of variables (people, institutions, and groups) capable of making decisions about values may be called a political system. Easton intends this definition to refer primarily to governments, because governments, more than other institutions in the modern age, are the agents that authoritatively allocate values. It is important to note that this is not universally true. For most of the Middle Ages, for example, it could be argued that the Roman Catholic Church was the primary agent for the authoritative allocation of values. Aristotle, in fact, begins a discussion of politics in his *The Politics* with a discussion of families, which are micrcosmic political systems and certainly allocate values. A strength of systems analysis is that it can be used to understand political systems at all levels. Political systems may include, for example, a social club, a local church, a national religious denomination, a school district, a city council, a regional planning commission, Congress, or the North Atlantic Treaty Organization (NATO).

Conducting systems analysis begins with an understanding of the standard components of any political system, which include:

- *people*, groups, or populations who interact in the system
- *gatekeepers*, those who set the agenda for making decisions
- *authorities*, those who speak for the system
- *inputs*, including
  - *demands* for actions and services
  - *supports* that help maintain and strengthen the system
- *outputs*, or decisions made by the system
- *intrasocietal* (inside the system) *environment*
- *extrasocietal* (outside the system) *environments*
- *disturbances*, things that cause stress in the system

Once the elements of a system have been identified, a *flow model*, a diagram which illustrates the relationships among the elements of the system, may be constructed. In addition to the basic elements listed above, a flow model will also include the following:

- major *transactions* (one-way actions) among the participants
- *exchanges* (two-way interactions) with other internal and external systems of the environment

- a *feedback loop*, the manner in which outputs return to the system as new inputs
- the *co-variance*, or manner in which changes in some elements in the system act in response to changes in other elements of the system
- the *interdependence* of some elements of the system upon each other.

A flow model of the political system of a local school district might be diagrammed as shown in the example presented below. The diagram represents, of course, a mere outline of the information, which the system analysis would produce.

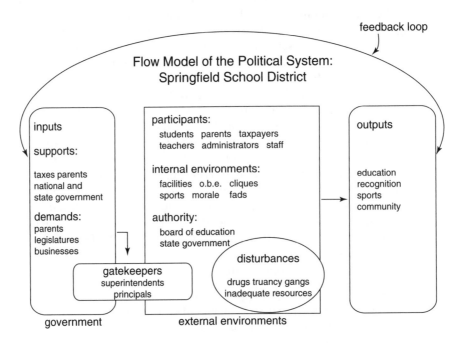

Systems analysis then proceeds to consider other factors, such as:

- levels and types of *stress* in the system; the way the system handles stress
- the *critical range*, or limits of the system's ability to handle stress
- the *openness* of the system to change
- *adaptibility* to new demands, stresses, and conditions
- *objectives* or purposes of the system
- the system's *potential* and *limitations* in respect to fulfilling its objectives
- *effectiveness* of the system in accomplishing its objectives
- *efficiency* of the system in converting inputs to outputs

Systems analysis is particularly useful in comparing political systems in different countries because while every system carries out the same functions, every political system handles those functions in different ways.

Structural-Functionalism

Gabriel Almond introduced structural and functional analysis to the study of comparative government in *The Politics of the Developing Areas* (1960).The political structures of any nation include political and legal institutions, such as executive, legislative, and judicial agencies; and the rules, such as the constitution and principal laws, under which the institutions operate. The political structures of the United States, for example, are first described in the U.S. Constitution, which establishes a federal system in which national, state, and local governments operate. The national government's institutions, including the presidency, the executive departments and agencies, Congress, the Supreme Court and other federal courts, operate under fundamental organizational principles, are also described in the Constitution, which includes checks and balances such as the president's veto power and judicial review.

A foundational principle of structural–functional analysis, as Almond points out, is that even though political structures differ from one country to the next, they all carry out the same basic functions. Almond presents four *input functions*, things that support a political system, and three *output functions*, things that the political system produces. Almond's four input functions are political socialization and recruitment, interest articulation, interest aggregation, and political communication.

Political socialization is the manner in which people learn the political values of their culture. Most political socialization is accomplished through mediating institutions such as families, schools, churches, clubs, and businesses. For example, for many years voting studies have indicated that a primary influence upon a person's choice of political party is the party of his or her parents. Families teach ideas and outlooks that are carried into the political arena by children brought up under them. The primary task of functional analysis, when studying the political systems of nations, is to determine the relative importance of various mediating institutions in shaping the political values and preferences of a nation. In some nations, such as Iran, people will be strongly influenced by a dominant religion. In other places, the political values of a person's social class will be more important.

Political recruitment is an extension of political socialization. It is the process through which society equips people for political roles by providing them with education and experience necessary to participate in the activities of government.

Interest articulation refers to the ways through which interests may be expressed. Functional analysis attempts to determine which groups are more effective at expressing their views than other groups, and the reasons for their relative effectiveness. Sometimes unwritten rules of expression are more important than the written laws of society in determining effectiveness of interest articulation. Because of these unwritten rules, some groups have less influence in the politics of the society than others. Native Americans provide an example of unwritten rules, which limit interest articulation. The culture of many native Americans is based on the concept of flowing with nature rather than trying to fight against it. Their religious beliefs incline them to quiet respect rather than aggressive confrontation. Their leaders are aware that because of their beliefs they are much less aggressive than other groups in politics, such as Christian fundamentalists, and that their articulation of their values in political issues is therefore sometimes less effective.

Interest aggregation, Almond's third input function, is the process by which interests compete, cooperate, and compromise to distribute the resources and make the rules of society. The American pattern is for interests to aggregate in political parties *before* elections. During the nominating process, presidential candidates attempt to draw into their parties as much support from as many groups as possible in order to form a coalition of interests large enough to get the 270 electoral college votes necessary for election. The United Kingdom, and other nations with parliamentary systems, however, aggregate interest *after* elections. After election of the members of parliament (MPs), the MPs elect one of their number as prime minister. When no political party elects a majority of the MPs, which is often the case, the party with the largest number of members must then make bargains with other parties and form coalitions which have sufficient votes to elect a prime minister. Interest aggregation takes place as parties agree to support each other's interests in the process of forming a majority coalition.

Political communication, the fourth input function, is the means by which political values in society are communicated. The primary concern of functional analysis with regard to political communication is the extent of openness in the system. Functionalists inquire about the extent of freedom of the press, the extent to which the major information services and media are either owned by a small group of people or dispersed among many people with a broad range of views. The first question functional analysts ask is, "Is there freedom of the press?" But they do not stop here. In the United States, we enjoy freedom of the press. But some commentators say that our abilities to influence opinion are far from equal. They point out that the major media organizations, newspapers, televisions, and radio stations are in the hands of a few powerful people. We note that individual citizens, like Ross Perot, may have a substantial effect upon a presidential election. But is such access available only to the wealthy?

Almond's three *output* functions are *rule making, rule application,* and *rule adjudication. Rule making* is a function, in democracies, first, of legislatures, and second, of executive agencies that implement the programs passed by legislatures. Rules may be made, however, by parents, school boards, city councils, state legislatures, and international organizations. Functionalist analysts identify the people who make the rules, examine the manner in which they are selected, describe the amount of authority they have, and estimate the extent of bargaining and compromise they must do.

Rule application is normally an executive function. Bureaucracies apply general rules to specific circumstances. The Department of Transportation, for example, makes regulations to apply the laws that Congress has passed to govern management of airports, highways, and navigable waters. Functionalist analysts describe the primary types of rule application structures, such as government department and regulatory agencies like the Interstate Commerce Commission. They then describe how a nation's customs and political culture affect the rule application process. Some bureaucracies apply rules efficiently, with a view to effective customer service. Others work through complicated procedures (known as red tape), and still others provide service only when bribes are paid.

Corruption and inefficiency can often be a critical impediment, such as in Zaire in 1995 when government operations were unable to respond quickly to the epidemic of the deadly ebola virus.

Rule adjudication, the final output function, is the responsibility of a judiciary. Functional analysts first compile a description of the court system, then examine the characters, qualifications, and cultural attributes of the participants in the judicial system, such as the judges, lawyers, and court administrators. The judicial process is examined next, including, for example, the extent to which most disputes are settled formally, through the courts, or in other settings. The analysts scrutinize the implications of such phenomena as a large number of lawyers in the general population and the extent to which the judicial system enjoys the respect of the people.

Communications Theory

Karl Deutsch applied cybernetics, the systematic study of human communication, to politics in *The Nerves of Government: Models of Human Communication and Control* (1963). According to Deutsch, the political system is a "self-conscious network" that is continuously self-responsive, which means that changes in one part of a system lead to adjustments in other parts of the system and to the system as a whole. He proposes that communication is the key to politics, and he compares communications systems in politics to the nervous system in the human body. Communications networks that produce political decisions are the eyes, ears, and nose of the corporate political body. Political systems are also "learning nets" or "self-modifying communications networks." Deutsch defines a learning net as "any system characterized by a relevant degree of organization, communication, and control, regardless of the particular processes by which its messages are transmitted and its functions carried out" (1963, 80). Information rather than political power is the essence of politics. Nations are essentially information networks in which power, instead of being an ongoing function of political systems, is normally employed only as a last resort.

Messages are the basic units of communication and are therefore the focus of cybernetic analysis. Messages are symbols which hold meaning, and are exchanged in many verbal and nonverbal forms.

For Deutsch and the cyberneticists what really counts is the process of decision making, rather than the implementation of the decisions. They believe that relatively small amounts of information, when utilized in decision making, keep organizations moving by providing needed direction. Deutsch compares the decision-making process in government to the steering mechanism in a ship. The small mechanism determines the direction the giant vessel will take. When Congress passes a wide-ranging tax reform law, for example, and it is signed by the president, only 535 people have produced a decision that will effect the personal lives of 260 million people.

Excessively rigid ideologies, such as extreme conservatism or extreme liberalism, induce a sort of selective deafness in the communication abilities of those who adhere to them because theses ideologies exclude certain types of accurate and valid information. Some communists long believed, for example, that the internal economic structures of capitalist systems were naturally bound to self-destruction as a result of inevitable revolutions by the working class. For decades, their ideology blinded them to the fact that, while communist revolutions did occur, they were by no means inevitable.

According to cybernetics, a political system's viability depends upon the system's ability to

- *absorb* information
- *process* it expeditiously
- *respond* appropriately
- *evaluate* its own response

Cyberneticists evaluate systems according to the above capacities by systematically describing:

- the individuals who are responsible for making decisions, their positions, and their responsibilities
- the laws, regulations, or rules that govern making decisions
- the steps in normal process through which the organization's decisions are made
- examples of decisions made by the organization's leadership, and the manner in which the decisions were made

The Hard Left

Dependency Theory

Political analysts of the hard left combines either a liberal or a radical ideology with a quantitative methodology. One example of an approach used by the hard left is "dependency theory," which applies a scientific methodology to propositions derived from a socialist analysis of the international political and economic system. Christopher Chase-Dunn, applying dependency theory, has attempted to objectively demonstrate that world capitalism consists of four interrelated classes:

1. the capitalist center (capitalists in the United States, Japan, and Western Europe)
2. the periphery of the center (exploited underclasses of the capitalist world)
3. the center of the periphery (dependent bourgeoisie in Latin America, Africa, and third world countries)
4. the periphery of the periphery (rural far Eastern and other peasant populations)

According to dependency theory, capitalist systems control the centers of economic activity. From this position, they continuously exploit the less-developed countries of the periphery by bringing resources from the periphery to the center in a pattern that keeps the periphery continually dependent upon the center. According to dependency theorists, only a transformation of the international regime from capitalism to socialism will eliminate dependency.

Gabriel Almond, the structure–function theorist mentioned earlier, is very critical of dependency theory. The portion of his response to dependency theory, which follows below, is exemplary of the discussion that is a continuous, necessary, and vibrant part of the discipline of political science.

> The analytic structure of dependency theory is relatively simple and straight-forward. World capitalism consists of four interrelated classes. . . . By comparison with Marxism and Leninism, dependency theory is incomplete and inconclusive. While it speaks of revolution and socialism as alternatives to the capitalist world system, the strategy, whether Marxist, Leninist, or some other, is left to implication. Marxist and Leninist theories are predictive theories. . . . Dependency theory is not very good Marxism or very good Leninism. Marx was far too good a historian and social scientist to have treated the world political economy as divisible into four class formations. The social periphery of metropolitan capitalism would not qualify as a Marxist proletariat, nor would the peripheral social groups of the dependent countries. A Marxist Revolution would have to occur in the capitalist industrialized world, and not in the backward, predominantly rural, agricultural periphery. . . . The dependency approach can best be characterized as a propaganda fragment of an ideology, a polemic against mainstream development theory. (Almond 1990, 231–33)

Almond's critique of dependency theory still provides a helpful overview of the philosophical and methodological controversies that abound in the era of eclecticism. You will find a much more sophisticated and detailed review of recent developments in political science in Ira Katznelson and Helen V. Milner's *Political Science: The State of the Discipline* (2002). Before concluding this historical overview, however, it is helpful to say a few words about the influence of postmodern thinking on political science.

3.3   POSTMODERNISM AND POLITICAL SCIENCE

Postmodernism is an approach to solving philosophical problems, perhaps best defined by French philosopher Francois Lyotard, who defined it as "suspicion of metanarratives." A metanarrative may be simplistically defined as a world view or ideology. It is a comprehensive perspective that answers the major questions of philosophy, such as ontology (What exists?), epistemology (How do we know what exists?), and What is the meaning of life? Many cultural, philosophical, religious, and psychological belief systems are metanarratives because they purport to have answers to these and other questions. Mormonism, Freudianism, Marxism, existentialism, and Hare Krishna are all metanarratives. Why are postmodern thinkers suspicious of metanarratives? They reject the idea that the

Truth will ever be found. Pointing to the vast variety of competing metanarratives in the world, they insist that no single Truth will ever be found that will gain the acceptance of even a majority, much less most of the world's population. Furthermore, metanarratives are political instruments that, while purporting to bring people freedom, actually subject people to political power. Therefore, while premodern and modern thinkers (e.g., St. Thomas Aquinas and Karl Marx) attempt to construct or support a particular metanarrative, postmodern thinkers have lost faith in metanarratives per se and are suspicious of the power structures that are supported by them. Instead of attempting to construct definitive philosophical systems, postmodern philosophers analyze the power relationships implicit in metanarratives and in the movements that subscribe to them. Along with Lyotard, Jacques Derrida and Michel Foucault are particularly prominent postmodern thinkers. Before briefly describing their contributions, however, it is helpful to understand how postmodern thinking evolved in the history of philosophy. The evolution began when philosophers (Hobbes, Locke, and others) recognized that adherents to the world's great religions not only opposed each other but held differing concepts of morality as well. The question then arose: Can human reason alone, without religion, construct a universally valid and acceptable system of morality?

Modern thinkers, Immanuel Kant (1724–1804) for example, answered in the affirmative. The basic question for Kant was "Can human reason alone, unaided by gods or religious traditions, tell us how to know what is right and what is wrong?" "Yes!" Kant answered. His primary philosophical tool for distinguishing right and wrong was the "categorical imperative," defined in his *Groundwork of the Metaphysics of Morals* (1785). The principle of the categorical imperative is that each person should "act only according to the maxim of action that you can at the same time will to be a universal law." Suppose, for example, that you propose to steal your neighbor's car. Can you will that obtaining articles by theft should be a universal law? If you cannot, you should change your behavior to conform to a principle that you would want to see universally applied. For Kant, moral law commands that we act rationally, that is, in our own long-term best interests. This command represents an imperative, which becomes categorical by applying it to all possible situations. Kant assumes that the value of human existence is, universally, the foundation of morality. The categorical imperative means, therefore, that you should "act so that you treat humanity, whether in your person or in that of another, always as an end and never as a means only." Kant, therefore, will not allow that any principle that you wish to universalize will meet the conditions of the categorical imperative. For example, Kant would reject the idea that the strong should dominate the weak because it treats part of humanity as means rather than ends. Although Kant's work has been highly influential among professional philosophers, it has failed to grasp the imagination of the general public, most of whom adhere to one religious tradition or another. Another problem with Kant's approach is that the categorical imperative does not instantly produce universally valid moral principles on all issues. Substantial disagreements arise among different people, honestly attempting to clearly define what principles should be adopted in particular cases.

The greatest challenge to modern thinking (metanarratives), however, was posed by Prussian philosopher Friedrich Nietzsche (1844–1900). If Nietzsche could have spoken a benediction for the nineteenth century, he would have called it sick. If the century could have responded, it might have placed a mirror before the German philosopher, and asked him if he was not merely projecting his own infirmity onto humanity, for Nietzsche had taken opium to relieve his migraine headaches and eventually died of what was probably syphilis after years of extreme mental instability. These problems, however, did not keep him from writing a condemnation of Western civilization and a vision for a new future that have had profound effects upon philosophy.

Nietzsche's philosophy has not yet ceased to shock and bewilder defenders of traditional Western culture, which he attacked with vigor and vituperation. For Nietzsche, Western civilization, at the close of the nineteenth century, had reached a state of almost total degeneration, a process that had started in ancient Greece. Before the time of Socrates (480–399 BCE), intelligent, creative and, above all, powerful men were honored by ordinary people. *Oedipus Rex* and the other great Greek tragedies of the pre–Socratic era expressed, for Nietzsche, an appreciation for the true character of life. In Nietzsche's interpretation, these tragedies portrayed life as inherently irrational and capricious. The true hero within them is not the naive optimist but rather the hard core pessimist who grasps the absurdity of life and bends it to his own will.

The degeneration of culture began in Greece with Socrates and his student Plato, who together proposed the idea, which Nietzsche found ridiculous and deceitful, that reason governs the universe. Even Socrates and Plato, however, could not surpass the damage done to Western civilization by Christianity, which Nietzsche called "Platonism for the people." For Nietzsche, Christianity was one of two forms of morality that vied for dominance of the world: slave morality and master morality. Christianity was the ultimate slave morality because it advocated meekness, altruism, and submission to authority. Such values produce weak, cowardly, and soft people, who perpetuate "defective, diseased, degenerating forms of life." The pre–Socratic Greeks had built a master morality with which they dominated inferior cultures. Western civilization, however, from Socrates forward, had followed Plato and Christianity and had thereby sunk into degradation.

In *Thus Spake Zarathustra* (1885), Nietzsche proclaimed that God is dead. A confirmed atheist, Nietzsche believed that God was once alive because people, particularly Christians, believed in him. God is now dead because modern science has demonstrated that there is no evidence for the existence of God and that God must therefore have been created by people who wanted to believe in him. Nietzsche hoped and believed that the death of God meant the death of Christian morality.

Christianity, further, promoted the rise of democracy, which to Nietzsche was rule by the mediocre, since most people are lazy and stupid. Western civilization in the nineteenth century had allowed the mediocre to rule not only through democracies but through the influence of public opinion upon the policies of monarchies as well. The values of democracy, such as equality, do not elevate the lowly. Instead, they bring the people who might have been great down to the lowest common denominator of education and culture.

With the death of God, people could discover their own creative possibilities because they could finally discover their own will to power, which would obliterate both Christianity and democracy. The will to power is the creative force that generates life. The will to power does not press people to seek out objective concepts of reality, truth, and goodness, because they do not exist. The will to power moves people to create their own forms and concepts of existence.

Nietzsche's ontology, his philosophy of what exists, is the aspect of his philosophy that has had the greatest direct effect on postmodernism. For Nietzsche, there is no objectively identifiable reality. Only differing perspectives of reality exist, and powerful people will create their own realities. In the future, these powerful men who create their own realities will become what Nietzsche called supermen. The superman will be the totally actualized human being who has created all things new for himself. The superman will be totally free and, living within the eternal return of time, will create new forms of philosophy that will transcend traditional concepts of good and evil and generate new forms of culture, which will surpass Christianity and democracy.

Ironically, Nietzsche thought that the superman may discover that the past, present, and future may exist in a continuous state, a form understood to primitive peoples as the myth of the eternal return (described in Chapter 2 of this book). He had always believed that philosophers of the nineteenth century had misunderstood the meaning of history. In *The Use and Abuse of History* (1874), Nietzsche argued against Hegel's idea of the meaning of history. For George Wilhelm Friedrich Hegel (1770–1831), history was the unfolding of reason, a process guided by a spiritual rationality, which had found its final fulfillment in Hegel's own time. For Nietzsche, history was anything but rational; in fact, it was highly irrational. Looking back through time, he found neither reason in history nor the likelihood of an ultimate end to history. The superman would continuously create new realities, and history, as his contemporaries saw it, would disappear.

For all his erratic rambling, Nietzsche was spectacularly successful, for he aimed a blow at modern secular philosophy from which it has never recovered. It might be simply stated like this. Why would anyone (if God is not in the picture) adopt any system of morality? The only answer is that he or she would expect it to be in his or her self-interest, that is, it would produce more good than bad. People choose not to cheat, steal, or kill, for example, because they do not want to be cheated, stolen from, or killed. Let us suppose, however, that you are stronger than others. You find that you can cheat, steal, and kill, taking all you want when you want it. Is it in your interest to act morally? Even if you personally would get immense satisfaction from simply doing what is good for others, many people, perhaps even most, will not. You do not have to look as far as Joseph Stalin or Mao Zedong (each of whom was responsible for the deaths of millions of people) for examples. Others live next door, work in your office, and attend your church. Nietzsche's insight was that moral systems are largely philosophical constructs employed by the powerful to keep the powerless subject to the ruling regime, and his influence is due to the fact that no one has successfully refuted him.

Postmodern thinkers accept Nietzsche's claim that systems of morality, no matter how well intended, are philosophical power structures. Postmodernists, therefore, attempt to help people to understand how these power structures affect them. Two of the most influential postmodern thinkers are Jacques Derrida and Michel Foucault.

Jacques Derrida (1930–2004) was born in El Biar, Nigeria, and for years directed the *Ecole des Hautes Etudes en Sciences Sociales* in Paris. He was a leading figure in the poststructuralist, deconstructionist movement, a school of philosophy that seeks to discover the multiple meanings and underlying assumptions in contemporary social thought. Derrida, building upon Nietzsche's and Heidegger's thought, with insights from Marx and Freud, held that language is inadequate to represent reality. He scrutinized texts for multiple meanings, which he found as *"differences"* in the meanings of words in the texts. To deconstruct a text is therefore to find the "differences" in meanings of the words in it, and to understand the implications of those differances. Deconstruction, therefore, opens our minds to new realms of possibilities, which in turn provide the freedom to explore new forms of knowledge and meaning.

Michel Foucault (1926–1984) was Professor of the History of Systems of Thought at the Collège de France. Although late in his career he became a political activist, he became most famous for his studies on French penal and health systems and on the history of sexuality. Among his most important works are *The History of Madness in the Classical Age* (1961), *The Birth of the Clinic* (1963), *The Order of Things*, and *Discipline and Punish* (1975).

Building on ideas from Nietzsche, Foucault constructed two new analytical tools that he called *archaeology* and *genealogy*. Rather than the science of excavating ruins and studying the artifacts of ancient cultures, Foucault's archaeology is a form of historiography (the study of how to study history). Foucault faulted historians for continuously constructing grand schemes of historical trends and then explaining specific historical events as manifestations of those trends. Instead, archaeology examines historical events within the narrow context of the places and times in which they occurred, and often finds that events are simply accidental.

Foucault's genealogy, similarly, is not finding ancestors to fill your family tree. Instead, it is a process of identifying *subjectification* and *objectification*. Subjectification is the process in which people become subject to norms, customs, and institutions. Foucault finds that society constructs elaborate systems of behavior control, some of the most powerful of which are *disciplines* (the discipline of political science, for example), which fix strict boundaries on acceptable behaviors and patterns of thought. To gain a better understanding of foucault's thought, read Section 14.3 of this manual, which describes Foucault's application of Jeremy Bentham's panopticon.

4

SOME QUANTITATIVE METHODS
IN POLITICAL SCIENCE

4.1 THE BASICS OF SCIENTIFIC KNOWLEDGE

In this chapter, we examine some quantitative methods commonly used for analyzing politics. Please note that some of the basic methods utilized by political scientists (surveys, policy analysis, and comparative analysis) are discussed in detail in other chapters and are therefore omitted here.

Quantitative methodology includes methods of study in which observations about politics are collected as data and then placed into categories that can be analyzed numerically. Paradigms of political exegesis are *specific* detailed methods of critical interpretation of political events. We are therefore about to study ways of conducting numerical analyses that help us to interpret political events.

Science, as it is understood at the end of the twentieth century, is the process of observing, categorizing, and analyzing empirical data. Relationships among empirical phenomena are discovered through counting, measuring, classifying, and organizing. Many of the qualitative approaches and perspectives on politics discussed in the previous chapter disregard quantitative measures in describing and evaluating political activities, and many of them are normative, that is, they bring value judgments to bear upon the subject matter. Quantitative measurements normally attempt to reduce the effects of normative judgments in the study of politics to a bare minimum, if not eliminate them all together in order to produce facts, which are observations that may be verified through recognized procedures.

Some commentators have argued that it is impossible to eliminate normative concerns completely from the study of politics. They claim, following the ideas of Karl Popper, that the act of choosing a subject to study itself includes a value judgment. Although quantitative political scientists are aware of these concerns, they attempt to reduce the effect of bias in their measurements as much as possible in order to make their studies value-free and objective as possible.

In addition to being nonnormative, scientific knowledge has several other characteristics. First, scientific knowledge is replicable. This means that the phenomena observed under a particular set of conditions will behave in the same manner whenever those same conditions exist. If two measurements of the same phenomena yield different results, then some significant variable in the process must have changed.

Second, scientific knowledge is also generalizable. The object of science is to discover principles or laws that apply from one situation to another, so that causes of phenomena can be found, and perhaps future events might be predicted.

Finally, as we discussed in the introduction to this book and in the previous chapter, science proceeds through a dialectical process of induction and deduction, wherein specific observations are generalized into principles from which further specific observations may be anticipated.

4.2 THE BASICS OF SOCIAL SCIENCE RESEARCH

Science is conducted primarily through the testing of hypotheses. A research hypothesis is a preliminary educated guess about the anticipated results of a scientific experiment. A hypothesis gives direction and purpose to a study before it has begun. If you do not know what it is you are trying to accomplish, how can you accomplish anything? A hypothesis is a declarative sentence that states that a specific *relationship* exists between two or more variables. *Variables* are the phenomena being observed, such as negative campaign ads or votes. A political scientist, for example, might develop the following research hypothesis: "Candidates who use negative campaign advertising are more likely to win elections." This hypothesis states that there is a specific relationship between two variables: (1) negative campaign advertising and (2) votes in elections. The hypothesis may or may not be true, but it serves as a starting place, giving direction to the inquiry.

The *dependent* variable is the phenomenon that is affected by other variables. In our example, voter turnout is the *dependent* variable. The *independent* variable is the phenomenon that may have some effect upon the dependent variable. Campaign advertising, therefore, is the independent variable in our example.

Antecedent variables are phenomena, which act upon or relate to independent variables. In our example, "candidates who use negative campaign advertising are more likely to win elections," antecedent variables could be factors that affect how negative the campaign ads are, such as the results of polls that show voter's reaction to previous ads, or the philosophy of the campaign manager concerning negative ads. Candidates who run negative campaign ads run the risk of going too far, creating sympathy for those they are trying to discredit.

Intervening variables are variables other than the independent variable that affect the dependent variable directly. In our example, since usually days or weeks pass between the time campaign, ads are published or broadcast, and at the time of the election, the response to the ad by the opposing candidate might be an intervening variable. Another intervening variable might be an endorsement of a particular candidate by an influential person.

Our example hypothesis, in a diagram that represents the relationships among the variables, looks like this:

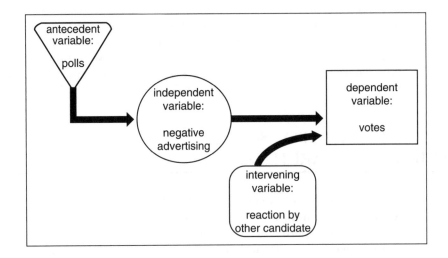

Identifying the dependent, independent, antecedent, and intervening variables helps researchers to carefully define the relationships they are examining. Hypotheses are constructed in order to find out what relationship, if any, exists between the independent and dependent variables. The hypothesis also states the nature of the relationship between the two variables. Relationships between variables are called correlations. Correlations between variables are of various types. Direct correlations are those in which as one variable increases, the other variable also increases. If, for example, candidates who are above average height tend to be elected more often than candidates who are below average height, then a direct correlation is observed between the height of the candidate and getting elected. Inverse correlations are those in which as one variable increases, the other variable decreases. If voters go to the polls less often when it rains, then rain and voting have an inverse correlation to one another. In a logarithmic correlation, one variable will increase or decrease at a different rate than the other variable in such a manner that eventually, as one variable increases, the other ceases to increase, or virtually ceases to increase. Suppose, for example, that a study of state legislative candidates finds that the more education candidates have, up through four years of college (sixteen years or education, or a bachelor's degree), the more likely they are to be elected; but candidates who have advanced degrees are no more likely to be elected than candidates who have just a bachelor's degree.

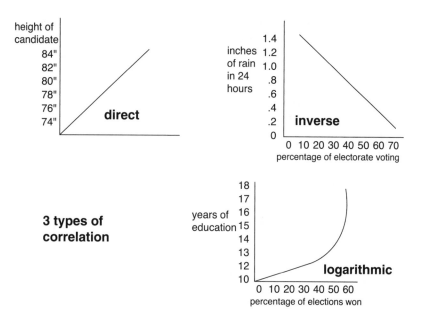

A hypothesis is said to be "true" if the relationship specified in the hypothesis is indeed found to exist between the variables that are being studied. Hypotheses are constructed for the sole purpose of testing whether or not they are true. Hypotheses are used to develop theories that help to explain how certain conditions lead to certain behaviors or results.

Testing a hypothesis requires the researcher to *measure* the amount of change in the dependent variable as change is observed in the independent variable. This requires making accurate measurements of the dependent and independent variables as they vary over time or in different circumstances.

Measurement of variables begins with a determination of the appropriate level of measurement. There are four levels of measurement: nominal, ordinal, interval, and ratio.

Nominal measurements are for types of information that are in no sequential or rank order; they are simply different. For example, if you are analyzing voter information by state of residence, some of your categories might be Washington, Oregon, California, Wyoming, and Montana.

Ordinal data is data for which one category is more or less than another, but the differences between categories are not exact, similar, or stable. For instance, "children" (ages 1–18), "adults" (ages 19–65), and "senior citizens" (ages 66–100) are categories that apply to age groupings that demonstrate an increase in age, but the number of years that defines each category is not the same.

Interval data has an arbitrary zero point, like years on a calendar, temperature, or the labels "liberal" and "conservative" on a political spectrum.

Ratio data is data for which the zero point actually represents an absence of the phenomena being studied. If one is comparing the number of votes received by two candidates, zero votes form a baseline of comparison, and we may accurately say that a particular candidate has received twice or three times as many votes as another candidate because we are using ratio data. If we were using interval data, such as a spectrum of ideology, we cannot say that one candidate is twice as conservative as another because no point on our ideological spectrum is objectively fixed. In ratio data, therefore, unlike nominal, ordinal, or interval data, the values that are quantified can be multiplied and divided.

To be called accurate, measurements must be *valid*, that is, they must measure the effects they are supposed to measure instead of measuring something else. Accurate measurements must also be *reliable*, which means that the same results can be obtained under similar circumstances when measurements are made at different points in time.

When doing nominal level analysis, validity is made possible only when the categories of analysis are exhaustive and mutually exclusive. To be exhaustive, there must be a category for every data element. In our example, there must be a state of residence for every voter. To be mutually exclusive means that a data element can be assigned to only one category, and therefore, in our example, residence should be defined so that voters may be a resident of only one state. If, therefore, some voters in the study have two or more homes in different states, a primary residence needs to be selected for each of these voters.

Accurate measurements require that the effects of antecedent and intervening variables upon the dependent variable be determined, and this is one of the most difficult areas of political science research. If a candidate issues a set of negative campaign advertisements (the independent variable), and that same week he or she is endorsed by an influential person (the intervening variable), how can a researcher tell if a rise in the polls after these events is due to the advertising (the independent variable), the endorsement (the intervening variable), both, or neither? Such variables can be measured if a study is properly constructed to test varying responses of voters over a period of time.

There are several kinds of validity. Face validity concerns whether a measurement seems reasonable. An instrument lacks face validity if it appears that there are good reasons to question it. Content validity concerns the comprehensiveness of the measurement. A measurement has content validity if all the relevant aspects of the specified subject are included in the research. Construct validity is obtained when a correlation is demonstrated between a measure of one concept and the measure of another concept. For example, if measurements of efficacy, the sense that a person's actions actually make a difference, and measurements of voter turnout demonstrate a significant correlation, then the comparison of efficacy and voter turnout has construct validity.

Reliability, the second major concern for effective measurement, concerns whether or not the measurement provides the same result when it is repeated. A measurement of opinions about universally available health care, for example, should provide the same results on rainy days or on sunny days, and from one week to the next with the same group of people, if nothing has happened to make the people change their minds.

The reliability of political science studies is difficult to determine for several reasons. Many problems may occur to make the data collected inaccurate.

People answering questions may give false or misleading answers because they secretly resent the intrusion of the questions, because they wish to conceal their ignorance, or because they misunderstand the questions. The people who are conducting the survey may be careless or fill in false answers merely to complete the assignment. Data entry provides another opportunity for mistakes. When people transfer the data to computers, mistakes are likely to be made.

Hypotheses help us to select specific aspects of a problem or question and explore them one at a time. Hypotheses that are too vague and general are difficult to test. In our example, we have proposed the following hypothesis: "Candidates who use negative campaign advertising are more likely to win elections." This hypothesis is so vague that it will be difficult to test. What is meant, for example, by "negative advertising"? A more specific hypothesis is needed, such as this: "Candidates whose advertising includes more references to faults of opponents than strengths of the candidate are more likely to win elections than candidates whose advertising contains more references to the candidate's strengths than to the faults of the other candidates." Furthermore, even if all the elections that we sample are the ones in which our hypothesis is confirmed, we have only a correlation between negative campaigning and voting, not a *causal* relationship. Our example hypothesis, that "candidates who use negative campaign advertising are more likely to win elections" is therefore a relational hypothesis, not a causal hypothesis. Relational hypotheses indicate whether or not two phenomena are related to one another in a specific way, without demonstrating that one causes the other.

Devising a good hypothesis is a difficult matter. Good hypotheses are

- plausible: they appear to be reasonable;
- specific: they are precisely stated in clearly defined terms;
- generalizable: they are applicable to other situations;
- empirical: they are nonnormative
- testable: they can be tested empirically to determine if they are true.

As mentioned earlier, causal hypotheses are very difficult to prove in political science. It is one thing to demonstrate that negative campaign ads are associated with votes for a candidate (direct correlation), but it is more difficult to prove that the ads caused the votes to be cast (causation). One way that political scientists, and scientist of all types, deal with the problem of the difficulty of proving causation is the null hypothesis. A null hypothesis is a hypothesis established precisely for the purpose of refuting it. The null hypothesis allows the researcher to make a statement of greater certainty. If we wanted to try, for example, to prove that negative campaign ads are associated with an increase in voter turnout, we would begin by testing a null hypothesis: "Negative campaign ads are not associated with an increase in voter turnout." If we can find a case in which voter turnout increases as negative campaign ads increase, then we will have disproved the null hypothesis. We will not have proved that voter turnout always increases as negative campaign ads increase, but we will have taken the first step by showing that negative campaign can be associated with an increase in voter turnout. Science thus proceeds by disproving successively specific null hypotheses.

Several difficulties frequently occur when testing hypotheses in political science. Sometimes sufficient data is not available. Necessary records are not consistent or accurate, or perhaps they have been compiled according to different systems or categories. Another problem is the multiplicity and ambiguity of variables. If we want to find out what influences presidential decisions, for example, we may need to try to sort out the competing influences of advisors, public opinion, attitudes of senators, Supreme Court opinions, or actions of foreign nations.

A third problem with the scientific study of politics has to do with the nature of knowledge itself. Testing hypotheses, an approach fundamental to the scientific method, is an inductive process and therefore shares the problems of induction in general. In *The Logic of Discovery* (1934), Karl Popper pointed out that to show that some examples of a certain phenomenon behave in a certain manner is not to demonstrate that others will also. Even if all known political candidates have spent money to obtain office, for example, there may be a candidate in the future who will win election without spending money. Even if all known national leaders have been effective orators, it is still possible that in the future, a national leader will arise who cannot speak at all.

Furthermore, according to Popper, scientific observation is always selective. We must choose what to observe, and what context we shall observe it in, before the actual observation takes place, and therefore hypotheses describe not reality, but only specific contexts of reality.

The next step is formulating a research question. A research question helps the analyst to clearly define exactly what he or she wants to know. Research questions, therefore, help analysts to focus their literature reviews. A research question may ask, for example, "what is the extent of registered voters' knowledge of Supreme Court decisions about abortion?" Research questions should be confined to a narrowly defined topic. Once the researcher has formulated a research question, stated a hypothesis, and supported the inquiry with a literature review, he or she is ready to conduct the research. Political scientists use a wide variety of research methods selected primarily for their appropriateness to the topic being studied. Several of the most common methods will be presented in this chapter.

4.3   CONTENT ANALYSIS

Content analysis is a method of analyzing written documents that allows researchers to transform nonquantitative data into quantitative data by counting and categorizing certain variables within the data. Content analysts look for certain types of words or references in the texts, categorize them, or count them. A content analyst of presidential speeches, for example, might count the number of times a selected president or several presidents refer to civil rights, or the economy, or foreign policy issues, or their mothers. This analysis can then be used as one indication of the relative importance of selected issues to presidents. Other content analyses determine if the news media has an ideological bias, or if published reports demonstrate a preoccupation with ethnic or religious issues.

Content analyses of "events data" focus on a particular event or a series of events over time. A number of content analyses have examined the major wars of this century and have attempted to identify factors that are common in situations of war. Compilations of events data, such as the *World Handbook of Political and Social Indicators*, provide a listing of the important political events (elections, coups, wars) for most countries of the world. These listings help to compare trends in selected types of events from one country to another. Press reports, statistics, televised and radio media reports, personal records, newspapers, and magazines provide inexhaustible mines of data for content analysis. Government documents are an especially rich source of material for political scientists. Different types of government documents include presidential papers; the Code of Federal Regulations; the Congressional Record; federal, state, and local election returns; historical records; judicial decisions; and legal records.

In her study of gender and statewide elections, Kim Fridkin Kahn, a political scientist at Arizona State University, used a content analysis:

> A content analysis of 26 U.S. Senate races and 21 gubernatorial races between male and female candidates was conducted to assess whether the media differentiate between male and female candidates in their coverage of statewide campaigns. . . . For the content analysis of news coverage, every day from September 1 through the day of the election was analyzed. Any item in the newspaper that mentioned either candidate was analyzed including news articles, columns, editorials, and "news analysis" articles. . . . I analyzed news characteristics known to be significant for a candidate's success [such as perceptions of] a candidate's viability. . . . Second, content was assessed by anticipated differences between male and female candidates. The content analysis also reveals consistent differences in the coverage of issues for male and female candidates—in both gubernatorial and senatorial campaigns. Women routinely receive less issue coverage than their male counterparts, and in some instances, these differences are quite dramatic. (1994, 167–69)

4.4 EXPERIMENTS

Experimentation is the fundamental method of acquiring knowledge in the physical sciences. As a research method, it has one primary and substantial advantage: experiments allow the researcher to control the variables, allowing the scientist to more easily determine the effect of the independent variable upon the dependent variable. In social sciences, experiments are more difficult to conduct than in physical sciences because the research subjects are human beings and the number of variables is normally large. In spite of these difficulties, however, political scientists are now successfully conducting more experiments than they have in the past.

Experiments in the social sciences are set up according to several different basic designs. The first is the simple posttest measurement. For example, a lecture on political ideologies may be followed by a test of the knowledge of the participants about ideology. The test–retest method is more accurate. The effects of a speech upon the attitudes of the people in an audience, for example, might be measured by having the members of the audience complete a survey, listen to the speech, and then complete the survey again. Researchers could then measure the differences in opinion registered before and after the survey. If no pretest is given, the researcher cannot be sure of the level of knowledge or the respondents' attitudes before the test was given, and the effects of the lecture or speech, then, are less certain.

The alternative form of the experiment uses two different measures of the same concept. If research concerns liberal and conservative attitudes, for example, the analyst could measure attitudes on defense, spending in one questionnaire and then measure attitudes on abortion in a separate questionnaire. The split-halves device is similar to the alternative forms measurement, except that two measures of the concept are applied (e.g., questions about defense and abortion in the same questionnaire) at the same time.

Kim Fridkin Kahn has used experimental methods in her studies of the effects of sex stereotypes in statewide campaigns:

> Do gender differences in news coverage and the candidates' sex influence people's perceptions of gubernatorial and senatorial candidates? To investigate this question, I conducted a series of experiments in which I manipulated both the type of coverage a candidate received and the candidate's sex. The results of these experiments suggest that people's perceptions of male and female candidates are influenced by patterns of news coverage and by people's sex stereotypes.
>
> This study suggests that women are uniquely advantaged in certain campaign environments, whereas disadvantaged in others. . . . During the 1992 senatorial campaigns, for instance, the end of the Cold War made foreign policy issues less central and the concurrent presidential campaign made such issues as health-care reform more prominent. Similarly, congressional scandals—like the White House banking scandal—made traits like integrity and trustworthiness especially relevant. The 1992 campaign, then, placed a premium on women's stereotypical strengths ("female" issues and "female" traits), thereby creating a favorable electoral setting for women candidates for the U.S. Senate. Given that people's sex stereotypes and patterns of news coverage make certain campaign environments especially desirable for women candidates, women should consider the prevailing political climate when seeking statewide office. (1994, 162)

As we have already mentioned, a number of problems are commonly associated with experimental designs. More specifically, they include

1. *Control of variables:* Can the environment be controlled to rule out other factors?
2. *Time passage:* People get tired, or for some other reason take a different attitude.
3. *Varying acts of measurement:* Poll takers may record responses differently.
4. *Statistical regression:* Someone who is on the high end of a test score range may register a high score only temporarily.
5. *Experimental mortality:* Subjects drop out.

6. Instrument decay: The instrument may not be used as carefully the second time.
7. Selection error: Control and experimental groups may not be equivalent.

In order to overcome these problems, a number of complex methodologies have been developed. Multigroup designs, for example, test multiple independent variables against the same dependent variable. Factorial designs may test the effects of several independent variables in different combinations. A simple "2 × 2" factorial design, for example, might test combinations of four possibilities that result from two different actions a candidate could take in conducting a campaign: (1) distributing a brochure and (2) mailing out personal letters to selected party activists. The chart below illustrates the four resultant possibilities:

	SEND PERSONAL LETTER	DO NOT SEND PERSONAL LETTER
Send Brochure	(1) Both brochure and letter	(2) Brochure but no letter
Do Not Send Brochure	(3) Letter but no brochure	(4) Neither letter nor brochure

A factorial design based upon the choices set forth in the above chart would test the results of voter activity according each of the four situations.

The factorial design is designed be used as a part of a field experiment, which is an experiment conducted within a natural setting (which in this case would be an actual political campaign). For each subject in the study, the researchers would have to be able to determine (1) who acted as a result of receiving information from the candidate (such as voting or making a contribution, or volunteering to assist in the campaign) and (2) to which of the four combinations of brochures and letters the voters had been exposed.

In her studies of the effects of sex stereotypes in statewide campaigns that we mentioned earlier, Kim Fridkin Kahn used a 2 × 4 factorial design, which, of course, results in eight categories of analysis.

> To investigate the effect of gender differences in coverage and the candidate's sex on people's evaluations of statewide candidates, I conducted a series of experiments. . . . I used a two-by-four factorial design, and the manipulated variables are the sex of the candidate (male or female) and the type of news coverage (male incumbent coverage, female incumbent coverage, male challenger coverage, female challenger coverage). . . . Selected residents of two local communities participated in these experiments, and each experimental session lasted approximately one hour. Volunteers came to a research setting at a major university campus to participate in the study, where they were randomly assigned to one of the experimental conditions. In each condition, the participants read a newspaper page that included the article about the statewide candidate as well as two other political articles. After reading the entire newspaper page, the participants completed a questionnaire. (1994, 174–75)

We wish to stress again that dozens of different types of experimental designs, using different combinations of strategies, are used in political science research. After reviewing more than 2,000 political science publications, Larry M. Bartels and Henry E. Brady, in their publication *The State of Quantitative Political Methodology,* conclude the following about experiments: "In the past decade, political scientists have found many new and exciting ways to do experimental work. Samples are more representative and treatments are more realistic, increasing greatly the external validity of experimental work" (1993, 122).

Bartels and Brady outline a number of these developments, including the experiments conducted by Michael Levine and Charles Plott (1977, 1978) in which they demonstrated that the work and decisions of committees can be altered by manipulating their agendas. Another study cited by Bartels and Brady is the work of Richard Johnston (1992), which demonstrated how, in Canadian elections, voters' perceptions of a free-trade agreement changed when particular candidates' names were attached to the title of the agreement. When voters asked about "[prime minister] *Mulroney's* free trade agreement," their answers were either more positive or negative, depending upon Mulroney's popularity at the time, than the answers of voters who were asked about a "free-trade agreement." In another experiment, Frolich and Oppenheimer demonstrated that under circumstances in which students set the rules under which their group will operate, acceptance of the rule is facilitated by participation in formulating the rule (Bartels and Brady, 1993, 123).

4.5   NONEXPERIMENTAL DESIGNS

Political scientists have used a wide variety of nonexperimental designs. Cross-sectional designs, for example, sample a cross-section of the population. Suppose that you want to determine if sermons in which pastors advocate political participation actually cause people to vote more often. Comparing voting records of people who have and who have not heard sermons could be one way of doing this. One of the main problems would be in isolating other variables. For example, did the people listening to the sermons previously vote more than those who did not?

Panel studies are cross-sectional designs done over time in which measurements are taken of the same variables on the same units at different points in time. Panel studies are like experiments, except that the researcher just lets the variable happen without introducing it. In an experimental design, for example, a group of voters could be subjected to a particular set of sermons selected by the researchers. In a panel study, however, the researcher would accumulate data on two series of voters' voting records, then wait as one group is exposed to the sermons, the other is not, and finally test the voting records of the two groups again.

A time series design takes multiple measures of a variable over a period of time. It may be used in experimental and nonexperimental designs. In a time series design of the effects of sermons on voting patterns, an experimental design could be constructed in which two groups of people's voting patterns are measured over a period of four years. The control group would not be exposed to sermons, and the experimental group would hear sermons at selected intervals.

4.6   INTERVIEWS

Interviews are used in studies in which it is important to get some depth in the observations taken, or to allow respondents to express views not anticipated by the interviewer. *Elite interviewing* selects a certain type of individual to interview, such as labor leaders, Congress people, or people with blue eyes. The elite can be any group of people specially selected for the purposes of the study. We may want the views of state court judges for example, if we were to conduct a study on the effects of limited jail space on the lengths of sentences that are given to people convicted of crimes. Interviews of any kind require considerable skill and preparation. Elite interviews, for example, often require the development of a standardized questions that are asked in a manner that does not sound like a set of standardized questions. This is because people often expect to be treated like individuals, and sometimes resent being asked standard questions.

4.7   CASE STUDIES

Case studies, which are in-depth examinations of particular situations, are conducted for the insights they reveal about the situations in question and generally upon political affairs. In his case study of the role of ethnicity in political developments surrounding the independence of Estonia after the demise of the Soviet Union, Andrus Park offers an explanation of the events that he had selected. He identifies political trends, provides an explanation of economic, social, and other factors associated with those trends, and draws conclusions from his findings. In 1989—at the time the independence process began—Estonia's population was approximately 62 percent Estonian, 30 percent Russian, and 8 percent other groups, including Ukrainians, Belarusians, and Finns. Previous to independence, however, the Russian population had enjoyed advantages that would no longer be honored in the new system ruled by the Estonian majority. Park's case study includes the following comments:

> In this article I argue that Estonia's ethnic developments in 1991–93 were characterized by the following features: after the independence declaration, there was (at least on the surface) a decline in the intensity of ethnic tensions; many public signs of ethnic conflict were displayed less vividly in 1991–93 than in 1988-91. . . . There were two main directions of international pressures in regard to Estonia's citizenship and the minorities policy in 1991–93; the governments of the Western countries and the main interstate organization were mostly friendly, while Russia was sharply critical. The Western media and human rights organizations also often expressed disapproval of Estonia's policies; compared with many other post-communist states (Moldova, former Yugoslavia, the Transcaucasian states, even former Czecho-Slovakia) the minorities and citizenship policy in Estonia in 1991–93 appeared to be quite successful: the visible signs of ethnic tensions diminished . . . violence or active

separatism on ethnic grounds was avoided. . . . Estonia's integration into European and other international organizations was generally successful. (1994, 69–87)

Case studies have gained increasing acceptance in recent years. They are flexible in that they may be used to study one particular phenomena or a single instance of a combination of phenomena. Even though it is difficult to confidently form generalizations directly from the results of case studies, they provide opportunities for testing hypotheses that are generated from theories.

Case studies are excellent educational tools. Law students gain much of their knowledge of legal precedents by reading the decisions and testimony of many actual cases filed in the courts. Business schools were pioneers in developing administrative case studies to help students understand actual management situations. Courses in public administration adopt the case study method as a primary teaching tool less often than business or law schools, but case studies have also become a common feature of many public administration courses.

4.8   DIRECT OBSERVATION

A number of other techniques are used for data collection. *Direct observation* of political phenomena is conducted by trained observers who carefully record selected behaviors. Observation may be structured, that is, a definite list of phenomena is noted, such as number of political contacts, political allusions in speech, or appeals to certain groups of voters. Or observation may be unstructured, in which case observation attempts to take in every action in a certain setting that may possibly be significant. In either case, successful observation for purposes of social science research always follows clear guidelines and standard procedures.

Although political scientists may make more use of direct observation in the future because it provides many opportunities for creative thinking which may lead to new discoveries, thus far analysts have been reluctant to use it widely for several reasons. First, observation data is said to be qualitative, and therefore subjective in nature. Although much of the data can be quantified, qualitative considerations are hard to avoid. Another problem is that political events can be difficult, time consuming and expensive to observe, and an entire event such as an election may require several observers whose activities are highly coordinated and regulated.

4.9   FOCUS GROUPS

Focus group methods are similar to direct observation techniques in that they produce qualitative data and are often used when little is known about the subject under study. Although substantial research exists on many topics in political science, research from which background knowledge can be drawn, there remain areas for which little is known. Focus groups make an excellent way to begin research into a new area because they provide opportunities for careful consideration of a topic in a setting that encourages creative thinking.

In a focus group, a moderator guides several carefully selected participants in a discussion of the topic under consideration. Let's suppose that a new religious group, with practices that are often unusual, has moved to a community, and the researcher wants to know how the newcomers have affected the local political climate. A focus group can help a researcher more carefully define both areas of topical concentration and methods for carrying on further research with respect to the newcomers in the community. To conduct a focus group, a moderator should be prepared with a clear conception of the goals and objectives that she or he wishes to accomplish, and a list of issues or questions to discuss which form a general guideline, not a strict agenda for the discussion. The moderator should guide the group by helping them stay on track, but she is there to help motivate discussion more than to define its direction. The moderator continually helps to clarify issues under discussion and to draw out the implications of observations made by participants in the group. An assistant to the moderator should take careful notes.

A major advantage of focus groups, compared to surveys, is that surveys will only take in the answers to the specific questions asked, whereas focus groups provide the opportunity to make sure that the correct questions are being asked in the first place.

CHAPTER

5

WRITING AS COMMUNICATION

5.1   WRITING TO LEARN

Writing is a way of ordering your experience. Think about it. No matter what you are writing—it may be a paper for your American government class, a short story, a limerick, a grocery list—you are putting pieces of your world together in new ways and making yourself freshly conscious of those pieces. This is one of the reasons why writing is so hard. From the infinite welter of data that your mind continually processes and locks in your memory, you are selecting only certain items significant to the task at hand, relating them to other items, and phrasing them with a new coherence. You are mapping a part of your universe that has hitherto been unknown territory. You are gaining a little more control over the processes by which you interact with the world around you.

This is why the act of writing, no matter what its result, is never insignificant. It is always *communication*—if not with another human being, then with yourself. It is a way of making a fresh connection with your world.

Writing therefore is also one of the best ways to learn. This statement may sound odd at first. If you are an unpracticed writer, you may share a common notion that the only purpose of writing is to express what you already know or think. According to this view, any learning that you as a writer might have experienced has already occurred by the time your pen meets the paper; your task is thus to inform and even surprise the reader. But, if you are a practiced writer, you know that at any moment as you write, you are capable of surprising yourself. And it is that surprise that you look for: the shock of seeing what happens in your own mind when you drop an old, established opinion into a batch of new facts or bump into a cherished belief from a different angle. Writing synthesizes new understanding for the writer. E. M. Forster's famous question "How do I know what I think until I see what I say?" is one that all of us could ask. We make meaning as we write, jolting ourselves by little, surprising discoveries into a larger and more interesting universe.

The Irony of Writing

Good writing, especially good writing about politics, helps the reader become aware of the ironies and paradoxes of human existence. One such paradox is that good writing expresses both that which is unique about the writer and that which the writer shares with every human being. Many of our most famous political statements share this double attribute of mirroring the singular and the ordinary simultaneously. For example, read the following excerpt from President Franklin Roosevelt's first inaugural address, spoken on March 4, 1933, in the middle of the Great Depression, and then answer this question: Is Roosevelt's speech famous because its expression is extraordinary or because it appeals to something that is basic to every human being?

This is pre-eminently the time to speak the truth, the whole truth, frankly and boldly. Nor need we shrink from honestly facing conditions in our country today. This great nation will endure as it has endured, will revive and will prosper.

So first of all let me assert my firm belief that the only thing we have to fear is fear itself—nameless, unreasoning, unjustified terror which paralyzes needed efforts to convert retreat into advance.

In every dark hour of our national life a leadership of frankness and vigor has met with that understanding and support of the people themselves which is essential to victory. I am convinced that you will again give that support to leadership in these critical days.

In such a spirit on my part and on yours we face our common difficulties. They concern, thank God, only material things. Values have shrunken to fantastic levels; taxes have risen; our ability to pay has fallen; government of all kinds is faced by serious curtailment of income; the means of exchange are frozen in the currents of trade; the withered leaves of industrial enterprise lie on every side; farmers find no markets for their produce; the savings of many years in thousands of families are gone.

More important, a host of unemployed citizens face the grim problem of existence, and an equally great number toil with little return. Only a foolish optimist can deny the dark realities of the moment.

Yet our distress comes from no failure of substance. We are stricken by no plague of locusts. Compared with the perils which our forefathers conquered because they believed and were not afraid, we have still much to be thankful for. Nature still offers her bounty and human efforts have multiplied it. Plenty is at our doorstep, but a generous use of it languishes in the very sight of the supply. . . .

The measure of the restoration lies in the extent to which we apply social values more noble than mere monetary profit.

Happiness lies not in the mere possession of money; it lies in the joy of achievement, in the thrill of creative effort.

The joy and moral stimulation of work no longer must be forgotten in the mad chase of evanescent profits. These dark days will be worth all they cost us if they teach us that our true destiny is not to be ministered unto but to minister to ourselves and to our fellow-men. (Roosevelt 1963, 240)

The help that writing gives us with learning and with controlling what we learn is one of the major reasons why your political science instructors will require a great deal of writing from you. Learning the complex and diverse world of the political scientist takes more than a passive ingestion of facts. You have to understand the processes of government, and come to grips with social issues and with your own attitudes toward them. When you write in a class on American government or public policy, you are entering into the world of political scientists in the same way they do—by testing theory against fact and fact against belief.

Writing is the means of entering political life. Virtually everything that happens in politics happens first on paper. Documents are wrestled into shape before their contents can affect the public. Great speeches are written before they are spoken. The written word has helped bring slaves to freedom, end wars, and shape the values of nations. Often, in politics as elsewhere, gaining recognition for ourselves and our ideas depends less on what we say than on how we say it. Accurate and persuasive writing is absolutely vital to the political scientist.

EXERCISE   Learning by Writing

One way of testing the notion that writing is a powerful learning tool is by rewriting your notes from a recent class lecture. The type of class does not matter; it can be history, chemistry, advertising, whatever. If possible, choose a difficult class, one in which you are feeling somewhat unsure of the material and for which you have taken copious notes.

As you rewrite, provide the transitional elements (connecting phrases such as *in order to, because of, and, but,* and *however*) that you were unable to supply in class because of the press of time. Furnish your own examples or illustrations of the ideas expressed in the lecture.

This experiment will force you to supply necessary coherence to your own thought processes. See if the time it takes you to rewrite the notes is not more than compensated for by your increased understanding of the lecture material.

Challenge Yourself

There is no way around it: writing is a struggle. Did you think you were the only one to feel this way? Take heart! Writing is hard for everybody, great writers included. Bringing order to the world is never easy. Isaac Bashevis Singer, winner of the 1978 Nobel Prize in literature, once wrote: "I believe in miracles in every area of life except writing. Experience has shown me that there are no miracles in writing. The only thing that produces good writing is hard work" (quoted in Lunsford and Connors 1992, 2).

Hard work was evident in the words of John F. Kennedy's inaugural address. Each word was crafted to embed an image in the listeners' mind. As you read the following excerpt from Kennedy's speech, what images does it evoke? Historians tend to consider a president "great" when his words live longer than his deeds in the minds of the people. Do you think this will be—or has been—true of Kennedy?

> We observe today not a victory of party but a celebration of freedom—
> symbolizing an end as well as a beginning—signifying renewal as well as

change. For I have sworn before you and Almighty God the same solemn oath our forebears prescribed nearly a century and three-quarters ago.

The world is very different now. For man holds in his mortal hands the power to abolish all forms of human poverty and all forms of human life. And yet the same revolutionary beliefs for which our forebears fought are still at issue around the globe—the belief that the rights of man come not from the generosity of the state but from the hand of God.

We dare not forget today that we are the heirs of that first revolution. Let the word go forth from this time and place, to friend and foe alike, that the torch has been passed to a new generation of Americans—born in this century, tempered by war, disciplined by a hard and bitter peace, proud of our ancient heritage—and unwilling to witness or permit the slow undoing of those human rights to which this nation has always been committed, and to which we are committed today at home and around the world. . . .

In the long history of the world, only a few generations have been granted the role of defending freedom in its hours of maximum danger. I do not shrink from this responsibility—I welcome it. I do not believe that any of us would exchange places with any other people or any other generation. The energy, the faith, the devotion which we bring to this endeavor will light our country and all who serve it—and the glow from that fire can truly light the world.

And so, my fellow Americans: ask not what your country can do for you— ask what you can do for your country.

My fellow citizens of the world: ask not what America will do for you, but what together we can do for the freedom of man. (Kennedy 1963, 688–89)

One reason that writing is difficult is that it is not actually a single activity at all but a process consisting of several activities that can overlap, with two or more sometimes operating simultaneously as you labor to organize and phrase your thoughts. (We will discuss these activities later in this chapter.) The writing process tends to be sloppy for everyone, an often-frustrating search for meaning and for the best way to articulate that meaning.

Frustrating though that search may sometimes be, it need not be futile. Remember this: the writing process uses skills that we all have. The ability to write, in other words, is not some magical competence bestowed on the rare, fortunate individual. Although few of us may achieve the proficiency of Isaac Bashevis Singer or John F. Kennedy, we are all capable of phrasing thoughts clearly and in a well-organized fashion. But learning how to do so takes practice.

The one sure way to improve your writing is to write.

One of the toughest but most important jobs in writing is to maintain enthusiasm for your writing project. Such commitment may sometimes be hard to achieve, given the difficulties that are inherent in the writing process and that can be made worse when the project is unappealing at first glance. How, for example, can you be enthusiastic about having to write a paper analyzing campaign financing for the 1998 congressional elections, when you have never once thought about campaign finances and can see no use in doing so now?

One of the worst mistakes that unpracticed student writers make is to fail to assume responsibility for keeping themselves interested in their writing. No matter how hard it may seem at first to drum up interest in your topic, you have to do it—that is, if you want to write a paper you can be proud of, one that contributes useful material and a fresh point of view to the topic. One thing is guaranteed: if you are bored with your writing, your reader will be, too. So what can you do to keep your interest and energy level high?

Challenge yourself. Think of the paper not as an assignment but as a piece of writing that has a point to make. To get this point across persuasively is the real reason you are writing, not because a teacher has assigned you a project. If someone were to ask you why you are writing your paper and your immediate, unthinking response is, "Because I've been given a writing assignment" or "Because I want a good grade" or some other nonanswer along these lines, your paper may be in trouble.

If, on the other hand, your first impulse is to explain the challenge of your main point—"I'm writing to show how campaign finance reform will benefit every taxpayer in America"—then you are thinking usefully about your topic.

Maintain Self-Confidence

Having confidence in your ability to write well about your topic is essential for good writing. This does not mean that you will always know what the result of a particular writing activity will be. In fact, you have to cultivate your ability to tolerate a high degree of uncertainty while weighing evidence, testing hypotheses, and experimenting with organizational strategies and wording. Be ready for temporary confusion and for seeming dead ends, and remember that every writer faces these obstacles. It is out of your struggle to combine fact with fact, to buttress conjecture with evidence, that order will arise.

Do not be intimidated by the amount and quality of work that others have already done in your field of inquiry. The array of opinion and evidence that confronts you in the literature can be confusing. But remember that no important topic is ever exhausted. There are always gaps—questions that have not been satisfactorily explored in either the published research or the prevailing popular opinion. It is in these gaps that you establish your own authority, your own sense of control.

Remember that the various stages of the writing process reinforce each other. Establishing a solid motivation strengthens your sense of confidence about the project, which in turn influences how successfully you organize and write. If you start out well, use good work habits, and allow ample time for the various activities to coalesce, you should produce a paper that will reflect your best work, one that your audience will find both readable and useful.

5.2   THE WRITING PROCESS

The Nature of the Process

As you engage in the writing process, you are doing many things at once. While planning, you are, no doubt, defining the audience for your paper at the same time that you are thinking about its purpose. As you draft the paper, you may organize your next sentence while revising the one you have just written. Different parts of the writing process overlap, and much of the difficulty of writing occurs because so many things happen at once. Through practice—in other words, through *writing*—it is possible to learn to control those parts of the process that can in fact be controlled and to encourage those mysterious, less controllable activities.

No two people go about writing in exactly the same way. It is important to recognize the routines—modes of thought as well as individual exercises—that help you negotiate the process successfully. It is also important to give yourself as much time as possible to complete the process. Procrastination is one of the writer's greatest enemies. It saps confidence, undermines energy, and destroys concentration. Writing regularly and following a well-planned schedule as closely as possible often make the difference between a successful paper and an embarrassment.

Although the various parts of the writing process are interwoven, there is naturally a general order in the work of writing. You have to start somewhere! What follows is a description of the various stages of the writing process—planning, drafting, revising, editing, and proofreading—along with suggestions on how to approach each most successfully.

Planning

Planning includes all activities that lead to the writing of the first draft of a paper. The particular activities in this stage differ from person to person. Some writers, for instance, prefer to compile a formal outline before writing the draft. Others perform brief writing exercises to jump-start their imaginations. Some draw diagrams; some doodle. Later, we will look at a few starting strategies, and you can determine which may help you.

Now, however, let us discuss certain early choices that all writers must make during the planning stage. These choices concern *topic, purpose, and audience,* elements that make up the writing context, or the terms under which we all write. Every time you write, even if you are only writing a diary entry or a note to the milkman, these elements are present. You may not give conscious consideration to all of them in each piece of writing that you do, but it is extremely important to think carefully about them when writing a political science paper. Some or all of these defining elements may be dictated by your assignment, yet you will always have a degree of control over them.

Selecting a Topic

No matter how restrictive an assignment may seem, there is no reason to feel trapped by it. Within any assigned subject you can find a range of topics to explore. What you are looking for is a topic that engages your own interest. Let your curiosity be your guide. If, for example, you have been assigned the subject of campaign finances, then guide yourself to find some issues concerning the topic that interests you. (For example, how influential are campaign finances in the average state senate race? What would be the repercussions of limiting financial contributions from special interest groups?) Any good topic comes with a set of questions; you may well find that your interest increases if you simply begin asking questions. One strong recommendation: ask your questions *on paper*. Like most mental activities, the process of exploring your way through a topic is transformed when you write down your thoughts as they come, instead of letting them fly through your mind unrecorded. Remember the words of Louis Agassiz: "A pen is often the best of eyes" (1958, 106).

Although it is vital to be interested in your topic, you do not have to know much about it at the outset of your investigation. In fact, having too heartfelt a commitment to a topic can be an impediment to writing about it; emotions can get in the way of objectivity. It is often better to choose a topic that has piqued your interest yet remained something of a mystery to you—a topic discussed in one of your classes, perhaps, or mentioned on television or in a conversation with friends.

Narrowing the Topic

The task of narrowing your topic offers you a tremendous opportunity to establish a measure of control over the writing project. It is up to you to hone your topic to just the right shape and size to suit both your own interests and the requirements of the assignment. Do a good job of it, and you will go a long way toward guaranteeing yourself sufficient motivation and confidence for the tasks ahead. However, if you do not do it well, somewhere along the way you may find yourself directionless and out of energy.

Generally, the first topics that come to your mind will be too large for you to handle in your research paper. For example, the subject of a national income security policy has recently generated a tremendous number of news reports. Yet despite all the attention, there is still plenty of room for you to investigate the topic on a level that has real meaning for you and that does not merely recapitulate the published research. What about an analysis of how one of the proposed income security policies might affect insurance costs in a locally owned company?

The problem with most topics is not that they are too narrow or have been too completely explored, but rather that they are so rich that it is often difficult to choose the most useful way to address them. Take some time to narrow your topic. Think through the possibilities that occur to you and, as always, jot down your thoughts.

Students in an undergraduate course on political theory were told to write an essay of 2,500 words on one of the following issues. Next to each general topic is an example of how students narrowed it into a manageable paper topic.

GENERAL TOPIC	NARROWED TOPIC
George W. Bush	Bush's view of the role of religion in politics
Freedom	A comparison of Jean Jacques Rousseau's concept of freedom with that of John Locke
Interest Groups	The political power of the National Rifle Association
Bart Simpson	Bart Simpson's political ideology

EXERCISE	**Narrowing Topics**

Without doing research, see how you can narrow the following general topics:

EXAMPLE

General topic	The United Nations
Narrowed topics	The United Nations' intervention in civil wars
	The United Nations' attempts to end starvation
	The role of the United Nations in stopping nuclear proliferation

GENERAL TOPICS

War in Iraq	Gun control	Freedom of marriage
International terrorism	Political corruption	Abortion rights
Education	Military spending	
Freedom of speech	The budget deficit	

Finding a Thesis

As you plan your writing, be on the lookout for an idea that can serve as your thesis. A *thesis* is not a fact, which can be immediately verified by data, but an assertion worth discussing, an argument with more than one possible conclusion. Your thesis sentence will reveal to your reader not only the argument you have chosen but also your orientation toward it and the conclusion that your paper will attempt to prove.

In looking for a thesis, you are doing many jobs at once:

1. You are limiting the amount and kind of material that you must cover, thus making them manageable.
2. You are increasing your own interest in the narrowing field of study.
3. You are working to establish your paper's purpose, the reason you are writing about your topic. (If the only reason you can see for writing is to earn a good grade, then you probably won't!)
4. You are establishing your notion of who your audience is and what sort of approach to the subject might best catch its interest.

In short, you are gaining control over your writing context. For this reason, it is a good idea to come up with a thesis early on, a *working thesis,* which will very probably change as your thinking deepens but which will allow you to establish a measure of order in the planning stage.

The Thesis Sentence.   The introduction of your paper will contain a sentence that expresses the task that you intend to accomplish. This *thesis sentence* communicates your main idea, the one you are going to prove, defend, or illustrate. It sets up an expectation in the reader's mind that it is your job to satisfy. But, in the planning stage, a thesis sentence is more than just the statement that informs your reader of your goal: it is a valuable tool to help you narrow your focus and confirm in your own mind your paper's purpose.

Developing a Thesis

Students in a class on public policy analysis were assigned a twenty-page paper on a problem currently being faced by the municipal authorities in their own city. The choice of the problem was left to the students. One, Richard Cory, decided to investigate the problem posed by the large number of abandoned buildings in a downtown neighborhood through which he drove on his way to the university. His first working thesis was as follows:

Abandoned houses result in negative social effects to the city.

The problem with this thesis, as Richard found out, was that it was not an idea that could be argued, but rather a fact that could be easily corroborated by the sources he began to consult. As he read reports from such groups as the Urban Land Institute and the City Planning Commission, and talked with representatives from the Community Planning Department, he began to get interested in the dilemma his city faced in responding to the problem of abandoned buildings. Richard's second working thesis was as follows:

Removal of abandoned buildings is a major problem facing the city.

While his second thesis narrowed the topic somewhat and gave Richard an opportunity to use material from his research, there was still no real comment attached to it. It still stated a bare fact, easily proved. At this point, Richard became interested in the even narrower topic of how building removal should best be handled. He found that the major issue was funding and that different civic groups favored different methods of accomplishing this. As Richard explored the arguments for and against the various funding plans, he began to feel that one of them might be best for the city. As a result, Richard developed his third working thesis:

Assessing a demolition fee on each property offers a viable solution to the city's building removal problem.

Note how this thesis narrows the focus of Richard's paper even further than the other two had, while also presenting an arguable hypothesis. It tells Richard what he has to do in his paper, just as it tells his readers what to expect.

At some time during your preliminary thinking on a topic, you should consult a library to see how much published work on your issue exists. This search has at least two benefits:

1. It acquaints you with a body of writing that will become very important in the research phase of your paper.
2. It gives you a sense of how your topic is generally addressed by the community of scholars you are joining. Is the topic as important as you think it is? Has there been so much research on the subject as to make your inquiry, in its present formulation, irrelevant?

As you go about determining your topic, remember that one goal of your political science writing in college is always to enhance your own understanding of the political process, to build an accurate model of the way politics works. Let this goal help you to direct your research into those areas that you know are important to your knowledge of the discipline.

Defining a Purpose

There are many ways to classify the purposes of writing, but in general most writing is undertaken either to inform or to persuade an audience. The goal of informative, or expository, writing is simply to impart information about a particular subject, whereas the aim of persuasive writing is to convince your reader of your point of view on an issue. The distinction between expository and persuasive writing is not hard and fast, and most writing in political science has elements of both types. Most effective writing, however, is clearly focused on either exposition or persuasion. Position papers (arguments for adopting particular policies), for example, are designed to persuade, whereas policy analysis papers (Chapter 12) are meant to inform. When you begin writing, consciously select a primary approach of exposition or persuasion, and then set out to achieve that goal.

EXERCISE   **To Explain or to Persuade**

Can you tell from the titles of these two papers, both on the same topic, which is an expository paper and which is a persuasive paper?

1. Social Services Funding in the Second George W. Bush Administration
2. How the Second George W. Bush Administration Shifted Shares of Wealth in America

---

Again taking up the subject of campaign finances, let us assume that you must write a paper explaining how finances were managed in the 2004 Republican presidential campaign. If you are writing an expository paper, your task could be to describe as coherently and impartially as possible the methods by which the Republicans administered their campaign funds. If, however, you are attempting to convince your readers that the 2004 Republican campaign finances were criminally mismanaged by an elected official, you are writing to persuade, and your strategy will be radically different. Persuasive writing seeks to influence the opinions of its audience toward its subject.

Learn what you want to say. By the time you write your final draft, you must have a very sound notion of the point you wish to argue. If, as you write that final draft, someone were to ask you to state your thesis, you should be able to give a satisfactory answer with a minimum of delay and no prompting. If, on the other hand, you have to hedge your answer because you cannot easily express your thesis, you may not yet be ready to write a final draft. You may have to write a draft or two or engage in various prewriting activities to form a secure understanding of your task.

EXERCISE   **Knowing What You Want to Say**

Two writers have been asked to state the thesis of their papers. Which one better understands the writing task?

Writer 1:   "My paper is about tax reform for the middle class."
Writer 2:   "My paper argues that tax reform for the middle class would be unfair to the upper and lower classes, who would then have to share more responsibility for the cost of government."

Watch out for bias! There is no such thing as pure objectivity. You are not a machine. No matter how hard you may try to produce an objective paper, the fact is that every choice you make as you write is influenced to some extent by your personal beliefs and opinions. What you tell your readers is truth, in other words, is influenced, sometimes without your knowledge, by a multitude of factors: your environment, upbringing, and education; your attitude toward your audience; your political affiliation; your race and gender; your career goals; and your ambitions for the paper you are writing. The influence of such factors can be very subtle, and it is something you must work to identify in your own writing as well as in the writing of others in order not to mislead or to be misled. Remember that one of the reasons for writing is *self-discovery.* The writing you will do in political science classes—as well as the writing you will do for the rest of your life—will give you a chance to discover and confront honestly your own views on your subjects. Responsible writers keep an eye on their own biases and are honest about them with their readers.

Defining Your Audience

In any class that requires you to write, you may sometimes find it difficult to remember that the point of your writing is not simply to jump through the technical hoops imposed by the assignment. The point is *communication*—the transmission of your knowledge and your conclusions to readers in a way that suits you. Your task is to pass on to your readers the spark of your own enthusiasm for your topic. Readers who were indifferent to your topic before reading your paper should look at it in a new way after finishing it. This is the great challenge of writing: to enter into a reader's mind and leave behind both new knowledge and new questions.

It is tempting to think that most writing problems would be solved if the writer could view the writing as if another person had produced it. The discrepancy between the understanding of the writer and that of the audience is the single greatest impediment to accurate communication. To overcome this barrier you must consider your audience's needs. By the time you begin drafting, most, if not all, of your ideas will have begun to attain coherent shape in your mind, so that virtually any words with which you try to express those ideas will reflect your thought accurately—to you. Your readers, however, do not already hold the conclusions that you have so painstakingly achieved. If you omit from your writing the material that is necessary to complete your readers' understanding of your argument, they may well be unable to supply that information themselves.

The potential for misunderstanding is present for any audience, whether it is made up of general readers, experts in the field, or your professor, who is reading in part to see how well you have mastered the constraints that govern the relationship between writer and reader. Make your presentation as complete as possible, bearing in mind your audience's knowledge of your topic.

Invention Strategies

We have discussed various methods of selecting and narrowing the topic of a paper. As your focus on a specific topic sharpens, you will naturally begin to think about the kinds of information that will go into the paper. In the case of papers that do not require formal research, this material will come largely from your own recollections. Indeed, one of the reasons instructors assign such papers is to convince you of the incredible richness of your memory, the vastness and variety of the "database" that you have accumulated and that, moment by moment, you continue to build.

So vast is your hoard of information that it can sometimes be difficult to find within it the material that would best suit your paper. In other words, finding out what you already know about a topic is not always easy. *Invention,* a term borrowed from classical rhetoric, refers to the task of discovering, or recovering from memory, such information. As we write, we go through some sort of invention procedure that helps us explore our topic. Some writers seem to have little problem coming up with material; others need more help. Over the centuries, writers have devised different exercises that can help locate useful material housed in memory. We will look at a few of these briefly.

Freewriting

Freewriting is an activity that forces you to get something down on paper. There is no waiting around for inspiration. Instead, you set a time limit—perhaps three to five minutes—and write for that length of time without stopping, not even to lift the pen from the paper or your hands from the keyboard. Focus on the topic, and do not let the difficulty of finding relevant material stop you from writing. If necessary, you may begin by writing, over and over, some seemingly useless phrase, such as, "I cannot think of anything to write," or perhaps the name of your topic. Eventually, something else will occur to you. (It is surprising how long a three-minute period of freewriting can seem to last!) At the end of the freewriting, look over what you have produced for anything you might be able to use. Much of the writing will be unusable, but there might be an insight or two that you did not know you had.

In addition to its ability to help you recover usable material from your memory for your paper, freewriting has certain other benefits. First, it takes little time, which means that you may repeat the exercise as often as you like. Second, it breaks down some of the resistance that stands between you and the act of writing. There is no initial struggle to find something to say; you just write.

Freewriting

For his second-year American government class, John Alexander had to write a paper on some aspects of local government. John, who felt his understanding of local government was slight, began the job of finding a topic that interested him with two minutes of freewriting. Thinking about local government, John wrote steadily for this period without lifting his pen from the paper. Here is the result of his freewriting:

Okay okay local government. Local, what does that mean? Like police? Chamber of Commerce? the mayor—whoever that is? judges? I got that parking ticket last year, went to court, had to pay it anyway, bummer. Maybe trace what happens to a single parking ticket—and my money. Find out the public officials who deal with it, from the traffic cop who gives it out to wherever it ends up. Point would be, what? Point point point. To find out how much the local government spends to give out and process a $35 parking ticket—how much do they really make after expenses, and where does that money go? Have to include cop's salary? judge's? Printing costs for ticket? Salary for clerk or whoever deals only with ticket. Is there somebody who lives whole life only processing traffic tickets? Are traffic tickets and parking tickets handled differently? Assuming the guy fights it. Maybe find out the difference in revenue between a contested and an uncontested ticket? Lots of phone calls to make. Who? Where to start?

Brainstorming

Brainstorming is simply the process of making a list of ideas about a topic. It can be done quickly and at first without any need to order items in a coherent pattern. The point is to write down everything that occurs to you as quickly and briefly as possible, using individual words or short phrases. Once you have a good-sized list of items, you can then group them according to relationships that you see among them. Brainstorming thus allows you to uncover both ideas stored in your memory and useful associations among those ideas.

Brainstorming

A professor in an international politics class asked his students to write a 700-word paper, in the form of a letter to be translated and published in a Warsaw newspaper, giving Polish readers useful advice about living in a democracy. One student, Melissa Jessup, started thinking about the assignment by brainstorming. First, she simply wrote down anything about life in a democracy that occurred to her:

voting rights	*welfare*	*freedom of press*
protest movements	*everybody equal*	*minorities*
racial prejudice	*American Dream*	*injustice*
the individual	*no job security*	*lobbyists and PACs*
justice takes time	*psychological factors*	*aristocracy of wealth*
size of bureaucracy		

Thinking through her list, Melissa decided to divide it into two separate lists: one devoted to positive aspects of life in a democracy; the other, to negative aspects. At this point she decided to discard some items that were redundant or did not seem to have much potential. As you can see, Melissa had some questions about where some of her items would fit:

POSITIVE	*NEGATIVE*
voting rights	*aristocracy of wealth*
freedom of the press	*justice takes time*
everybody equal	*racial prejudice*
American Dream	*welfare*
psychological factors	*lobbyists and PACs*
protest movements (positive?)	*size of bureaucracy*

At this point, Melissa decided that her topic would be about the ways in which money and special interests affect a democratically elected government. Which items on her lists would be relevant to her paper?

Asking Questions

It is always possible to ask most or all of the following questions about any topic: *Who? What? When? Where? Why? How?* They force you to approach the topic as a journalist does, setting it within different perspectives that can then be compared.

Asking Questions

A professor asked her class on the judicial process to write a paper describing the impact of Supreme Court clerks on the decision-making process. One student developed the following questions as he began to think about a thesis:

Who are the Supreme Court's clerks? (How old? What is their racial and gender mix? What are their politics?)

What are their qualifications for the job?

What exactly is their job?

When during the court term are they most influential?

Where do they come from? (Is there any geographical or religious pattern in the way they are chosen? Do certain law schools contribute a significantly greater number of clerks than others?)

How are they chosen? (Are they appointed? elected?)

When in their careers do they serve?

Why are they chosen as they are?

Who have been some influential court clerks? (Have any gone on to sit on the bench themselves?)

Can you think of other questions that would make for useful inquiry?

Maintaining Flexibility

As you engage in invention strategies, you are also performing other writing tasks. You are still narrowing your topic, for example, as well as making decisions that will affect your choice of tone or audience. You are moving forward on all fronts with each decision you make affecting the others. This means that you must be flexible enough to allow for slight adjustments in your understanding of the paper's development and of your goal. Never be so determined to prove a particular theory that you fail to notice when your own understanding of it changes. Stay objective.

Organizing Your Writing

A paper that contains all the necessary facts but presents them in an ineffective order will confuse rather than inform or persuade. Although there are various methods of grouping ideas, none is potentially more effective than outlining. Unfortunately, no organizing process is more often misunderstood.

Outlining for Yourself

Outlining can do two jobs. First, it can force you, the writer, to gain a better understanding of your ideas by arranging them according to their interrelationships. There is one primary rule of outlining: ideas of equal weight are placed on the same level within the outline. This rule requires you to determine the relative importance of your ideas. You have to decide which ideas are of the same type or order, and into which subtopic each idea best fits.

If, in the planning stage, you carefully arrange your ideas in a coherent outline, your grasp of your topic will be greatly enhanced. You will have linked your ideas logically together and given a basic structure to the body of the paper. This sort of subordinating and coordinating activity is difficult, however, and as a result, inexperienced writers sometimes begin to write their first draft without an effective outline, hoping for the best. This hope is usually unfulfilled, especially in complex papers involving research.

EXERCISE   **Organizing Thoughts**

Rodrigo, a student in a second-year class in government management, researched the impact of a worker-retraining program in his state and came up with the following facts and theories. Number them in logical order:

___ A growing number of workers in the state do not possess the basic skills and education demanded by employers.

___ The number of dislocated workers in the state increased from 21,000 in 1997 to 32,000 in 2006.

___ A public policy to retrain uneducated workers would allow them to move into new and expanding sectors of the state economy.

___ Investment in high technology would allow the state's employers to remain competitive in the production of goods and services in both domestic and foreign markets.

___ The state's economy is becoming more global and more competitive.

Outlining for Your Reader

The second job an outline can perform is to serve as a reader's blueprint to the paper, summarizing its points and their interrelationships. By consulting your outline, a busy policymaker can quickly get a sense of your paper's goal and the argument you have used to promote it. The clarity and coherence of the outline help determine how much attention your audience will give to your ideas.

As political science students, you will be given a great deal of help with the arrangement of your material into an outline to accompany your paper. A look at the formats presented in Chapter 3 of this manual will show you how strictly these formal outlines are structured. But, although you must pay close attention to these requirements, do not forget how powerful a tool an outline can be in the early planning stages of your paper.

The Formal Outline Pattern

Following this pattern accurately during the planning stage of your paper helps to guarantee that your ideas are placed logically:

Thesis sentence (precedes the formal outline)

I. First main idea
   A. First subordinate idea
      1. Reason, example, or illustration
         a. Supporting detail
         b. Supporting detail
         c. Supporting detail
      2. Reason, example, or illustration
         a. Supporting detail
         b. Supporting detail
         c. Supporting detail
   B. Second subordinate idea
II. Second main idea

Notice that each level of the paper must have more than one entry; for every A there must be at least a B (and, if required, a C, a D, and so on), and for every 1 there must be a 2. This arrangement forces you to *compare ideas,* looking carefully at each one to determine its place among the others. The insistence on assigning relative values to your ideas is what makes an outline an effective organizing tool.

The Patterns of Political Science Papers

The structure of any particular type of political science paper is governed by a formal pattern. When rigid external controls are placed on their writing, some writers feel that their creativity is hampered by a kind of "paint-by-numbers" approach to structure. It is vital to the success of your paper that you never allow yourself to be overwhelmed by the pattern rules for any type of paper. Remember that such controls exist not to limit your creativity but to make the paper immediately and easily useful to its intended audience. It is as necessary to write clearly and confidently in a position paper or a policy analysis paper as in a term paper for English literature, a résumé, a short story, or a job application letter.

Drafting

The Rough Draft

The planning stage of the writing process is followed by the writing of the first draft. Using your thesis and outline as direction markers, you must now weave your amalgam of ideas, data, and persuasion strategies into logically ordered sentences and paragraphs. Although adequate prewriting may facilitate drafting, it still will not be easy. Writers establish their own individual methods of encouraging themselves to forge ahead with the draft, but here are some tips:

1. *Remember that this is a rough draft, not the final paper.* At this stage, it is not necessary that every word be the best possible choice. Do not put that sort of pressure on yourself. You must not allow anything to slow you down now. Writing is not like sculpting in stone, where every chip is permanent; you can always go back to your draft and add, delete, reword, and rearrange. *No matter how much effort you have put into planning, you cannot be sure how much of this first draft you will eventually keep.* It may take several drafts to get one that you find satisfactory.

2. *Give yourself sufficient time to write.* Do not delay the first draft by telling yourself there is still more research to do. You cannot uncover all the material there is to know on a particular subject, so do not fool yourself into trying. Remember that writing is a process of discovery. You may have to begin writing before you can see exactly what sort of research you need to do. Keep in mind that there are other tasks waiting for you after the first draft is finished, so allow for them as you determine your writing schedule.

More importantly, give yourself time to write, because the more time that passes after you have written a draft, the better your ability to view it with objectivity. It is very difficult to evaluate your writing accurately soon after you complete it. You need to cool down, to recover from the effort of putting all those words together. The "colder" you get on your writing, the better you are able to read it as if it were written by someone else and thus acknowledge the changes you will need to make to strengthen the paper.

3. *Stay sharp.* Keep in mind the plan you created as you narrowed your topic, composed a thesis sentence, and outlined the material. But, if you begin to feel a strong need to change the plan a bit, do not be afraid to do so. Be ready for surprises dealt you by your own growing understanding of your topic. Your goal is to record your best thinking on the subject as accurately as possible.

Language Choices

To be convincing, your writing has to be authoritative; that is, you have to sound as if you have complete confidence in your ability to convey your ideas in words. Sentences that sound stilted, or that suffer from weak phrasing or the use of clichés, are not going to win supporters for the positions that you express in your paper. So a major question becomes, How can I sound confident?

Here are some points to consider as you work to convey to your reader that necessary sense of authority:

Level of Formality.   Tone is one of the primary methods by which you signal to the readers who you are and what your attitude is toward them and toward your topic. Your major decision is which level of language formality is most appropriate to your audience. The informal tone you would use in a letter to a friend might well be out of place in a paper on "Waste in Military Spending" written for your government professor. Remember that tone is only part of the overall decision that you make about how to present your information. Formality is, to some extent, a function of individual word choices and phrasing. For example, is it appropriate to

use contractions such as *isn't* or *they'll*? Would the strategic use of a sentence fragment for effect be out of place? The use of informal language, the personal *I*, and
the second-person *you* is traditionally forbidden—for better or worse—in certain
kinds of writing. Often, part of the challenge of writing a formal paper is simply
how to give your prose impact while staying within the conventions.

Jargon.   One way to lose readers quickly is to overwhelm them with
jargon—phrases that have a special, usually technical meaning within your discipline but that are unfamiliar to the average reader. The very occasional use of
jargon may add an effective touch of atmosphere, but anything more than that
will severely dampen a reader's enthusiasm for the paper. Often the writer uses
jargon in an effort to impress the reader by sounding lofty or knowledgeable.
Unfortunately, all jargon usually does is cause confusion. In fact, the use of jargon indicates a writer's lack of connection to the audience.

Political science writing is a haven for jargon. Perhaps writers of policy
analyses and position papers believe their readers are all completely attuned to
their terminology. Or some may hope to obscure damaging information or
potentially unpopular ideas in confusing language. In other cases, the problem
could simply be unclear thinking by the writer. Whatever the reason, the fact is
that political science papers too often sound like prose made by machines to be
read by machines.

Students may feel that, to be accepted as political scientists, their papers
should conform to the practices of their published peers. *This is a mistake.*
Remember that it is never better to write a cluttered or confusing sentence than
a clear one, and burying your ideas in jargon defeats the effort that you went
through to form them.

EXERCISE   **Revising Jargon**

What words in the following sentence, from an article in a political science journal, are
jargon? Can you rewrite it to clarify its meaning?

> The implementation of statute-mandated regulated inputs exceeds the conceptual-
> ization of the administrative technicians.

Clichés.   In the heat of composition, as you are looking for words to help you
form your ideas, it is sometimes easy to plug in a *cliché*—a phrase that has attained
universal recognition by overuse. (*Note:* Clichés differ from jargon in that clichés are
part of the general public's everyday language, whereas jargon is specific to the language of experts in a field.) Our vocabularies are brimming with clichés:

It's *raining cats and dogs.*
That issue is as *dead as a doornail.*
It's time for the governor to *face the music.*
Angry voters *made a beeline* for the ballot box.

The problem with clichés is that they are virtually meaningless. Once colorful means of expression, they have lost their color through overuse, and they tend to bleed energy and color from the surrounding words. When revising, replace clichés with fresh wording that more accurately conveys your point.

Descriptive Language.   Language that appeals to readers' senses will always engage their interest more fully than language that is abstract. This is especially important for writing in disciplines that tend to deal in abstracts, such as political science. The typical political science paper, with its discussions of principles, demographics, or points of law, is usually in danger of floating off into abstraction, with each paragraph drifting further away from the felt life of the readers. Whenever appropriate, appeal to your readers' sense of sight, hearing, taste, touch, or smell.

EXERCISE   **Using Descriptive Language**

Which of these two sentences is more effective?

1. The housing project had deteriorated badly since the last inspection.
2. The housing project had deteriorated badly since the last inspection; stench rose from the plumbing, grime coated the walls and floors, and rats scurried through the hallways.

Sexist Language.   Language can be a very powerful method of either reinforcing or destroying cultural stereotypes. By treating the sexes in subtly different ways in your language, you may unknowingly be committing an act of discrimination. A common example is the use of the pronoun *he* to refer to a person whose gender has not been identified.

Some writers, faced with this dilemma, alternate the use of male and female personal pronouns; others use the plural to avoid the need to use a pronoun of either gender:

SEXIST	**NONSEXIST**
A lawyer should always treat his client with respect.	A lawyer should always treat his or her client with respect.
	Lawyers should always treat their clients with respect.
Man is a political animal.	People are political animals.

Remember that language is more than the mere vehicle of your thoughts. Your words shape perceptions for your readers. How well you say something will profoundly affect your readers' response to what you say. Sexist language denies to a large number of your readers the basic right to fair and equal treatment. Make sure your writing is not guilty of this form of discrimination.

Revising

Revising is one of the most important steps in ensuring the success of your essay. Although unpracticed writers often think of revision as little more than making sure all the *i*'s are dotted and *t*'s are crossed, it is much more than that. Revising is *reseeing* the essay, looking at it from other perspectives, trying always to align your view with the one that will be held by your audience. Research indicates that we are actually revising all the time, in every phase of the writing process, as we reread phrases, rethink the placement of an item in an outline, or test a new topic sentence for a paragraph. Subjecting your entire hard-fought draft to cold, objective scrutiny is one of the toughest activities to master, but it is absolutely necessary. You have to make sure that you have said everything that needs to be said clearly and logically. One confusing passage will deflect the reader's attention from where you want it to be. Suddenly the reader has to become a detective, trying to figure out why you wrote, what you did, and what you meant by it. You do not want to throw such obstacles in the path of understanding.

Here are some tips to help you with revision:

1. *Give yourself adequate time for revision.* As discussed above, you need time to become "cold" on your paper in order to analyze it objectively. After you have written your draft, spend some time away from it. Then try to reread it as if someone else had written it.

2. *Read the paper carefully.* This is tougher than it sounds. One good strategy is to read it aloud yourself or to have a friend read it aloud while you listen. (Note, however, that friends are usually not the best critics. They are rarely trained in revision techniques and are often unwilling to risk disappointing you by giving your paper a really thorough examination.)

3. *Have a list of specific items to check.* It is important to revise in an orderly fashion, in stages, first looking at large concerns, such as the overall organization, and then at smaller elements, such as paragraph or sentence structure.

4. *Check for unity*—the clear and logical relation of all parts of the essay to its thesis. Make sure that every paragraph relates well to the whole of the paper and is in the right place.

5. *Check for coherence.* Make sure there are no gaps between the various parts of the argument. Look to see that you have adequate transitions everywhere they are needed. Transitional elements are markers indicating places where the paper's focus or attitude changes. Such elements can take the form of one word—*however, although, unfortunately, luckily*—or an entire sentence or a paragraph: *In order to fully appreciate the importance of democracy as a shaping presence in post–Cold War Polish politics, it is necessary to examine briefly the Poles' last historical attempt to implement democratic government.*

Transitional elements rarely introduce new material. Instead, they are direction pointers, either indicating a shift to new subject matter or signaling how the writer wishes certain material to be interpreted by the reader. Because you, the writer, already know where and why your paper changes direction and how you want particular passages to be received, it can be very difficult for you to catch those places where transition is needed.

6. *Avoid unnecessary repetition.* Two types of repetition can annoy a reader: repetition of content and repetition of wording.

Repetition of content occurs when you return to a subject you have already discussed. Ideally, you should deal with a topic once, memorably, and then move on to your next subject. Organizing a paper is a difficult task, however, which usually occurs through a process of enlightenment in terms of purposes and strategies, and repetition of content can happen even if you have used prewriting strategies. What is worse, it can be difficult for you to be aware of the repetition in your own writing. As you write and revise, remember that any unnecessary repetition of content in your final draft is potentially annoying to your readers, who are working to make sense of the argument they are reading and do not want to be distracted by a passage repeating material they have already encountered. You must train yourself, through practice, to look for material that you have repeated unnecessarily.

Repetition of wording occurs when you overuse certain phrases or words. This can make your prose sound choppy and uninspired, as the following examples demonstrate:

> The subcommittee's report on education reform will surprise a number of people. A number of people will want copies of the report.

> The chairman said at a press conference that he is happy with the report. He will circulate it to the local news agencies in the morning. He will also make sure that the city council has copies.

> I became upset when I heard how the committee had voted. I called the chairman and expressed my reservations about the committee's decision. I told him I felt that he had let the teachers and students of the state down. I also issued a press statement.

The last passage illustrates a condition known by composition teachers as the *I-syndrome.* Can you hear how such duplicated phrasing can hurt a paper? Your language should sound fresh and energetic. Make sure, before you submit your final draft, to read through your paper carefully, looking for such repetition. However, not all repetition is bad. You may wish to repeat a phrase for rhetorical effect or special emphasis: "*I came. I saw. I conquered.*" Just make sure that any repetition in your paper is intentional, placed there to produce a specific effect.

Editing

Editing is sometimes confused with the more involved process of revising. But editing is done later in the writing process, after you have wrestled through your first draft—and maybe your second and third—and arrived at the final draft. Even though your draft now contains all the information you want to impart and has the information arranged to your satisfaction, there are still many factors to check, such as sentence structure, spelling, and punctuation.

It is at this point that an unpracticed writer might be less than vigilant. After all, most of the work on the paper is finished, as the "big jobs" of discovering, organizing, and drafting information have been completed. *But watch out!*

Editing is as important as any other part of the writing process. Any error that you allow in the final draft will count against you in the mind of the reader. This may not seem fair, but even a minor error—a misspelling or confusing placement of a comma—will make a much greater impression on your reader than perhaps it should. Remember that everything about your paper is your responsibility, including performing even the supposedly little jobs correctly. Careless editing undermines the effectiveness of your paper. It would be a shame if all the hard work you put into prewriting, drafting, and revising were to be damaged because you carelessly allowed a comma splice!

Most of the tips given above for revising hold for editing as well. It is best to edit in stages, looking for only one or two kinds of errors each time you reread the paper. Focus especially on errors that you remember committing in the past. If, for instance, you know that you have a tendency to misplace commas, go through your paper looking at each comma carefully. If you have a weakness for writing unintentional sentence fragments, read each sentence aloud to make sure that it is indeed a complete sentence. Have you accidentally shifted verb tenses anywhere, moving from past to present tense for no reason? Do all the subjects in your sentences agree in number with their verbs? *Now is the time to find out.*

Watch out for *miscues*—problems with a sentence that the writer simply does not see. Remember that your search for errors is hampered in two ways:

1. As the writer, you hope not to find any errors in your work. This desire can cause you to miss mistakes when they do occur.
2. Because you know your material so well, it is easy, as you read, to unconsciously supply missing material—a word, a piece of punctuation—as if it were present.

How difficult is it to see that something is missing in the following sentence?

Unfortunately, legislators often have too little regard their constituents.

We can guess that the missing word is probably *for,* which should be inserted after *regard.* It is quite possible, however, that the writer of the sentence would automatically supply the missing *for* as if it were on the page. This is a miscue, which can be hard for writers to spot because they are so close to their material.

One tactic for catching mistakes in sentence structure is to read the sentences aloud, starting with the last one in the paper and then moving to the next-to-last, then to the previous sentence, and thus going backward through the paper (reading each sentence in the normal, left-to-right manner, of course) until you reach the first sentence of the introduction. This backward progression strips each sentence of its rhetorical context and helps you focus on its internal structure.

Editing is the stage in which you finally answer those minor questions that you had put off when you were wrestling with wording and organization. Any ambiguities regarding the use of abbreviations, italics, numerals, capital letters, titles (When do you capitalize the title *president*, for example?), hyphens, dashes (usually created on a typewriter or computer by striking the hyphen key twice), apostrophes, and quotation marks have to be cleared up now. You must also check to see that you have used the required formats for footnotes, endnotes, margins, page numbers, and the like.

Guessing is not allowed. Sometimes unpracticed writers who realize that they do not quite understand a particular rule of grammar, punctuation, or format do nothing to fill that knowledge gap. Instead they rely on guesswork and their own logic—which is not always up to the task of dealing with so contrary a language as English—to get them through problems that they could solve if they referred to a writing manual. Remember that it does not matter to the reader why or how an error shows up in your writing. It only matters that you have dropped your guard. You must not allow a careless error to undo all the good work that you have done.

Proofreading

Before you hand in the final version of your paper, it is vital that you check it one more time to make sure there are no errors of any sort. This job is called *proofreading,* or *proofing.* In essence, you are looking for many of the same things you had checked for during editing, but now you are doing it on the last draft, which is about to be submitted to your audience. Proofreading is as important as editing; you may have missed an error that you still have time to find, or an error may have been introduced when the draft was recopied or typed for the last time. Like every other stage of the writing process, proofreading is your responsibility.

At this point, you must check for typing mistakes: transposed or deleted letters, words, phrases, or punctuation. If you have had the paper professionally typed, you still must check it carefully. Do not rely solely on the typist's proofreading. If you are creating your paper on a computer or a word processor, it is possible for you to unintentionally insert a command that alters your document drastically by slicing out a word, line, or sentence at the touch of a key. Make sure such accidental deletions have not occurred.

Above all else, remember that your paper represents you. It is a product of your best thinking, your most energetic and imaginative response to a writing challenge. If you have maintained your enthusiasm for the project and worked through the stages of the writing process honestly and carefully, you should produce a paper you can be proud of, one that will serve its readers well.

CHAPTER
6

WRITING COMPETENTLY

6.1 GRAMMAR AND STYLE

The Competent Writer

Good writing places your thoughts in your readers' minds in exactly the way you want them to be there. Good writing tells your readers just what you want them to know without telling them anything you do not want them to know. This may sound odd, but the fact is that writers have to be careful not to let unwanted messages slip into their writing. Look, for example, at the passage below, taken from a paper analyzing the impact of a worker-retraining program. Hidden within the prose is a message that jeopardizes the paper's success. Can you detect the message?

Recent articles written on the subject of dislocated workers have had little to say about the particular problems dealt with in this paper. Because few of these articles focus on the problem at the state level.

Chances are, when you reached the end of the second "sentence," you felt that something was missing and perceived a gap in logic or coherence, so you went back through both sentences to find the place where things had gone wrong. The second sentence is actually not a sentence at all. It does have certain features of a sentence—for example, a subject (*few*) and a verb (*focus*)—but its first word (*Because*) subordinates the entire clause that follows, taking away its ability to stand on its own as a complete idea. The second "sentence," which is properly called a *subordinate clause*, merely fills in some information about the first sentence, telling us why recent articles about dislocated workers fail to deal with problems discussed in the present paper.

The sort of error represented by the second "sentence" is commonly called a *sentence fragment*, and it conveys to the reader a message that no writer wants to send: that the writer either is careless or, worse, has not mastered the language. Language errors such as fragments, misplaced commas, or shifts in verb tense send out warnings in readers' minds. As a result, readers lose some of their concentration on the issue being discussed; they become distracted and begin to wonder about the language competency of the writer. The writing loses effectiveness.

NOTE. Whatever goal you set for your paper—be it to persuade, describe, analyze, or speculate—you must also set one other goal: *to display language competence.* If your paper does not meet this goal, it will not completely achieve its other aims. Language errors spread doubt like a virus; they jeopardize all the hard work you have done on your paper.

Language competence is especially important in political science, for credibility in politics depends on such skill. Anyone who doubts this should remember the beating that Vice President Dan Quayle took in the press for misspelling the word *potato* at a 1992 spelling bee. His error caused a storm of humiliating publicity for the hapless Quayle, adding to an impression of his general incompetence.

Correctness Is Relative

Although they may seem minor, the sort of language errors we are discussing—often called *surface errors*—can be extremely damaging in certain kinds of writing. Surface errors come in a variety of types, including misspellings, punctuation problems, grammar errors, and the inconsistent use of abbreviations, capitalization, and numerals. These errors are an affront to your readers' notion of correctness, and therein lies one of the biggest problems with surface errors. Different audiences tolerate different levels of correctness. You know that you can get away with surface errors in, say, a letter to a friend, who will probably not judge you harshly for them, whereas those same errors in a job application letter might eliminate you from consideration for the position. Correctness depends to an extent on context.

Another problem is that the rules governing correctness shift over time. What would have been an error to your grandmother's generation—the splitting of an infinitive, for example, or the ending of a sentence with a preposition—is taken in stride by most readers today.

So how do you write correctly when the rules shift from person to person and over time? Here are some tips:

Consider Your Audience

One of the great risks of writing is that even the simplest of choices regarding wording or punctuation can sometimes prejudice your audience against you in ways that may seem unfair. For example, look again at the old grammar rule forbidding the splitting of infinitives. After decades of telling students to never split an infinitive (something just done in this sentence), most composition experts now concede that a split infinitive is *not* a grammar crime. But suppose you have written a position paper trying to convince your city council of the need to hire security personnel for the library, and half of the council members—the people you wish to convince—remember their eighth-grade grammar teacher's warning about splitting infinitives. How will they respond when you tell them, in your introduction, that librarians are compelled "to always accompany" visitors to the rare book room because of the threat of vandalism? How much of their attention have you suddenly lost because of their automatic recollection of what is now a nonrule? It is possible, in other words, to write correctly and still offend your readers' notions of language competence.

Make sure that you tailor the surface features and the degree of formality of your writing to the level of competency that your readers require. When in doubt, take a conservative approach. Your audience might be just as distracted by a contraction as by a split infinitive.

Aim for Consistency

When dealing with a language question for which there are different answers—such as whether to use a comma before the conjunction in a series of three ("The mayor's speech addressed taxes, housing for the poor, and the job situation.")—always use the same strategy throughout your paper. If, for example, you avoid splitting one infinitive, avoid splitting *all* infinitives.

Have Confidence in What You Know About Writing!

It is easy for unpracticed writers to allow their occasional mistakes to shake their confidence in their writing ability. The fact is, however, that most of what we know about writing is correct. We are all capable, for example, of writing grammatically sound phrases, even if we cannot list the rules by which we achieve coherence. Most writers who worry about their chronic errors make fewer mistakes than they think. Becoming distressed about errors makes writing even more difficult.

Grammar

As various composition theorists have pointed out, the word *grammar* has several definitions. One meaning is "the formal patterns in which words must be arranged in order to convey meaning." We learn these patterns very early in life and use them spontaneously, without thinking. Our understanding of grammatical patterns is extremely sophisticated, despite the fact that few of us can actually cite the rules by which the patterns work. Patrick Hartwell tested grammar learning by asking native English speakers of different ages and levels of education, including high school teachers, to arrange these words in natural order:

French the young girls four

Everyone could produce the natural order for this phrase: "the four young French girls." Yet none of Hartwell's respondents said they knew the rule that governs the order of the words (Hartwell 1985, 111).

Eliminate Chronic Errors

But if just thinking about our errors has a negative effect on our writing, how do we learn to write more correctly? Perhaps the best answer is simply to write as often as possible. Give yourself lots of practice in putting your thoughts into written shape—and then in revising and proofing your work. As you write and revise, be honest with yourself—and patient. Chronic errors are like bad habits; getting rid of them takes time.

You probably know of one or two problem areas in your writing that you could have eliminated but have not. Instead, you may have "fudged" your writing at the critical points, relying on half-remembered formulas from past English classes or trying to come up with logical solutions to your writing problems. (*Warning:* The English language does not always work in a way that seems logical.) You may have simply decided that comma rules are unlearnable or that you will never understand the difference between the verbs *lay* and *lie*. And so you guess, and you come up with the wrong answer a good part of the time. What a shame, when just a little extra work would give you mastery over those few gaps in your understanding and boost your confidence as well.

Instead of continuing with this sort of guesswork and living with the holes in your knowledge, why not face the problem areas now and learn the rules that have heretofore escaped you? What follows is a discussion of those surface features of writing in which errors most commonly occur. You will probably be familiar with most if not all of the rules discussed, but there may well be a few you have not yet mastered. Now is the time to do so.

6.2   PUNCTUATION

Apostrophes

An apostrophe is used to show possession. When you wish to say that something belongs to someone or something, you add either an apostrophe and an *s* or an apostrophe alone to the word that represents the owner.

When the owner is singular (a single person or thing), the apostrophe precedes an added *s:*

According to Mayor Anderson's secretary, the news broadcast has been canceled.

The union's lawyers challenged the government's policy in court.
Somebody's briefcase was left in the auditorium.

The same rule applies if the word showing possession is a plural that does not end in *s:*

The women's club sponsored several debates during the last presidential campaign.

Governor Smith has proven himself a tireless worker for children's rights.

When the word expressing ownership is a plural ending in *s*, the apostrophe follows the *s:*

The new legislation was discussed at the secretaries' conference.

There are two ways to form the possessive for two or more nouns:

1. To show joint possession (both nouns owning the same thing or things), the last noun in the series is possessive:

   The president and first lady's invitations were sent out yesterday.

2. To indicate that each noun owns an item or items individually, each noun must show possession:

   Mayor Scott's and Mayor MacKay's speeches took different approaches to the same problem.

The importance of the apostrophe is obvious when you consider the difference in meaning between the following two sentences:

Be sure to pick up the senator's bags on your way to the airport.
Be sure to pick up the senators' bags on your way to the airport.

In the first sentence, you have only one senator to worry about, whereas in the second, you have at least two!

A Prepostrophe?

James Swanson, political commentator and editor of the *Gesundheit Gazette*, occasionally encounters political statements that he finds to be preposterous. He believes that journalists should warn us when they print one of these statements by placing a "prepostrophe" (^) at the end of a preposterous sentence. Consider, for example, how a prepostrophe might assist the reader in the following statement: "We can cut taxes without reducing services ^" For even more preposterous statements, we add more prepostrophes, as in, "I never had sex with that woman ^ ^"

Capitalization

Here is a brief summary of some hard-to-remember capitalization rules:

1. You may, if you choose, capitalize the first letter of the first word in a sentence that follows a colon. However, make sure you use one pattern consistently throughout your paper:

> Our instructions are explicit: *Do not* allow anyone into the conference without an identification badge.

> Our instructions are explicit: *do not* allow anyone into the conference without an identification badge.

2. Capitalize *proper nouns* (names of specific people, places, or things) and *proper adjectives* (adjectives made from proper nouns). A common noun following a proper adjective is usually not capitalized, nor is a common adjective preceding a proper adjective (such as *a, an,* or *the*):

PROPER NOUNS	PROPER ADJECTIVES
Poland	Polish officials
Iraq	the Iraqi ambassador
Shakespeare	a Shakespearean tragedy

Proper nouns include:

- *Names of monuments and buildings:* the Washington Monument, the Empire State Building, the Library of Congress
- *Historical events, eras, and certain terms concerning calendar dates:* the Civil War, the Dark Ages, Monday, December, Columbus Day
- *Parts of the country:* North, Southwest, Eastern Seaboard, the West Coast, New England.

NOTE. When words like *north, south, east, west,* and *northwest* are used to designate direction rather than geographical region, they are not capitalized: "We drove east to Boston and then made a tour of the East Coast."

- *Words referring to race, religion, and nationality:* Islam, Muslim, Caucasian, White (or white), Asian, Negro, Black (or black), Slavic, Arab, Jewish, Hebrew, Buddhism, Buddhists, Southern Baptists, the Bible, the Koran, American
- *Names of languages:* English, Chinese, Latin, Sanskrit
- *Titles of corporations, institutions, universities, and organizations:* Dow Chemical, General Motors, the National Endowment for the Humanities, University of Tennessee, Colby College, Kiwanis Club, American Association of Retired Persons, Oklahoma State Senate

NOTE. Some words once considered proper nouns or adjectives have, over time, become common and are no longer capitalized, such as *french fries, pasteurized milk, arabic numerals, and italics.*

3. Titles of individuals may be capitalized if they precede a proper name; otherwise, titles are usually not capitalized:

The committee honored Senator Jones.

The committee honored the senator from Kansas.

We phoned Doctor Jessup, who arrived shortly afterward.

We phoned the doctor, who arrived shortly afterward.

A story on Queen Elizabeth's health appeared in yesterday's paper.

A story on the queen's health appeared in yesterday's paper.

Pope John Paul's visit to Colorado was a public relations success.

The pope's visit to Colorado was a public relations success.

When Not to Capitalize

In general, you do not capitalize nouns when your reference is nonspecific. For example, you would not capitalize *the senator*, but you would capitalize *Senator Smith*. The second reference is as much a title as it is a term of identification, whereas the first reference is a mere identifier. Likewise, there is a difference in degree of specificity between *the state treasury* and *the Texas State Treasury*.

NOTE. The meaning of a term may change somewhat depending on its capitalization. What, for example, might be the difference between a *Democrat* and a *democrat*? When capitalized, the word refers to a member of a specific political party; when not capitalized, it refers to someone who believes in the democratic form of government.

Capitalization depends to some extent on the context of your writing. For example, if you are writing a policy analysis for a specific corporation, you may capitalize words and phrases that refer to that corporation—such as *Board of Directors, Chairman of the Board,* and *the Institute* —that would not be capitalized in a paper written for a more general audience. Likewise, in some contexts, it is not unusual to see the titles of certain powerful officials capitalized even when not accompanying a proper noun:

The President took few members of his staff to Camp David with him.

Colons

We all know certain uses for the colon. A colon can, for example, separate the parts of a statement of time (*4:25 A.M.*), separate chapter and verse in a biblical quotation (*John 3:16*), and close the salutation of a business letter (*Dear Senator Keaton:*). But the colon has other, less well-known uses that can add extra flexibility to sentence structure.

The colon can introduce into a sentence certain kinds of material, such as a list, a quotation, or a restatement or description of material mentioned earlier:

LIST

The committee's research proposal promised to do three things: (1) establish the extent of the problem, (2) examine several possible solutions, and (3) estimate the cost of each solution.

QUOTATION

In his speech, the mayor challenged us with these words: "How will your council's work make a difference in the life of our city?"

RESTATEMENT OR DESCRIPTION

Ahead of us, according to the senator's chief of staff, lay the biggest job of all: convincing our constituents of the plan's benefits.

Commas

The comma is perhaps the most troublesome of all marks of punctuation, no doubt because its use is governed by so many variables, such as sentence length, rhetorical emphasis, and changing notions of style. The most common problems are outlined below.

The Comma Splice

A *comma splice* is the joining of two complete sentences with only a comma:

An impeachment is merely an indictment of a government official, actual removal usually requires a vote by a legislative body.

An unemployed worker who has been effectively retrained is no longer an economic problem for the community, he has become an asset.

It might be possible for the city to assess fees on the sale of real estate, however, such a move would be criticized by the community of real estate developers.

In each of these passages, two complete sentences (also called *independent clauses*) have been spliced together by a comma, which is an inadequate break between the two sentences.

One foolproof way to check your paper for comma splices is to read the structures on both sides of each comma carefully. If you find a complete sentence on each side, and if the sentence following the comma does not begin with a coordinating conjunction (*and, but, for, nor, or, so, yet*), then you have found a comma splice.

Simply reading the draft to try to "hear" the comma splices may not work because the rhetorical features of your prose—its "movement"—may make it hard to detect this kind of error in sentence completeness. There are five commonly used ways to correct comma splices:

1. Place a period between the two independent clauses:

   INCORRECT   A political candidate receives many benefits from his or her affiliation with a political party, there are liabilities as well.

   CORRECT   A political candidate receives many benefits from his or her affiliation with a political party. There are liabilities as well.

2. Place a comma and a coordinating conjunction (*and, but, for, or, nor, so, yet*) between the independent clauses:

   INCORRECT   The councilman's speech described the major differences of opinion over the economic situation, it also suggested a possible course of action.

   CORRECT   The councilman's speech described the major differences of opinion over the economic situation, and it also suggested a possible course of action.

3. Place a semicolon between the independent clauses:

   INCORRECT   Some people feel that the federal government should play a large role in establishing a housing policy for the homeless, many others disagree.

   CORRECT   Some people feel that the federal government should play a large role in establishing a housing policy for the homeless; many others disagree.

4. Rewrite the two clauses as one independent clause:

   INCORRECT   Television ads played a big part in the campaign, however they were not the deciding factor in the challenger's victory over the incumbent.

   CORRECT   Television ads played a large but not a decisive role in the challenger's victory over the incumbent.

5. Change one of the independent clauses into a dependent clause by beginning it with a subordinating word (*although, after, as, because, before, if, though, unless, when, which, where*), which prevents the clause from being able to stand on its own as a complete sentence.

   INCORRECT   The election was held last Tuesday, there was a poor voter turnout.

CORRECT   When the election was held last Tuesday, there was a
poor voter turnout.

Commas in a Compound Sentence

A *compound sentence* is composed of two or more independent clauses—two
complete sentences. When these two clauses are joined by a coordinating conjunction, the conjunction should be preceded by a comma to signal the reader that
another independent clause follows. (This is method number 2 for fixing a comma
splice, described above.) When the comma is missing, the reader is not expecting to
find the second half of a compound sentence and may be distracted from the text.

As the following examples indicate, the missing comma is especially a problem in longer sentences or in sentences in which other coordinating conjunctions
appear. Notice how the comma sorts out the two main parts of the compound
sentence, eliminating confusion:

INCORRECT   The senator promised to visit the hospital and investigate the
problem and then he called the press conference to a close.

CORRECT   The senator promised to visit the hospital and investigate the
problem, and then he called the press conference to a close.

INCORRECT   The water board can neither make policy nor enforce it nor
can its members serve on auxiliary water committees.

CORRECT   The water board can neither make policy nor enforce it, nor can
its members serve on auxiliary water committees.

An exception to this rule arises in shorter sentences, where the comma may
not be necessary to make the meaning clear:

The mayor phoned and we thanked him for his support.

However, it is never wrong to place a comma after the conjunction between
independent clauses. If you are the least bit unsure of your audience's notion of
"proper" grammar, it is a good idea to take the conservative approach and use
the comma:

The mayor phoned, and we thanked him for his support.

Commas with Restrictive and Nonrestrictive Elements

A *nonrestrictive element* is a part of a sentence—a word, phrase, or clause—that
adds information about another element in the sentence without restricting or limiting its meaning. Although this information may be useful, the nonrestrictive element is not needed for the sentence to make sense. To signal its inessential nature,
the nonrestrictive element is set off from the rest of the sentence with commas.

The failure to use commas to indicate the nonrestrictive nature of a sentence element can cause confusion. See, for example, how the presence or
absence of commas affects our understanding of the following sentence:

The mayor was talking with the policeman, who won the outstanding service award last year.

The mayor was talking with the policeman who won the outstanding service award last year.

Can you see that the comma changes the meaning of the sentence? In the first version of the sentence, the comma makes the information that follows it incidental: *The mayor was talking with the policeman, who happens to have won the service award last year.* In the second version of the sentence, the information following the word *policeman* is vital to the sense of the sentence; it tells us specifically *which* policeman—presumably there are more than one—the mayor was addressing. Here, the lack of a comma has transformed the material following the word *policeman* into a *restrictive element,* which means that it is necessary to our understanding of the sentence.

Be sure that you make a clear distinction in your paper between nonrestrictive and restrictive elements by setting off the nonrestrictive elements with commas.

Commas in a Series

A series is any two or more items of a similar nature that appear consecutively in a sentence. These items may be individual words, phrases, or clauses. In a series of three or more items, the items are separated by commas:

> *The senator, the mayor, and the police chief* all attended the ceremony.

> Because of the new zoning regulations, *all trailer parks must be moved out of the neighborhood, all small businesses must apply for recertification and tax status, and the two local churches must repave their parking lots.*

The final comma in the series, the one before *and*, is sometimes left out, especially in newspaper writing. This practice, however, can make for confusion, especially in longer, complicated sentences like the second example above. Here is the way this sentence would read without the final, or serial, comma:

> Because of the new zoning regulations, all trailer parks must be moved out of the neighborhood, all small businesses must apply for recertification and tax status and the two local churches must repave their parking lots.

Notice that, without a comma, the division between the second and third items in the series is not clear. This is the sort of ambiguous structure that can cause a reader to backtrack and lose concentration. You can avoid such confusion by always using that final comma. Remember, however, that if you do decide to include it, do so consistently; make sure it appears in every series in your paper.

Dangling Modifiers

A *modifier* is a word or group of words used to describe, or modify, another word in the sentence. A *dangling modifier* appears at either the beginning or the end of a sentence and seems to be describing some word other than the one the writer obviously intended. The modifier therefore "dangles," disconnected from its correct meaning. It is often hard for the writer to spot a dangling modifier, but readers can—and will—find them, and the result can be disastrous for the sentence, as the following examples demonstrate:

INCORRECT	Flying low over Washington, the White House was seen.
CORRECT	Flying low over Washington, we saw the White House.
INCORRECT	Worried at the cost of the program, sections of the bill were trimmed in committee.
CORRECT	Worried at the cost of the program, the committee trimmed sections of the bill.
INCORRECT	To lobby for prison reform, a lot of effort went into the television ads.
CORRECT	The lobby group put a lot of effort into the television ads advocating prison reform.
INCORRECT	Stunned, the television broadcast the defeated senator's concession speech.
CORRECT	The television broadcast the stunned senator's concession speech.

Note that, in the first two incorrect sentences above, the confusion is largely due to the use of *passive-voice* verbs: "the White House *was seen*," "sections of the bill *were trimmed*." Often, although not always, a dangling modifier results because the actor in the sentence—*we* in the first sentence, *the committee* in the second—is either distanced from the modifier or obliterated by the passive-voice verb. It is a good idea to avoid using the passive voice unless you have a specific reason for doing so.

One way to check for dangling modifiers is to examine all modifiers at the beginning or end of your sentences. Look especially for to be phrases or for words ending in -*ing* or -*ed* at the start of the modifier. Then see if the modified word is close enough to the phrase to be properly connected.

Parallelism

Series of two or more words, phrases, or clauses within a sentence should have the same grammatical structure, a situation called *parallelism*. Parallel structures can add power and balance to your writing by creating a strong rhetorical rhythm. Here is a famous example of parallelism from the Preamble to the U.S. Constitution. (The capitalization follows that of the original eighteenth-century document. Parallel structures have been italicized:)

> We the People of the United States, in Order to *form a more perfect Union, Establish justice, insure Domestic Tranquillity, provide for the common defense, promote the general Welfare,* and *secure the Blessings of Liberty to ourselves and our Posterity,* do *ordain* and *establish* this Constitution for the United States of America.

There are actually two series in this sentence: the first, composed of six phrases, each of which completes the infinitive phrase beginning with the word to [*to form,* (*to*) *Establish,* (*to*) *insure,* (*to*) *provide,* (*to*) *promote,* and (*to*) *secure*]; the second, consisting of two verbs (*ordain* and *establish*). These parallel series appeal to our love of balance and pattern, and give an authoritative tone to the sentence.

The writer, we feel, has thought long and carefully about the matter at hand and has taken firm control of it.

Because we find a special satisfaction in balanced structures, we are more likely to remember ideas phrased in parallelisms than in less highly ordered language. For this reason, as well as for the sense of authority and control that they suggest, parallel structures are common in political utterances:

> *We hold these truths to be self-evident, that all men are created equal, that they are endowed by their Creator with certain unalienable rights, that among these are life, liberty, and the pursuit of happiness.*
> —The Declaration of Independence, 1776

> *But in a larger sense, we cannot dedicate, we cannot consecrate, we cannot hallow this ground. The brave men, living and dead, who struggled here, have consecrated it far above our poor power to add or detract. The world will little note, nor long remember what we say here; but it can never forget what they did here.*
> —ABRAHAM LINCOLN, GETTYSBURG ADDRESS, 1863

> *Ask not what your country can do for you, ask what you can do for your country.*
>
> —JOHN F. KENNEDY, Inaugural Address, 1961

Faulty Parallelism

If the parallelism of a passage is not carefully maintained, the writing can seem sloppy and out of balance. Scan your writing to make sure that all series and lists have parallel structures. The following examples show how to correct faulty parallelism:

INCORRECT	The mayor promises not only *to reform* the police department but also *the giving of raises* to all city employees. (Connective structures such as *not only . . . but also* and *both . . . and* introduce elements that should be parallel.)
CORRECT	The mayor promises not only *to reform* the police department but also *to give* raises to all city employees.
INCORRECT	The cost *of doing nothing* is greater than the cost *to renovate* the apartment block.
CORRECT	The cost *of doing nothing* is greater than the cost *of renovating* the apartment block.
INCORRECT	Here are the items on the committee's agenda: (1) *to discuss* the new property tax; (2) *to revise* the wording of the city charter; (3) *a vote* on the city manager's request for an assistant.
CORRECT	Here are the items on the committee's agenda: (1) *to discuss* the new property tax; (2) *to revise* the wording of the city charter; (3) *to vote* on the city manager's request for an assistant.

Fused (Run-On) Sentences

A *fused sentence* is one in which two or more independent clauses (passages that can stand as complete sentences) have been run together without the aid of any suitable connecting word, phrase, or punctuation. There are several ways to correct a fused sentence:

INCORRECT	The council members were exhausted they had debated for two hours.
CORRECT	The council members were exhausted. They had debated for two hours. (The clauses have been separated into two sentences.)
CORRECT	The council members were exhausted; they had debated for two hours. (The clauses have been separated by a semicolon.)
CORRECT	The council members were exhausted, having debated for two hours. (The second clause has been rephrased as a dependent clause.)
INCORRECT	Our policy analysis impressed the committee it also convinced them to reconsider their action.
CORRECT	Our policy analysis impressed the committee and also convinced them to reconsider their action. (The second clause has been rephrased as part of the first clause.)
CORRECT	Our policy analysis impressed the committee, and it also convinced them to reconsider their action. (The clauses have been separated by a comma and a coordinating word.)

Although a fused sentence is easily noticeable to the reader, it can be maddeningly difficult for the writer to catch. Unpracticed writers tend to read through the fused spots, sometimes supplying the break that is usually heard when sentences are spoken. To check for fused sentences, read the independent clauses in your paper carefully, making sure that there are adequate breaks among all of them.

Pronoun Errors

Its Versus *It's*

Do not make the mistake of trying to form the possessive of *it* in the same way that you form the possessive of most nouns. The pronoun *it* shows possession by simply adding an *s*.

The prosecuting attorney argued the case on its merits.

The word *it's* is a contraction of *it is*:

It's the most expensive program ever launched by the council.

What makes the *its/it's* rule so confusing is that most nouns form the singular possessive by adding an apostrophe and an *s:*

The jury's verdict startled the crowd.

When proofreading, any time you come to the word *it's,* substitute the phrase *it is* while you read. If the phrase makes sense, you have used the correct form. If you have used the word *it's,*

> The newspaper article was misleading in *it's* analysis of the election.

then read it as *it is:*

> The newspaper article was misleading in *it is* analysis of the election.

If the phrase makes no sense, substitute *its* for *it's:*

> The newspaper article was misleading in *its* analysis of the election.

Vague Pronoun References

Pronouns are words that take the place of nouns or other pronouns that have already been mentioned in your writing. The most common pronouns include *he, she, it, they, them, those, which,* and *who.* You must make sure there is no confusion about the word to which each pronoun refers:

> The mayor said that *he* would support our bill if the city council would also back it.

The word that the pronoun replaces is called its *antecedent.* To check the accuracy of your pronoun references, ask yourself, "To what does the pronoun refer?" Then answer the question carefully, making sure that there is not more than one possible antecedent. Consider the following example:

> Several special interest groups decided to defeat the new health care bill. *This* became the turning point of the government's reform campaign.

To what does the word *This* refer? The immediate answer seems to be the word *bill* at the end of the previous sentence. It is more likely that the writer was referring to the attempt of the special interest groups to defeat the bill, but there is no word in the first sentence that refers specifically to this action. The pronoun reference is thus unclear. One way to clarify the reference is to change the beginning of the second sentence:

> Several special *interest groups* decided to defeat the new health care bill. *Their attack on the bill* became the turning point of the government's reform campaign.

This point is further demonstrated by the following sentence:

> When John F. Kennedy appointed his brother Robert to the position of U.S. attorney general, *he* had little idea how widespread the corruption in the Teamsters Union was.

To whom does the word *he* refer? It is unclear whether the writer is referring to John or Robert Kennedy. One way to clarify the reference is simply to repeat the antecedent instead of using a pronoun:

> When John F. Kennedy appointed his brother Robert to the position of U.S. attorney general, Robert had little idea how widespread the corruption in the Teamsters Union was.

Pronoun Agreement

A pronoun must agree with its antecedent in both gender and number, as the following examples demonstrate:

Mayor Smith said that *he* appreciated our club's support in the election.

One reporter asked the senator what *she* would do if the president offered *her* a cabinet post.

Having listened to our case, the judge decided to rule on *it* within the week.

Engineers working on the housing project said *they* were pleased with the renovation so far.

Certain words, however, can be troublesome antecedents because they may look like plural pronouns but are actually singular:

anyone	each	either	everybody	everyone
nobody	no one	somebody	someone	

A pronoun referring to one of these words in a sentence must be singular too:

INCORRECT	*Each* of the women in the support group brought *their* children.
CORRECT	*Each* of the women in the support group brought *her* children.
INCORRECT	*Has* everybody received *their* ballot?
CORRECT	*Has* everybody received *his or her* ballot? (The two gender-specific pronouns are used to avoid sexist language.)
CORRECT	Have *all the delegates* received *their* ballots? (The singular antecedent has been changed to a plural one.)

A Shift in Person

It is important to avoid shifting unnecessarily among first person (*I, we*), second person (*you*), and third person (*she, he, it, one, they*). Such shifts can cause confusion:

INCORRECT	*Most people* (third person) who run for office find that if *you* (second person tell the truth during *your* campaign, *you* will gain the voters' respect.
CORRECT	*Most people* who run for office find that if *they* tell the truth during *their* campaigns, *they* will gain the voters' respect.
INCORRECT	*One* (first person) cannot tell whether *they* (third person) are suited for public office until *they* decide to run.
CORRECT	*One* cannot tell whether *one* is suited for public office until *one* decides to run.

Quotation Marks

It can be difficult to remember when to use quotation marks and where they go in relation to other punctuation. When faced with these questions, unpracticed writers often try to rely on logic rather than on a rule book, but the rules do not always seem to rely on logic. The only way to make sure of your use of quotation marks is to memorize the rules. Luckily, there are not many.

The Use of Quotation Marks

Use quotation marks to enclose direct quotations that are not longer than four typed lines:

> In his farewell address to the American people, George Washington warned, "The great rule of conduct for us, in regard to foreign nations, is, in extending our commercial relations, to have with them as little political connection as possible."

Longer quotes are placed in a double-spaced indented block, *without* quotation marks:

> Lincoln clearly explained his motive for continuing the Civil War in his August 22, 1862, response to Horace Greeley's open letter:
>
> > I would save the Union. I would save it the shortest way under the Constitution. The sooner the National authority can be restored, the nearer the Union will be the Union as it was. If there be those who would not save the Union unless they could at the same time save Slavery, I do not agree with them. If there be those who would not save the Union unless they could at the same time destroy Slavery, I do not agree with them. (Lincoln 1946, 652)

Use single quotation marks to set off quotations within quotations:

> "I intend," said the senator, "to use in my speech a line from Frost's poem, 'The Road Not Taken.'"

NOTE. When the quote occurs at the end of the sentence, both the single and double quotation marks are placed outside the period.

Use quotation marks to set off titles of the following:

> Short poems (those not printed as a separate volume)
> Short stories
> Articles or essays
> Songs
> Episodes of television or radio shows

Use quotation marks to set off words or phrases used in special ways:

1. To convey irony:

   The "liberal" administration has done nothing but cater to big business.

2. To indicate a technical term:

   To "filibuster" is to delay legislation, usually through prolonged speech-making. The last notable filibuster occurred just last week in the Senate. (Once the term is defined, it is not placed in quotation marks again.)

Quotation Marks in Relation to Other Punctuation

Place commas and periods *inside* closing quotation marks:

"My fellow Americans," said the president, "there are tough times ahead of us."

Place colons and semicolons *outside* closing quotation marks:

In his speech on voting, the governor warned against "an encroaching indolence"; he was referring to the middle class.

There are several victims of the government's campaign to "Turn Back the Clock": the homeless, the elderly, the mentally impaired.

Use the context to determine whether to place question marks, exclamation points, and dashes inside or outside closing quotation marks. If the punctuation is part of the quotation, place it inside the quotation mark:

"When will Congress make up its mind?" asked the ambassador.
The demonstrators shouted, "Free the hostages!" and "No more slavery!"

If the punctuation is not part of the quotation, place it outside the quotation mark:

Which president said, "We have nothing to fear but fear itself"? (Although the quote is a complete sentence, you do not place a period after it. There can only be one piece of terminal punctuation, or punctuation that ends a sentence.)

Semicolons

The semicolon is a little-used punctuation mark that you should learn to incorporate into your writing strategy because of its many potential applications. For example, a semicolon can be used to correct a comma splice:

INCORRECT	The union representatives left the meeting in good spirits, their demands were met.
CORRECT	The union representatives left the meeting in good spirits; their demands were met.

INCORRECT   Several guests at the fundraiser had lost their invitations, how-
              ever, we were able to seat them anyway.

CORRECT   Several guests at the fundraiser had lost their invitations; how-
              ever, we were able to seat them anyway. [Conjunctive adverbs
              such as *however, therefore,* and *thus* are not coordinating
              words (such as *and, but, or, for, so, yet*) and cannot be used
              with a comma to link independent clauses. If the second inde-
              pendent clause begins with *however,* it must be preceded by
              either a period or a semicolon.]

As you can see from the second example above, connecting two independent
clauses with a semicolon instead of a period strengthens their relationship.

Semicolons can also separate items in a series when the series items themselves contain commas:

The newspaper account of the rally stressed the march, which drew the
biggest crowd; the mayor's speech, which drew tremendous applause; and
the party in the park, which lasted for hours.

Avoid misusing semicolons. For example, use a comma, not a semicolon, to separate an independent clause from a dependent clause:

INCORRECT   Students from the college volunteered to answer phones during
              the pledge drive; which was set up to generate money for the
              new arts center.

CORRECT   Students from the college volunteered to answer phones during
              the pledge drive, which was set up to generate money for the
              new arts center.

Do not overuse semicolons. Although they are useful, too many semicolons in
your writing can distract your readers' attention. Avoid monotony by using semicolons sparingly.

Sentence Fragments

A *fragment* is an incomplete part of a sentence that is punctuated and capitalized as if it were an entire sentence. It is an especially disruptive error because
it obscures the connections that the words of a sentence must make in order to
complete the reader's understanding.

Students sometimes write fragments because they are concerned that a sentence needs to be shortened. Remember that cutting the length of a sentence
merely by adding a period somewhere often creates a fragment. When checking
a writing for fragments, it is essential that you read each sentence carefully to

determine whether it has (1) a complete subject and a verb; and (2) a subordinating word before the subject and verb, which makes the construction a subordinate clause rather than a complete sentence.

Types of Sentence Fragments

Some fragments lack a verb:

INCORRECT	The chairperson of our committee, receiving a letter from the mayor. (Watch out for words that look like verbs but are being used in another way.)
CORRECT	The chairperson of our committee received a letter from the mayor.

Some fragments lack a subject:

INCORRECT	Our study shows that there is broad support for improvement in the health-care system. And in the unemployment system.
CORRECT	Our study shows that there is broad support for improvement in the health care system and in the unemployment system.

Some fragments are subordinate clauses:

INCORRECT	After the latest edition of the newspaper came out. [This clause has the two major components of a complete sentence: a subject (*edition*) and a verb (*came*). Indeed, if the first word (*After*) were deleted, the clause would be a complete sentence. But that first word is a *subordinating word*, which prevents the following clause from standing on its own as a complete sentence. Watch out for this kind of construction. It is called a *subordinate clause*, and it is not a sentence.]
CORRECT	After the latest edition of the newspaper came out, the mayor's press secretary was overwhelmed with phone calls. (A common method of correcting a subordinate clause that has been punctuated as a complete sentence is to connect it to the complete sentence to which it is closest in meaning.)
INCORRECT	Several representatives asked for copies of the vice president's position paper. Which called for reform of the Environmental Protection Agency.

CORRECT   Several representatives asked for copies of the vice president's
                 position paper, which called for reform of the Environmental
                 Protection Agency.

Spelling

All of us have problems spelling certain words that we have not yet committed to memory. But most writers are not as bad at spelling as they believe they
are. Usually an individual finds only a handful of words troubling. It is important
to be as sensitive as possible to your own particular spelling problems—and to
keep a dictionary handy. There is no excuse for failing to check spelling.

What follows are a list of commonly confused words and a list of commonly
misspelled words. Read through the lists, looking for those words that tend to
give you trouble. If you have any questions, consult your dictionary.

Commonly Confused Words

accept/except
advice/advise
affect/effect
aisle/isle
allusion/illusion
an/and
angel/angle
ascent/assent
bare/bear
brake/break
breath/breathe
buy/by
capital/capitol
choose/chose
cite/sight/site
complement/
  compliment
conscience/
  conscious
corps/corpse
council/counsel
dairy/diary
descent/dissent
desert/dessert
device/devise
die/dye
dominant/dominate
elicit/illicit

eminent/immanent/
  imminent
envelop/envelope
every day/everyday
fair/fare
formally/formerly
forth/fourth
hear/here
heard/herd
hole/whole
human/humane
its/it's
know/no
later/latter
lay/lie
lead/led
lessen/lesson
loose/lose
may be/maybe
miner/minor
moral/morale
of/off
passed/past
patience/patients
peace/piece
personal/personnel
plain/plane
precede/proceed

presence/presents
principal/principle
quiet/quite
rain/reign/rein
raise/raze
reality/realty
respectfully/respectively
reverend/reverent
right/rite/write
road/rode
scene/seen
sense/since
stationary/stationery
straight/strait
taught/taut
than/then
their/there/they're
threw/through
too/to/two
track/tract
waist/waste
waive/wave
weak/week
weather/whether
were/where
which/witch
whose/who's
your/you're

Commonly Misspelled Words

acceptable	gauge	peaceable
accessible	guaranteed	performance
accommodate	guard	pertain
accompany	harass	practical
accustomed	hero	preparation
acquire	heroes	probably
against	humorous	process
annihilate	hurried	professor
apparent	hurriedly	prominent
arguing	hypocrite	pronunciation
argument	ideally	psychology
authentic	immediately	publicly
before	immense	pursue
begin	incredible	pursuing
beginning	innocuous	questionnaire
believe	intercede	realize
benefited	interrupt	receipt
bulletin	irrelevant	received
business	irresistible	recession
cannot	irritate	recommend
category	knowledge	referring
committee	license	religious
condemn	likelihood	remembrance
courteous	maintenance	reminisce
definitely	manageable	repetition
dependent	meanness	representative
desperate	mischievous	rhythm
develop	missile	ridiculous
different	necessary	roommate
disappear	nevertheless	satellite
disappoint	no one	scarcity
easily	noticeable	scenery
efficient	noticing	science
environment	nuisance	secede
equipped	occasion	secession
exceed	occasionally	secretary
exercise	occurred	senseless
existence	occurrences	separate
experience	omission	sergeant
fascinate	omit	shining
finally	opinion	significant
foresee	opponent	sincerely
forty	parallel	skiing
fulfill	parole	stubbornness

studying	tendency	until
succeed	therefore	vacuum
success	tragedy	valuable
successfully	truly	various
susceptible	tyranny	vegetable
suspicious	unanimous	visible
technical	unconscious	without
temporary	undoubtedly	women

CHAPTER

7

PAPER FORMATS

Your format makes your paper's first impression. Justly or not, accurately or not, it announces your professional competence—or lack of competence. A well-executed format implies that your paper is worth reading. More importantly, however, a proper format brings information to your readers in a familiar form that has the effect of setting their minds at ease. Your paper's format should therefore impress your readers with your academic competence as a political scientist by following accepted professional standards. Like the style and clarity of your writing, your format communicates messages that are often more readily and profoundly received than the content of the document itself.

The formats described in this chapter are in conformance with generally accepted standards in the discipline of political science, including instructions for the following elements:

General page formats	Table of contents
Title page	Reference page
Abstract	List of tables and figures
Executive summary	Text
Outline page	Appendixes

Except for special instructions from your instructor, follow the directions in this manual exactly.

7.1 GENERAL PAGE FORMATS

Political science assignments should be printed on 8-by-11-inch premium white bond paper, 20 pound or heavier. Do not use any other size or color except to comply with special instructions from your instructor, and do not use off-white or poor quality (draft) paper. Political science that is worth the time to write and read is worth good paper.

Always submit to your instructor an original typed or computer-printed manuscript. Do not submit a photocopy! Always make a second paper copy and back up your electronic copy for your own files in case the original is lost.

Margins, except in theses and dissertations, should be one inch on all sides of the paper. Unless otherwise instructed, all papers should be *double-spaced* in a 12-point word-processing font or typewriter pica type. Typewriter elite type may be used if another is not available. Select a font that is plain and easy to read, such as Helvetica, Courier, Garamond, or Times Roman. Do not use script, stylized, or elaborate fonts.

Page numbers should appear in the upper right-hand corner of each page, starting immediately after the title page. No page number should appear on the title page or on the first page of the text. Page numbers should appear one inch from the right side and one-half inch from the top of the page. They should proceed consecutively beginning with the title page (although the first number is not actually printed on the title page). You may use lowercase roman numerals (i, ii, iii, iv, v, vi, vii, viii, ix, x, and so on) for the pages, such as the title page, table of contents, and table of figures, that precede the first page of text, but if you use them, the numbers must be placed at the center of the bottom of the page.

Ask your instructor about bindings. In the absence of further directions, *do not bind* your paper or enclose it within a plastic cover sheet. Place one staple in the upper left-hand corner, or use a paper clip at the top of the paper. Note that a paper to be submitted to a journal for publication should not be clipped, stapled, or bound in any form.

Title Page

The following information will be centered on the title page:

Title of the paper
Name of writer
Course name, section number, and instructor
College or university
Date

```
                    The Second Bush Presidency
                              by
                    Nicole Ashley Linscheid


                    The American Presidency
                            POL213
                    Dr. Bushrod Collyflour
                    St. Johnswort College
                      January 1, 2006
```

As the sample title page shows, the title should clearly describe the problem addressed in the paper. If the paper discusses juvenile recidivism in Albemarle County jails, for example, the title "Recidivism in the Albemarle County Criminal Justice System" is professional, clear, and helpful to the reader. "Albemarle County," "Juvenile Justice," or "County Jails" are all too vague to be effective. Also, the title should not be "cute." A cute title may attract attention for a play on Broadway, but it will detract from the credibility of a paper in political science. "Inadequate Solid Waste Disposal Facilities in Denver" is professional. "Down in the Dumps" is not.

In addition, title pages for position papers and policy analysis papers must include the name, title, and organization of the public official who has the authority and responsibility to implement the recommendation of your paper. The person to whom you address the paper should be the person who has the responsibility and the authority to make the decision that is called for in your paper. The "address" should include the person's name, title, and organization, as shown in the example of a title page for a position paper that follows. To identify the appropriate official, first carefully define the problem and the best solution. Then ascertain the person or persons who have the authority to solve the problem. If you recommend installation of a traffic signal at a particular intersection, for example, find out who makes the decisions regarding such actions in your community. It may be the public safety director, a transportation planning commission, or a town council.

Oak City Police Department Personnel Policy Revisions

submitted to

Farley Z. Simmons

Director of Personnel

Police Department

Oak City, Arkansas

by

Luke Tyler Linscheid

American National Government

GOV 1001

Dr. Prospect Pigeon

Perpetual Homework University

January 21, 2006

Abstract

An abstract is a brief summary of a paper written primarily to allow potential readers to see if the paper contains information of sufficient interest for them to read. People conducting research want specific kinds of information, and they often read dozens of abstracts looking for papers that contain relevant data. Abstracts have the designation "Abstract" centered near the top of the page. Next is the title, also centered, followed by a paragraph that precisely states the paper's topic, research and analysis methods, and results and conclusions. The abstract should be written in one paragraph of no more than 150 words. Remember, an abstract is not an introduction; instead, it is a summary, as demonstrated in the sample below.

Abstract

Bertrand Russell's View of Mysticism

This paper reviews Bertrand Russell's writings on religion, mysticism, and science, and defines his perspective of the contribution of mysticism to scientific knowledge. Russell drew a sharp distinction between what he considered to be (1) the essence of religion, and (2) dogma or assertions attached to religion by theologians and religious leaders. Although some of his writings, including *Why I Am Not a Christian,* appear hostile to all aspects of religion, Russell actually asserts that religion, freed from doctrinal encumbrances, not only fulfills certain psychological needs but evokes many of the most beneficial human impulses. He believes that religious mysticism generates an intellectual disinterestedness that may be useful to science, but that it is not a source of a special type of knowledge beyond investigation by science.

Executive Summary

An executive summary, like an abstract, summarizes the content of a paper but does so in more detail. A sample executive summary is given on next page. Whereas abstracts are read by people who are doing research, executive summaries are more likely to be read by people who need some or all of the information in the paper in order to make a decision. Many people, however, will read the executive summary to fix clearly in their mind the organization and results of a paper before reading the paper itself.

Executive Summary

Municipal parks in Springfield are deteriorating because of inadequate maintenance, and one park in particular, Oak Ridge Community Park, needs immediate attention. The problem is that parking, picnic, and restroom facilities at Oak Ridge Community Park have deteriorated as a result of normal wear, adverse weather, and vandalism, and are inadequate to meet public demand. The park was established as a public recreation "Class B" facility in 1967. Only one major renovation has occurred: in the summer of 1987 general building repair was done, and new swing sets were installed. The Park Department estimates that 10,000 square feet of new parking space, fourteen items of playground equipment, seventeen new picnic tables, and repairs on current facilities would cost about $43,700.

Three possible solutions have been given extensive consideration in this paper. One option is to do nothing. Area residents will use the area less as deterioration continues, but no immediate outlay of public funds will be necessary. The first alternative solution is to make all repairs immediately. Area residents will enjoy immediate and increased use of facilities. Taxpayers have turned down the last three tax increase requests. Revenue bonds may be acceptable to a total of $20,000, according to the City Manager, but no more than $5,000 per year is available from general city revenues.

A second alternative is to make repairs, according to a priority list, over a five-year period, using a combination of general city revenues and a $20,000 first-year bond issue that will require City Council and voter approval. Residents will enjoy the most needed improvements immediately.

The recommendation of this report is that the second alternative be adopted by the City Council. The City Council should, during its May 15 meeting, (1) adopt a resolution of intent to commit $5,000 per year for five years from the general revenue fund, dedicated to this purpose; and (2) approve for submission to public vote in the November 2007 election a $20,000 bond issue.

Outline Page

An outline page is a specific type of executive summary. Most often found in position papers and policy analysis papers, an outline page provides more information about the organization of the paper than does an executive summary. The outline shows clearly the sections in the paper and the information in each. An outline page is an asset because it allows busy decision-makers to understand the entire content of a paper without reading it all or to refer quickly to a specific part for more information. Position papers and policy analysis papers are written for people in positions of authority who normally need to make a variety of decisions in a short period. Outline pages reduce the amount of time they need to understand a policy problem, the alternative solutions, and the author's preferred solution. Outline pages sequentially list the complete topic sentences of the major paragraphs of a paper, in outline form. In a position paper, for example, you will be stating a problem, defining possible solutions, and then recommending the best solution. These three steps will be the major headings in your outline. (See Chapter 5 for instructions on writing an outline.) Wait until you have completed the paper before writing the outline page. Take the topic sentences from the leading (most important) paragraph in each section of your paper and place them in the appropriate places in your outline. A sample outline page is given on page 147.

Table of Contents

A table of contents does not provide as much information as an outline, but it does include the titles of the major divisions and subdivisions of a paper. Tables of contents are not normally required in student papers or papers presented at professional meetings but may be included. They are normally required, however, in books, theses, and dissertations. The table of contents should consist of the chapter or main section titles, and the headings used in the text, with one additional level of titles, along with their page numbers, as the sample on page 150 demonstrates.

Reference Page

The format for references is discussed in detail in Chapter 8. Sample reference pages for two formats, the author-date system and the documentary-note system, appear in Chapter 8.

7.2 TABLES, ILLUSTRATIONS, FIGURES, AND APPENDIXES

List of Tables, Illustrations, and Figures

A list of tables, illustrations, or figures contain their titles as used in the paper, in the order in which they appear, along with their page numbers. You may list tables, illustrations, and figures together under the title "Figures" (and

Outline of Contents

I. The problem is that parking, picnic, and restroom facilities at Oak Ridge Community Park have deteriorated as a result of normal wear, adverse weather, and vandalism, and are inadequate to meet public demand.

    A. Only one major renovation has occurred since 1967, when the park was opened.

    B. The Park Department estimates that 10,000 square feet of new parking space, fourteen items of playground equipment, seventeen new picnic tables, and repairs on current facilities would cost about $43,700.

II. Three possible solutions have been given extensive consideration:

    A. One option is to do nothing. Area residents will use the area less as deterioration continues, but no immediate outlay of public funds will be necessary.

    B. The first alternative solution is to make all repairs immediately. Area residents will enjoy immediate and increased use of facilities. $43,700 in funds will be needed. Sources include: (1) Community Development Block Grant funds; (2) increased property taxes; (3) revenue bonds; and (4) general city revenues.

    C. A second alternative is to make repairs according to a priority list over a five-year period, using a combination of general city revenues and a $20,000 first-year bond issue. Residents will enjoy the most needed improvements immediately. The bond issue will require City Council and voter approval.

III. The recommendation of this report is that alternative C be adopted by the City Council. The benefit/cost analysis demonstrates that residents will be satisfied if basic improvements are made immediately. The City Council should, during its May 15 meeting, (1) adopt a resolution of intent to commit $5,000 per year for five years from the general revenue fund, dedicated to this purpose; and (2) approve for submission to public vote in the November 2007 election a $20,000 bond issue.

Contents

call them all "Figures" in the text), or if you have more than a half page of entries, you may have separate lists for tables, illustrations, and figures (and title them accordingly in the text). An example of the format for such lists is given in this page.

Figures

Tables

Tables are used in the text to show relationships among data, to help the reader come to a conclusion or understand a certain point. Tables that show simple results or "raw" data should be placed in an appendix. Tables should not reiterate the content of the text. They should say something new, and they should stand on their own. In other words, the reader should be able to understand the table without reading the text. Clearly label the columns and rows in the table. Each word in the title (except articles, prepositions, and conjunctions) should be capitalized. The source of the information should be shown immediately below the table, not in a footnote or endnote. A sample table is shown below.

Table 1. Projections of the Total Population of Selected States, 2005–2035 (in thousands)

State	2005	2015	2025	2030	2035
Alabama	4,253	4,451	4,631	4,956	5,224
Illinois	11,830	12,051	12,266	12,808	13,440
Maine	1,241	1,259	1,285	1,362	1,423
New Mexico	1,685	1,860	2,016	2,300	2,612
Oklahoma	3,278	3,373	3,491	3,789	4,057
Tennessee	5,256	5,657	5,966	6,365	6,665
Virginia	6,618	6,997	7,324	7,921	8,466

Source: U.S. Census Bureau.

Illustrations and Figures

Illustrations are not normally inserted in the text of a political science paper, even in an appendix, unless they are necessary to explain the content. If illustrations are necessary, do not paste or tape photocopies of photographs or similar materials to the text or the appendix. Instead, photocopy each one on a separate sheet of paper and center it, along with its typed title, within the normal margins of the paper. The format of illustration titles should be the same as that for tables and figures.

Figures in the form of charts and graphs may be very helpful in presenting certain types of information, as the example shows on page 150.

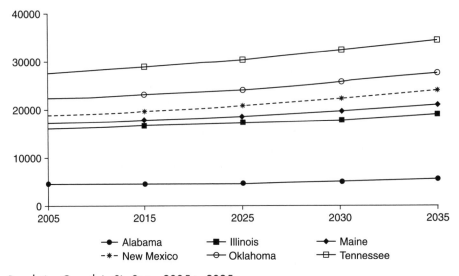

Population Growth in Six States 2005 to 2035

Appendixes

Appendixes are reference materials provided for the convenience of the reader at the back of the paper, after the text. Providing information that supplements the important facts in the text, they may include maps, charts, tables, and selected documents. Do not place materials that are merely interesting or decorative in your appendix. Use only items that will answer questions raised by the text or are necessary to explain the text. Follow the guidelines for formats for tables, illustrations, and figures when adding material in an appendix. At the top center of the page, label your first appendix "Appendix A," your second appendix "Appendix B," and so on. Do not append an entire government report, journal article, or other publication, but only the portions of such documents that are necessary to support your paper. The source of the information should always be evident on the appended pages.

7.3   TEXT

Ask your instructor for the number of pages required for the paper you are writing. The text should follow the directions explained in Chapters 5 and 6 of this manual and should conform to the format of the facsimile page shown on page 151.

Chapter Headings

Your paper should include no more than three levels of headings:

1. *Primary,* which should be centered, with each word except articles, prepositions, and conjunctions capitalized

Sample Passage of Text

The problem is that parking, picnic, and restroom facilities at Oak Ridge Community Park have deteriorated as a result of normal wear, adverse weather, and vandalism, and are of inadequate quantity to meet public demand. The paved parking lot has crumbled and eroded. As many as two hundred cars park on the lawn during major holidays. Only one of the five swing sets is in safe operating condition. Each set accommodates four children, but during weekends and holidays many children wait turns for the available sets. Spray paint vandalism has marred the rest room facilities, which are inadequate to meet major holiday demands.

The Department of Parks and Recreation established the park as a public recreation Class B facility in 1963. In the summer of 1987, the department conducted general building repair and installed new steel swing sets. Only minimal annual maintenance has occurred since that time.

The department estimates that 10,000 square feet of new parking lot space, fourteen items of playground equipment, seventeen new picnic tables, and repairs on current facilities would cost about $43,700 (Department of Parks and Recreation 2005). Parking lot improvements include a new surface of coarse gravel on the old paved lot and expansion of the new paved lot by 10,000 square feet. The State Engineering Office estimates the cost of parking lot improvements to be $16,200.

---

2. *Secondary,* which begin at the left margin, also with each word except articles, prepositions, and conjunctions capitalized
3. *Tertiary,* which should be written in sentence style (with only the first word and proper nouns capitalized), with a period at the end, underlined

The following illustration shows the proper use of chapter headings:

The House of Representatives   (Primary Heading)
Impeachment Procedures of the House   (Secondary Heading)
<u>Rules for debate in impeachment proceedings.</u> (Tertiary Heading)

CHAPTER

8

CITING SOURCES

8.1 THE APSA AUTHOR-DATE SYSTEM

One of your most important jobs as a research writer is to document your use of source material carefully and clearly. Failure to do so will cause your reader confusion, damage the effectiveness of your paper, and perhaps make you vulnerable to a charge of plagiarism. Proper documentation is more than just good form. It is a powerful indicator of your own commitment to scholarship and the sense of authority that you bring to your writing. Good documentation demonstrates your expertise as a researcher and increases your reader's trust in you and your work.

Unfortunately, as anybody who has ever written a research paper knows, getting the documentation right can be a frustrating, confusing job, especially for the writer who is not familiar with the documentation system he or she is trying to use. Positioning each element of a single reference citation accurately can require a lot of time looking through the style manual. Even before you begin to work on the specific citations for your paper, there are important questions of style and format to answer.

What to Document

You must always credit direct quotes, as well as certain kinds of paraphrased material. Information that is basic—important dates, universally acknowledged facts, or commonly held opinions—need not be cited. Information that is not widely known, however, should receive documentation. This type of material includes ideas, evaluations, critiques, and descriptions original to your source.

What if you are unsure whether a certain fact is an academic "given" or sufficiently unique to warrant a citation? You are, after all, probably a new-comer to the field in which you are conducting your research. If in doubt, *supply the documentation.* It is better to overdocument than to fail to do justice to a source.

The Choice of Style

There are several documentation styles available, each designed to meet the needs of researchers in particular fields. The reference systems approved by the *Modern Language Association* (MLA) and the *American Psychological Association* (APA) are often used in the humanities and the social sciences and could serve the needs of the political science writer, but this manual offers the style most likely to be appropriate for political science papers: the APSA Author-Date System.

The American Political Science Association (APSA) has adopted a modification of the style elaborated in the *Chicago Manual of Style* (*CMS*), perhaps the most universally approved of all documentation authorities. One of the advantages of using the APSA style, which is outlined in an APSA pamphlet entitled *Style Manual for Political Science* (1993, revised 2005), is that it is designed to guide the professional political scientist in preparing a manuscript for submission to the *American Political Science Review,* the journal of the American Political Science Association and the most influential political science journal in publication. Learning the APSA documentation style, then, offers you as a student another crucial connection to the world of the political scientist. For this reason, there are models below of formats described in the APSA *Style Manual* in addition to other models found only in the *CMS.*

NOTE. The APSA *Style Manual* for Political Science covers only certain basic reference and bibliographical models. For other models and for more detailed suggestions about referencing format, the 2005 revised edition of the APSA *Style Manual* refers readers to the "latest edition" of the *CMS* (fifteenth ed, 2003). The formats below are based on APSA guidelines, whenever such guidelines are available. Otherwise, the formats follow models taken from the fifteenth (2003) edition of the *CMS,* and, when necessary, from the more exhaustive fourteenth (1993) edition. Models based on the *CMS* are identified as such, with section numbers for relevant passages in the *CMS* given in parentheses, preceded by the number of the edition. For example, *CMS* 15 (17.288) refers to the 288th section of Chapter 17 in the fifteenth edition of the *Chicago Manual of Style,* a section that shows how to cite source material taken from the U.S. Constitution.

The Importance of Consistency

The most important rule regarding documentation of your work is to *be consistent.* Sloppy referencing undermines your reader's trust and does a disservice to the writers whose work you are incorporating into your own argument. And from a purely practical standpoint, inconsistent referencing can severely damage your grade.

Using the Style Manual

Read through the guidelines in the following pages before trying to use them to structure your notes. Unpracticed student researchers tend to ignore this section of the style manual until the moment the first note has to be worked out, and then they skim through the examples looking for the one that perfectly corresponds to the immediate case in hand. But most style manuals do not include every possible documentation model, so the writer must piece together a coherent reference out of elements from several examples. Reading through all the examples before using them can give you a feel for the placement of information in citations for different kinds of sources—such as magazine articles, book chapters, government documents, and electronic texts—as well as for how the referencing system works in general.

When you use the author-date system of citation, you place a note, in parentheses, within the text, following the passage where your source material appears. In order not to distract the reader from the argument, make the reference as brief as possible, containing just enough information to refer the reader to the full citation in the reference list following the text. Usually the minimum information necessary is the author's last name, the date of the publication of the source, and if you are referring to a specific passage instead of the entire work, the page number(s) of the passage you are using. As indicated by the models below, this information can be given in a number of ways.

Models of full citations that correspond to these parenthetical text references are given in the subsection that begins on page 160. A sample reference list appears on page 168.

The Author-Date System: Citations

Author, Date, and Page in Parentheses

> Several critics found the senator's remarks to be, in the words of one, "hopelessly off the mark and dangerously incendiary" (Northrup 2006, 28).

Note that, when it appears at the end of a sentence, the parenthetical reference is placed inside the period.

Page and Chapter in Notes

A text citation may refer to an entire article, in which case you need not include page numbers, since they are given in the reference list at the end of the paper. However, you will sometimes need to cite specific page and chapter numbers, which follow the date and are preceded by a comma and, in the case of a chapter, the abbreviation *chap.* Note that you do not use the abbreviation *p.* or *pp.* when referring to page numbers.

Page Numbers

Randalson (2004, 84–86) provides a brief but coherent description of the bill's evolution.

Chapter Numbers

Collins (2006, chaps. 9, 10) discusses at length the structure of the Roman senate.

Author and Date in Text

The following example focuses the reader's attention on Northrup's article:

For a highly critical review of the senator's performance, see Northrup 2006 (28).

Author in the Text, Date and Page in Parentheses

Here the emphasis is on the author, for only Northrup's name is within the grammar of the sentence:

Northrup (2006, 28) called the senator's remarks "hopelessly off the mark and dangerously incendiary."

Source with Two Authors

The administration's efforts at reforming the education system are drawing more praise than condemnation (Younger and Petty 2005).

Notice that the names are not necessarily arranged alphabetically. Use the order that the authors themselves sanctioned on the title page of the book or article.

Source with Three Authors

Most of the farmers in the region support the cooperative's new pricing plan (Moore, Macrory, and Traylor 2004, 132).

Source with Four or More Authors

Place the Latin phrase *et al.,* meaning "and others," after the name of the first author. Note that the phrase appears in roman type, not italics, and is followed by a period:

According to Herring et al. (2004, 42), five builders backed out of the project due to doubts about the local economy.

More Than One Source

Note that the references are arranged alphabetically:

Several commentators have supported the council's decision to expand the ruling (Barrere 2004; Grady 2004; Payne 2004).

Two Authors with the Same Last Name

Use a first initial to differentiate two authors with the same last name.

Research suggests that few taxpayers will appreciate the new budget cuts (B. Grady 2005; L. Grady 2004).

Two Works by the Same Author

If two references by the same author appear in the same note, place a comma between the publication dates:

George (2005, 2004) argues for sweeping tax reform on the national level.

If the two works were published in the same year, differentiate them by adding lowercase letters to the publication dates. Be sure to add the letters to the reference list, too:

The commission's last five annual reports pointed out the same weaknesses in the structure of the city government (Estrada 2004a, 2004b).

Reprints

It is sometimes significant to note the date when an important text was first published, even if you are using a reprint of that work. In this case, the date of the first printing appears in brackets before the date of the reprint:

During that period, there were three advertising campaign strategies that were deemed potentially useful to political campaigners (Adams [1960] 2004, 12).

Classic Texts

You may use the author-date system to structure notes for classic texts, such as the Bible, standard translations of ancient Greek works, or numbers of *The Federalist Papers,* by citing the date and page numbers of the edition you are using. Or you may refer to these texts by using the systems by which they are subdivided. Since all editions of a classic text employ the same standard subdivisions, this reference method has the advantage of allowing your reader to find the citation in any published version of the text. For example, you may cite a biblical passage by referring to the particular book, chapter, and verse, all in roman type, with the translation given after the verse number. Titles of books of the Bible should be abbreviated.

"But the path of the just is as the shining light, that shineth more and more unto the perfect day" (Prov. 4:18 King James Version).

The Federalist Papers may be cited by their standard numbers:

Madison addresses the problem of factions in a republic (*Federalist* 10).

Public Documents

According to the 2005 revised edition of the APSA *Style Manual,* you may cite public documents using the standard author-date technique. The *Style Manual* recommends consulting the fourteenth edition of *CMS* (16.148–98) and

Chapter 12 of the latest edition of Kate L. Turabian's *Manual for Writers of Term Papers, Theses, and Dissertations* (Univ. of Chicago Press, 2004) for more detailed information. While the 2005 APSA *Style Manual* provides models of reference list entries for a few types of government documents, neither it nor the fifteenth edition of *CMS* (2003) offers corresponding examples of parenthetical text citations. The following models are based, therefore, on information taken from the APSA *Style Manual* and from Chapters 15 and 16 of the fourteenth edition of *CMS* (1993).

Congressional Journals.   Parenthetical text references to either the *Senate Journal* or the *House Journal* start with the journal title in place of the author, the session year, and, if applicable, the page:

> Senator Jones endorsed the proposal as reworded by Senator Edward's committee (*U.S. Senate Journal* 2006, 24).

Congressional Debates.   Congressional debates are printed in the daily issues of the *Congressional Record,* which are bound biweekly and then collected and bound at the end of the session. Whenever possible, you should consult the bound yearly collection instead of the biweekly compilations. Your parenthetical reference should begin with the title *Congressional Record* (or *Cong. Rec.*) in place of the author's name and include the year of the congressional session, the volume and part of the *Congressional Record,* and finally the page:

> Rep. Valentine and Rep. Beechnut addressed the question of funding for secondary education (*Cong. Rec.* 1930, 72, pt. 8: 9012).

Congressional Reports and Documents.   References to these reports and documents, which are numbered sequentially in one- or two-year periods, include the name of the body generating the material, the year, and the page:

> Rep. Slavin promised from the floor to answer the charges against him within the next week (U.S. Congress. House 2006, 12–13).

NOTE. You may omit the *U.S.,* if it is clear from the context that you are referring to the United States. Whichever form you use, be sure to use it consistently, in both the notes and the reference list.

Bills and Resolutions.

The recent ruling prohibits consular officials from rejecting visa requests out of hand (U.S. Congress. Senate. 2005).

Statutes.

Citing to the Statutes at Large

Congress stipulates that any book deposited for copyright in the Library of Congress that suffers serious damage or deterioration due to age be rebound in library cloth (*Book Preservation Act,* 2006, *Statutes*).

Citing to the United States Code

Congress stipulates that any book deposited for copyright in the Library of Congress that suffers serious damage or deterioration due to age be rebound in library cloth (*Book Preservation Act*, 2006, *U.S. Code*).

United States Constitution.   According to *CMS* 14 (15.367), references to the U.S. Constitution include the number of the article or amendment, the section number, and the clause, if necessary:

> The president has the power, in extraordinary circumstances, either to convene or to dismiss Congress (U.S. Constitution, art. 3, sec. 3).

It is not necessary to include the Constitution in the reference list.

Executive Department Documents.   A reference to a report, bulletin, circular, or any other type of material issued by the executive department starts with the name of the agency issuing the document, although you may use the name of the author, if known:

> Recent demographic projections suggest that city growth will continue to be lateral for several more years, as businesses flee downtown areas for the suburbs (Department of Labor 2004, 334).

Legal References.

Supreme Court.   As with laws, court decisions are rarely given their own parenthetical text citation and reference list entry, but are instead identified in the text. If you wish to use a formal reference, however, you may place within the parentheses the title of the case, in italics, followed by the source (for cases after 1875 this is the *United States Supreme Court Reports,* abbreviated *U.S.*), which is preceded by the volume number and followed by the page number.

> The judge ruled that Ms. Warren did have an obligation to offer assistance to the survivors of the wreck, an obligation which she failed to meet (*State of Nevada v. Goldie Warren* 324 U.S. 123).

Before 1875, Supreme Court decisions were published under the names of official court reporters. The reference below is to William Cranch, *Reports of Cases Argued and Adjudged in the Supreme Court of the United States, 1801–1815,* 9 vols. (Washington, DC, 1804–17). The number preceding the clerk's name is the volume number; the last number is the page:

> The first case in which the Supreme Court ruled a law of Congress to be void was *Marbury v. Madison,* in 1803 (1 Cranch 137).

For most of these parenthetical references, it is possible to move some or all of the material outside the parentheses simply by incorporating it in the text:

> In 1969, in *State of Nevada v. Goldie Warren* (324 U.S. 123), the judge ruled that an observer of a traffic accident has an obligation to offer assistance to survivors.

Lower Courts.   Decisions of lower federal courts are published in the *Federal Reporter*. The note should give the volume of the *Federal Reporter* (*F.*), the series, if it is other than the first (*2d,* in the model below), the page, and, in brackets, an abbreviated reference to the specific court (the example below is to the Second Circuit Court) and the year:

> One ruling takes into account the bias that often exists against the defendant in certain types of personal injury lawsuits (*United States v. Sizemore,* 183 F.2d 201 [2d Cir. 1950]).

Publications of Government Commissions.   According to *CMS* 14 (15.368), references to bulletins, circulars, reports, and study papers that are issued by various government commissions should include the name of the commission, the date of the document, and the page:

> This year saw a sharp reaction among large firms to the new tax law (Securities and Exchange Commission 2004, 57).

Corporate Authors.   Because government documents are often credited to a corporate author with a lengthy name, you may devise an acronym or a shortened form of the name and indicate in your first reference to the source that this name will be used in later citations:

> Government statistics over the last year showed a continuing leveling of the inflation rate (*Bulletin of Labor Statistics* 2006, 1954; *hereafter BLS*).

The practice of using a shortened name in subsequent references to any corporate author, whether a public or private organization, is sanctioned in most journals, including the *American Political Science Review,* and approved in *CMS* 14 (15.252). Thus, if you refer often to the *U.N. Monthly Bulletin of Statistics,* you may, after giving the publication's full name in the first reference, use a shortened form of the title—perhaps an acronym such as *UNMBS*—in all later cites.

Publications of State and Local Governments.   According to *CMS* 14 (15.377), references to state and local government documents are similar to those for the corresponding national government sources:

> In arguing for the legality of cockfighting, Senator Lynd actually suggested that the "sport" served as a deterrent to crime among the state's young people (Oklahoma Legislature 2004, 24).

CMS 14 (16.178) restricts bibliographical information concerning state laws or municipal ordinances to the running text.

Electronic Sources

Parenthetical references to electronic sources should present the same sorts of information as references to printed sources, when possible. In other words, include the author's last name, the year of publication, and the relevant page number from the source, if given. However, some types of information that appear in standard text citations, such as the author's name and relevant page numbers, are often missing in electronic sources and so cannot appear in the reference. If the author's name is missing, the parenthetical reference can include the title of the document, in quotation marks. If the online article has numbered paragraphs, you may supply numbers for paragraphs bearing the relevant passages:

> The election results that November may have been what startled Congress into taking such an action ("Effects of Landmark Elections" 2004, para. 12–14).

Interviews

According to the revised 2005 edition of the APSA *Style Manual,* unpublished interviews should be identified within the text of a sentence rather than in a parenthetical citation. Include in the sentence the name of the interviewee, the means of communication (whether by telephone, written correspondence, or a formal, face-to-face interview), the date, and, if relevant, the location. If the interview is published, however, it should be given both a text citation and an entry in the reference list at the end of the paper.

Published Interview.

> In an interview last March, Simon criticized the use of private funds to build such city projects as the coliseum (Fox 2005, 58–59).

Unpublished Interview Conducted by the Writer of the Paper.   If you are citing material from an interview that you conducted, you should identify yourself as the author and give the date of the interview:

> In an interview with the author on 23 April 2004, Dr. Kennedy expressed her disappointment with the new court ruling.

The Author-Date System: Reference List

In a paper using the author-date bibliographic system, the parenthetical references point the reader to the full citations in the reference list. This list, which always follows the text of the paper, is arranged alphabetically according to the first element in each citation. Usually this element is the last name of the author or editor, but in the absence of such information, the citation is alphabetized according to the title of the work, which is then the first element in the citation.

The bibliography is double-spaced throughout, even between entries. As with most alphabetically arranged bibliographies, there is a kind of reverse indentation system called a "hanging indent": after the first line of a citation, all subsequent lines are indented five spaces.

Capitalization

The APSA *Style Manual* uses standard, or "headline style," capitalization rules for titles in the bibliographical citations. In this style, all first and last words in a title, and all other words except articles (*a, an, the*), coordinating words (*and, but, or, for, nor*), and all prepositions, are capitalized.

Books

One Author.

Northrup, Alan K. 2004. *Living High Off the Hog: Recent Pork Barrel Legislation in the Senate.* Cleveland: Johnstown.

First comes the author's name, inverted, then the date of publication, followed by the title of the book, the place of publication, and the name of the publishing house. For place of publication, do not identify the state unless the city is not well known. In that case, use postal abbreviations to denote the state (e.g., *OK, AR*).

Periods are used to divide most of the elements in the citation, although a colon is used between the place of publication and publisher. Custom dictates that the main title and subtitle be separated by a colon, even though a colon may not appear in the title as printed on the title page of the book.

Two Authors. The name of only the first author is reversed, since it is the one by which the citation is alphabetized:

Spence, Michelle, and Kelly Rudd. 2005. *Education and the Law.* Boston: Tildale.

Three Authors.

Moore, J. B., Jeannine Macrory, and Natasha Traylor. 2004. *Down on the Farm: Renovating the Farm Loan.* Norman: Univ. of Oklahoma Press.

According to *CMS* 15 (17.104), you may abbreviate the word *University* if it appears in the name of the press.

Four or More Authors.

Herring, Ralph, et al. 2004. *Funding City Projects.* Atlanta: Jessup Institute for Policy Development.

Editor, Compiler, or Translator as Author. When no author is listed on the title page, *CMS* 15 (17.41) calls for you to begin the citation with the name of the editor, compiler, or translator, followed by the appropriate phrase—*ed., comp,* or *trans.:*

Trakas, Dylan, comp. 2004. *Making the Road-Ways Safe: Essays on Highway Preservation and Funding.* El Paso: Del Norte Press.

Editor, Compiler, or Translator with Author. Place the name of the editor, compiler, or translator after the title, prefaced by the appropriate phrase—*Ed., Comp., or Trans.:*

Pound, Ezra. 1953. *Literary Essays.* Ed. T. S. Eliot. New York: New Directions.

Stomper, Jean. 1973. *Grapes and Rain.* Trans. and ed. John Picard. New York: Baldock.

Two or More Works by the Same Author.   The revised 2005 edition of the APSA *Style Manual* prohibits the replacement of an author's name in entries after the first by a three-em dash. Instead all entries by the same author must bear his or her name, and they must be arranged chronologically by publication date rather than alphabetically by title:

> Russell, Henry. 1978. *Famous Last Words: Notable Supreme Court Cases of the Last Five Years.* New Orleans: Liberty Publications.

> Russell, Henry, ed. 1988. *Court Battles to Remember.* Denver: Axel & Myers.

Chapter in a Multiauthor Collection.

> Gray, Alexa North. 2005. "Foreign Policy and the Foreign Press." In *Current Media Issues,* ed. Barbara Bonnard. New York: Boulanger.

The parenthetical text reference may include the page reference:

> (Gray 2005, 191)

If the author and the editor are the same person, you must repeat the name:

> Farmer, Susan A. 2004. "Tax Shelters in the New Dispensation: How to Save Your Income." In *Making Ends Meet: Strategies for the Nineties,* ed. Susan A. Farmer. Nashville: Burkette and Hyde.

Author of a Foreword or Introduction.   There is no need, according to *CMS* 15 (17.46, 17.74–75), to cite the author of a foreword or introduction in your bibliography, unless you have used material from that author's contribution to the volume. In that case, the bibliography entry is listed under the name of the author of the foreword or introduction. Place the name of the author of the work itself after the title of the work:

> Farris, Carla. 2004. Foreword to *Marital Stress and the Professoriat: A Case Study,* by Basil Givan. New York: Galapagos.

The parenthetical text reference cites the name of the author of the foreword or introduction, not the author of the book:

> (Farris 2004)

Subsequent Editions.   If you are using an edition of a book other than the first, you must cite the number of the edition or the status, such as *Rev. ed.* for *Revised edition,* if there is no edition number:

> Hales, Sarah. 2004. *The Coming Water Wars.* 2d ed. Pittsburgh: Blue Skies.

Multivolume Work.   If you are citing a multivolume work in its entirety, use the following format:

> Graybosch, Charles. 1988–89. *The Rise of the Unions.* 3 vols. New York: Starkfield.

If you are citing only one of the volumes in a multivolume work, use the following format:

Ronsard, Madeleine. 2005. *Monopolies.* Vol. 2 of *A History of Capitalism.* Ed.
Joseph M. Sayles. Boston: Renfrow.

Reprints.

Adams, Sterling R. [1964] 1988. *How to Win an Election: Promotional
Campaign Strategies.* New York: Starkfield.

Modern Editions of Classics. If the original year of publication is known,
include it, in brackets, before the publication date for the edition used:

Burke, Edmond. [1790] 1987. *Reflections on the Revolution in France.* Ed. J.
G. A. Pocock. Indianapolis: Hackett.

Remember, if the classic text is divided into short, numbered sections (such
as the chapter and verse divisions of the Bible), you do not need to include the
work in your bibliography unless you wish to specify a particular edition.

Periodicals

Journal Articles. Journals are periodicals, usually published either
monthly or quarterly, that specialize in serious scholarly articles in a particular
field. The revised 2005 edition of the APSA *Style Manual* stipulates that a
reference for a journal article must include either the month, the season, or
the issue number (in that order of preference), placed just after the volume
number.

Hunzecker, Joan. 2004. "Teaching the Toadies: Cronyism in Municipal
Politics." *Review of Local Politics* 4 (June): 250–62.

Note that the name of the journal, which is italicized, is followed without
punctuation by the volume number. A colon separates the name of the month, in
parentheses, from the inclusive page numbers. Do not use *p.* or *pp.* to introduce
the page numbers.

Magazine Articles. Magazines, which are usually published weekly,
bimonthly, or monthly, appeal to the popular audience and generally have a wider
circulation than journals. *Newsweek* and *Scientific American* are examples of magazines.

Monthly Magazine. The name of the magazine is separated from the month
of publication by a comma:

Stapleton, Bonnie. 1981. "How It Was: On the Campaign Trail with Ike."
Lifetime Magazine, April, 16–21.

Weekly or Bimonthly Magazine. The day of the issue's publication appears
before the month:

Bruck, Connie. 2006. "The World of Business: A Mogul's Farewell." *The
New Californian,* 18 October.

Newspaper Articles. While the revised 2005 edition of the APSA *Style
Manual* does not discuss reference list entries for newspaper articles, *CMS* 15

(15.234–42, 16.117–18) deals with the topic in some detail. Here are two typical models:

> *New York Times.* 2006. Editorial, 10 August.

> Fine, Austin. 2005. "Hoag on Trial." *Carrollton (Texas) Tribune,* 24 November.

Note that *The* is omitted from the newspaper's title. If the name of the city in which an American newspaper is published does not appear in the paper's title, it should be appended, in italics. If the city is not well known, the name of the state is added, in italics, in parentheses, as in the second model above.

Public Documents

Congressional Journals.   References to either the *Senate Journal* or the *House Journal* begin with the journal's title and include the years of the session, the number of the Congress and session, and the month and day of the entry:

> *U.S. Senate Journal.* 2006. 105th Cong., 1st sess., 10 December.

The ordinal numbers *second* and *third* may be represented as *d* (52d, 103d) or as *nd* and *rd,* respectively.

Congressional Debates.

> *Congressional Record.* 1930. 72st Cong., 2d sess., vol. 72, pt. 8.

Congressional Reports and Documents.   Following the designation of Senate or House, include as many of the following items as possible, in this order: committee title, year, title of report or document, Congress, session, and report or document number or committee print number.

> U.S. Congress. House. Committee on the Budget. 2006. *Report on Government Efficiency As Perceived by the Public.* 105th Cong., 2d sess. H. Rept. 225.

Bills and Resolutions.

> U.S. Congress. Senate. 2005. *Visa Formalization Act of 2005.* 105th Cong. 1st sess. S.R. 1437.

The abbreviation *S.R.* in the model above stands for *Senate Resolutions,* and the number following is the bill or resolution number. For references to House bills, the abbreviation is *H.R.*

Statutes.

> *Citing to the* Statutes at Large

> Book Preservation Act. 2006. *Statutes at Large.* Vol. 82, sec. 6, p. 184.

> *Citing to the* United States Code

> Book Preservation Act. 2006. *U.S. Code.* Vol. 38, sec. 1562, p. 265.

United States Constitution.   While the revised 2005 edition of the APSA *Style Manual* does not discuss references for the U.S. Constitution, *CMS* 14 (16.172) states that the Constitution is not listed in the bibliography.

Executive Department Documents. Include the name of the corporate author, the year, title, city, and publisher.

> Department of Labor. 2004. *Report on Urban Growth Potential Projections.* Washington, DC: GPO.

The abbreviation for the publisher in the above model, *GPO,* stands for the *Government Printing Office,* which prints and distributes most government publications. According to *CMS* 15 (15.327), you may use any of the following formats to refer to the GPO:

> Washington, DC: U.S. Government Printing Office, 2005
> Washington, DC: Government Printing Office, 2005
> Washington, DC: GPO, 2005
> Washington, DC, 2005

Remember to be consistent in using the form you choose.

Legal References.

Supreme Court. Use the same format as for the parenthetical text citation, only add the date after the name of the case:

> *State of Nevada v. Goldie Warren.* 1969. 324 U.S. 123.

For a case prior to 1875, use the following format:

> *Marbury v. Madison.* 1803. 1 Cranch 137.

Lower Courts. Include the volume of the *Federal Reporter* (*F.*), the series, if it is other than the first (*2d,* in the model below), the page, and, in parentheses, an abbreviated reference to the specific district.

> *United States v. Sizemore.* 1950. 183 F.2d 201 (2d Cir.).

Publications of Government Commissions.

> U.S. Securities and Exchange Commission. 1984. *Annual Report of the Securities and Exchange Commission for the Fiscal Year.* Washington, DC: GPO.

Publications of State and Local Governments. Remember that references for state and local government publications are modeled on those for corresponding national government documents:

> Oklahoma Legislature. 2006. Joint Committee on Public Recreation. *Final Report to the Legislature, 2006, Regular Session, on Youth Activities.* Oklahoma City.

Electronic Sources

If a source is available in both print and electronic forms, it is preferable to use the print form, which is probably more readily available to readers than the electronic form. But if you have used the electronic version and it is different from the print version, the general practice is to make your reference to the electronic source as similar as possible to that for the print version, adding the full retrieval path (the electronic address) and the date of your last access of the material.

Electronic Book.   Begin with the author's name, reversed, followed if possible by date of publication, then the title of the work, the retrieval path, and the date of your last access to the work, in parentheses.

> Amshiral, Sretas. 2004. *Aviation in the Far East.*http://www.flight_easthist.org (January 3, 2005).

Chapter in an Electronic Book.

> Burris, Akasha. 2004. "Experiments in Transubstantiation." *Surviving Global Disaster.* http://www.meekah/exit/paleoearth.html (March 5, 2005).

Note that you may continue a lengthy URL on the next line of the reference. Do not add a hyphen at the end of the first line.

Electronic Journals.   Include all of the following information that you can find, in this order: name of author, reversed; year of publication; title of article, in quotation marks; title of journal, in italics; any further publication information, such as volume number, day or month; full retrieval path; and date of your last access, in parentheses:

> Zoheret, Jeanie. 2003. "The Politics of Social Deprivation." *B & N Digest* 3 (February). http://postmodern/tsu/b&n.edu (December 5, 2004).

Material from a World Wide Web (WWW) Site.   The author's name (reversed) and year of publication are followed by the title of the article, in quotation marks; the title, if applicable, of the complete work or Web page, in italics; the full Web address (URL); and, finally, the date on which you last accessed the page, in parentheses:

> Squires, Lawrence. 2004. "A Virtual Tour of the White House, circa 1900." *National Landmarks: Then and Now.* http://www.natlandmk.com/hist (August 21, 2004).

E-Mail Material.   The revised 2005 edition of the APSA *Style Manual* suggests that e-mail, bulletin board, and electronic discussion group messages be cited as personal communication in the text and left out of the reference list.

Interviews

Published Interviews.

Untitled Interview in a Book.

> Jorgenson, Mary. 2004. Interview by Alan McAskill. In *Hospice Pioneers.* Ed. Alan McAskill, 62–86. Richmond: Dynasty Press.

Titled Interview in a Periodical.

> Simon, John. 2004. "Picking the Patrons Apart: An Interview with John Simon." By Selena Fox. *Media Week,* March 14, 40–46.

Interview on Television.

Snopes, Edward. 2004. Interview by Klint Gordon. *Oklahoma Politicians.*
    WKY Television, 4 June.

Unpublished Interview.   According to the revised 2005 edition of the
APSA *Style Manual,* unpublished interviews should be identified within the text
of a sentence rather than in a parenthetical citation and left out of the reference list.

Unpublished Sources.

Theses and Dissertations.   If the work has a sewn or glued binding,
place the title in italics, like a book; otherwise designate the title by quotation
marks:

Hochenauer, Art. 2005. *Populism and the Free Soil Movement.* Ph.D. diss.
    University of Virginia.

Sharpe, Ellspeth Stanley. 2003. "Black Women in Politics: A Troubled
    History." Master's thesis. Oregon State University.

Paper Presented at a Meeting.

Zelazny, Kim, and Ed Gilmore. 2005. "Art for Art's Sake: Funding the NEA
    in the Twenty-First Century." Presented at the Annual Meeting of the
    Conference of Metropolitan Arts Councils, San Francisco.

Manuscript in the Author's Possession.

Borges, Rita V. 1969. "Mexican-American Border Conflicts, 1915–1970."
    University of Texas at El Paso. Photocopy.

The entry includes the institution with which the author is affiliated and
ends with a description of the format of the work (typescript, photocopy, etc.).

Sample Bibliography: APSA Author-Date System

NOTE. Most of the sources used as models in this chapter are not references to
actual publications.

8.2   AVOIDING PLAGIARISM

You want to use your source material as effectively as possible. This will
sometimes mean that you should quote from a source directly, whereas at other
times you will want to express such information in your own words. At all times,
you should work to integrate the source material skillfully into the flow of your
written argument.

Ariès, Philippe. 1962. <u>Centuries of Childhood: A Social History of Family Life.</u> Trans. Robert Baldock. New York: Knopf.

Cesbron, Henry. 1909. <u>Histoire critique de l'hystérie</u>. Paris: Asselin et Houzeau.

Farmer, Susan A. 2004. "Tax Shelters in the New Dispensation: How to Save Your Income." In <u>Making Ends Meet: Strategies for the Nineties</u>, ed. Susan A. Farmer. Nashville: Burkette and Hyde.

Herring, Ralph, et al. 2004. <u>Funding City Projects</u>. Atlanta: Jessup Institute for Policy Development.

Hunzecker, Joan. 2004. "Teaching the Toadies: Cronyism in Municipal Politics." <u>Review of Local Politics</u> 4:250–62.

Moore, J. B., Jeannine Macrory, and Natasha Traylor. 2004. <u>Down on the Farm: Renovating the Farm Loan</u>. Norman: Univ. of Oklahoma Press.

Northrup, Alan K. 2004. <u>Living High Off the Hog: Recent Pork Barrel Legislation in the Senate</u>. Cleveland: Johnstown.

Skylock, Browning. 1991. "'Fifty-Four Forty or Fight!': Sloganeering in Early America." <u>American History Digest</u> 28(3): 25–34.

Squires, Lawrence. 2006. "A Virtual Tour of the White House, circa 1900." *National Landmarks: Then and Now.* http://www.natlandmk.com/hist (21 August 2004).

Stapleton, Bonnie. 1981. "How It Was: On the Campaign Trail with Ike." <u>Lifetime Magazine</u>, April.

U.S. Securities and Exchange Commission. 1984. <u>Annual Report of the Securities and Exchange Commission for the Fiscal Year</u>. Washington, 2005.

When to Quote

You should quote directly from a source when the original language is distinctive enough to enhance your argument, or when rewording the passage would lessen its impact. In the interest of fairness, you should also quote a passage to which you will take exception. Rarely, however, should you quote a source at great length (longer than two or three paragraphs). Nor should your paper, or any substantial section of it, be merely a string of quoted passages. The more language you take from the writings of others, the more the quotations will disrupt the rhetorical flow of your own words. Too much quoting creates a choppy patchwork of varying styles and borrowed purposes in which your sense of your own control over your material is lost.

Quotations in Relation to Your Writing

When you do use a quotation, make sure that you insert it skillfully. According to the APSA *Style Manual,* quotations of four lines or fewer should be integrated into your text and set off with quotation marks:

> "In the last analysis," Alice Thornton argued in 2006, "we cannot afford not to embark on a radical program of fiscal reform" (12).

Quotations longer than four lines should begin on a new line, be indented five spaces from the left margin and not be enclosed in quotation marks.

Blake's outlook for the solution to the city's problem of abandoned buildings is anything but optimistic:

> If the trend in demolitions due to abandonment continues, the cost of doing nothing may be too high. The three-year period from 2004 to 2007 shows an annual increase in demolitions of roughly twenty percent. Such an upward trend for a sustained period of time would eventually place a disastrous hardship on the city's resources. And yet the city council seems bent on following the tactic of inaction. (2004, 8)

Acknowledge Quotations Carefully

Failing to signal the presence of a quotation skillfully can lead to confusion or choppiness:

> The U.S. Secretary of Labor believes that worker retraining programs have failed because of a lack of trust within the American business culture. "The American business community does not visualize the need to invest in its workers" (Winn 2004, 11).

The first sentence in the above passage seems to suggest that the quote that follows comes from the Secretary of Labor. Note how this revision clarifies the attribution:

> According to reporter Fred Winn, the U.S. Secretary of Labor believes that worker retraining programs have failed because of a lack of trust within the American business culture. Summarizing the secretary's view, Winn writes, "The American business community does not visualize the need to invest in its workers" (2004, 11).

The origin of each quote must be indicated within your text at the point where the quote occurs as well as in the list of works cited, which follows the text.

Quote Accurately

If your transcription of a quotation introduces careless variants of any kind, you are misrepresenting your source. Proofread your quotations very carefully, paying close attention to such surface features as spelling, capitalization, italics, and the use of numerals.

Occasionally, in order to make a quotation fit smoothly into a passage, to clarify a reference, or to delete unnecessary material, you may need to change the original wording slightly. You must, however, signal any such change to your reader. Some alterations may be noted by brackets:

> "Several times in the course of his speech, the attorney general said that his stand [on gun control] remains unchanged" (McAffrey 2004, 2).

Ellipses indicate that words have been left out of a quote:

> "The last time voters refused to endorse one of the senator's policies . . . was back in 1982" (Laws 2005, 143).

When you integrate quoted material with your own prose, it is unnecessary to begin the quote with ellipses:

> Benton raised eyebrows with his claim that "nobody in the mayor's office knows how to tie a shoe, let alone balance a budget" (Williams 2006, 12).

Paraphrasing

Your writing has its own rhetorical attributes, its own rhythms and structural coherence. Inserting several quotations into one section of your paper can disrupt the patterns of your prose and diminish its effectiveness. Paraphrasing, or recasting source material in your own words, is one way to avoid the choppiness that can result from a series of quotations.

Remember that a paraphrase is to be written in your language; it is not a near-copy of the source writer's language. Merely changing a few words of the original does justice to no one's prose and frequently produces stilted passages. This sort of borrowing is actually a form of plagiarism. To integrate another's material into your own writing fully, use your own language.

Paraphrasing may actually increase your comprehension of source material, because in recasting a passage you will have to think very carefully about its meaning—more carefully, perhaps, than if you had merely copied it word for word.

Avoiding Plagiarism When Paraphrasing

Paraphrases require the same sort of documentation as direct quotes. The words of a paraphrase may be yours, but the idea belongs to someone else. Failure to give that person credit, in the form of references within the text and in the bibliography, may make you vulnerable to a charge of plagiarism.

Plagiarism is the use of someone else's words or ideas without proper credit. Although some plagiarism is deliberate, produced by writers who understand that they are guilty of a kind of academic thievery, much of it is unconscious, committed by writers who are not aware of the varieties of plagiarism or who are careless in recording their borrowings from sources. Plagiarism includes:

- Quoting directly without acknowledging the source
- Paraphrasing without acknowledging the source
- Constructing a paraphrase that closely resembles the original in language and syntax

One way to guard against plagiarism is to keep careful notes of when you have directly quoted source material and when you have paraphrased—making sure that the wording of the paraphrases is yours. Be sure that all direct quotes in your final draft are properly set off from your own prose, either with quotation marks or in indented blocks.

What kind of paraphrased material must be acknowledged? Basic material that you find in several sources need not be documented by a reference. For example, it is unnecessary to cite a source for the information that Franklin Delano Roosevelt was elected to a fourth term as president of the United States shortly before his death, because this is a commonly known fact. However, Professor Smith's opinion, published in a recent article, that Roosevelt's winning of a fourth term hastened his death is not a fact, but a theory based on Smith's research and defended by her. If you wish to use Smith's opinion in a paraphrase, you need to credit her, as you should all judgments and claims from another source. Any information that is not widely known, whether factual or open to dispute, should be documented. This includes statistics, graphs, tables, and charts taken from sources other than your own primary research.

CHAPTER

9

ORGANIZING THE RESEARCH PROCESS

9.1   GAINING CONTROL OF THE RESEARCH PROCESS

The research paper is where all your skills as an interpreter of details, an organizer of facts and theories, and a writer of clear prose come together. Building logical arguments on the twin bases of fact and hypothesis is the way things are done in political science, and the most successful political scientists are those who master the art of research.

Students new to the writing of research papers sometimes find themselves intimidated by the job ahead of them. After all, the research paper adds what seems to be an extra set of complexities to the writing process. As any other expository or persuasive paper does, a research paper must present an original thesis using a carefully organized and logical argument. But it also investigates a topic that is outside the writer's own experience. This means that writers must locate and evaluate information that is new, thus, in effect, educating themselves as they explore their topics. A beginning researcher sometimes feels overwhelmed by the basic requirements of the assignment or by the authority of the source material being investigated.

As you begin a research project, it may be difficult to establish a sense of control over the different tasks you are undertaking. You may have little notion of where to search for a thesis or even for the most helpful information. If you do not carefully monitor your own work habits, you may find yourself unwittingly abdicating responsibility for the paper's argument by borrowing it wholesale from one or more of your sources.

Who is in control of your paper? The answer must be you—not the instructor who assigned you the paper, and certainly not the published writers and interviewees whose opinions you solicit. If all your paper does is paste together the opinions of others, it has little use. It is up to you to synthesize an original idea from a judicious evaluation of your source material. At the beginning of your research project, you will, of course, be unsure about many elements of your paper. For example, you will probably not yet have a definitive thesis sentence or even much understanding of the shape of your argument. But you can establish a measure of control over the process you will go through to complete the paper. And, if you work regularly and systematically, keeping yourself open to new ideas as they present themselves, your sense of control will grow. Here are some suggestions to help you establish and maintain control of your paper:

1. *Understand your assignment.* It is possible for a research assignment to go badly simply because the writer did not read the assignment carefully. Considering how much time and effort you are about to put into your project, it is a very good idea to make sure you have a clear understanding of what your instructor wants you to do. Be sure to ask your instructor about any aspect of the assignment that is unclear to you—but only after you have read it carefully. Recopying the assignment in your own handwriting is a good way to start, even though your instructor may have already given it to you in writing. Before you dive into the project, make sure that you have considered the questions listed below.

2. *What is your topic?* The assignment may give you a great deal of specific information about your topic, or you may be allowed considerable freedom in establishing one for yourself. In a government class in which you are studying issues affecting American foreign policy, your professor might give you a very specific assignment—a paper, for example, examining the difficulties of establishing a viable foreign policy in the wake of the collapse of international communism—or he or she may allow you to choose for yourself the issue that your paper will address. You need to understand the terms, as set up in the assignment, by which you will design your project.

3. *What is your purpose?* Whatever the degree of latitude you are given in the matter of your topic, pay close attention to the way your instructor has phrased the assignment. Is your primary job to *describe* a current political situation or to *take a stand* on it? Are you to *compare* political systems, and if so, to what end? Are you to *classify, persuade, survey,* or *analyze*? To determine the purpose of the project, look for such descriptive terms in the assignment.

4. *Who is your audience?* Your own orientation to the paper is profoundly affected by your conception of the audience for whom you are writing. Granted that your main reader is your instructor, who else would be interested in your paper? Are you writing for the voters of a community, a governor, or a city council? A paper that describes the proposed renovation of city buildings may justifiably contain much more technical jargon for an audience of contractors than for a council of local business and civic leaders.

5. *What kind of research are you doing?* You will be doing one if not both of the following kinds of research:

• *Primary research*, which requires you to discover information firsthand, often by conducting interviews, surveys, or polls. In primary research, you are collecting and sifting through raw data—data that have not already been interpreted by researchers—which you will then study, select, arrange, and speculate on. These raw data may be the opinions of experts or of people on the street, historical documents, the published letters of a famous politician, or material collected from other researchers. It is important to set up carefully the methods by which you collect your data. Your aim is to gather the most accurate information possible, from which sound observations may be made later, either by you or by other writers using the material you have uncovered.

• *Secondary research*, which uses published accounts of primary materials. Although the primary researcher might poll a community for its opinion on the outcome of a recent bond election, the secondary researcher will use the material from the poll to support a particular thesis. Secondary research, in other words, focuses on interpretations of raw data. Most of your college papers will be based on your use of secondary sources.

PRIMARY SOURCE	SECONDARY SOURCE
A published collection of Thurgood Marshall's letters	A journal article arguing that the volume of letters illustrates Marshall's attitude toward the media
An interview with the mayor	A character study of the mayor based on the interview
Material from a questionnaire	A paper basing its thesis on the results of the questionnaire

6. *Keep your perspective.* Whichever type of research you perform, you must keep your results in perspective. There is no way that you, as a primary researcher, can be completely objective in your findings. It is not possible to design a questionnaire that will net you absolute truth, nor can you be sure that the opinions you gather in interviews reflect the accurate and unchanging opinions of the people you question. Likewise, if you are conducting secondary research, you must remember that the articles and journals you are reading are shaped by the aims of their writers, who are interpreting primary materials for their own ends. The farther you are removed from a primary source, the greater the possibility for distortion. Your job as a researcher is to be as accurate as possible, which means keeping in view the limitations of your methods and their ends.

9.2   EFFECTIVE RESEARCH METHODS

In any research project, there will be moments of confusion, but you can prevent this confusion from overwhelming you by establishing an effective research procedure. You need to design a schedule that is as systematic as possible, yet flexible enough so that you do not feel trapped by it. By always showing you what to do next, a schedule will help keep you from running into dead ends.

At the same time, the schedule helps you retain the focus necessary to spot new ideas and new strategies as you work.

Give Yourself Plenty of Time

You may feel like delaying your research for many reasons: unfamiliarity with the library, the press of other tasks, a deadline that seems comfortably far away. But do not allow such factors to deter you. Research takes time. Working in a library seems to speed up the clock, so that the hour you expected it would take you to find a certain source becomes two. You must allow yourself the time needed not only to find material but also to read it, assimilate it, and set it in the context of your own thoughts. If you delay starting, you may well find yourself distracted by the deadline, having to keep an eye on the clock while trying to make sense of a writer's complicated argument.

The following schedule lists the steps of a research project in the order in which they are generally accomplished. Remember that each step is dependent on the others and that it is quite possible to revise earlier decisions in light of later discoveries. After some background reading, for example, your notion of the paper's purpose may change, a fact that may in turn alter other steps. One of the strengths of a good schedule is its flexibility. Note that this schedule lists tasks for both primary and secondary research; you should use only those steps that are relevant to your project.

Do Background Reading

Whether you are doing primary or secondary research, you need to know what kinds of work have already been done in your field. A good way to start is by consulting general reference works, though you do not want to overdo it (see below). Chapters 10 and 11 list specialized reference works on topics of interest to political scientists on the Internet. You might find help in such sources even for specific local problems, such as how to restructure a city council or finance an antidrug campaign in area schools.

WARNING Be very careful not to rely too heavily on material in general encyclopedias, such as the *Wikipedia, Encyclopaedia Britannica* or *Collier's Encyclopedia.* You may wish to consult one for an overview of a topic with which you are unfamiliar, but students new to research are often tempted to import large sections, if not entire articles, from such volumes, and this practice is not good scholarship. One major reason your instructor has assigned a research paper is to let you experience the kinds of books and journals in which the discourse of political science is conducted. Encyclopedias are good places for instant introductions to subjects; some even include bibliographies of reference works at the ends of their articles. But to write a useful paper, you will need much more detailed information about your subject. Once you have learned what you can from a general encyclopedia, move on to other sources.

A primary rule of source hunting is to *use your imagination*. Determine what topics relevant to your study might be covered in general reference works. If, for example, you are looking for introductory readings to help you with a research paper on antidrug campaign financing, you might look into such specialized reference tools as the *Encyclopedia of Social Work*. Remember to check articles in such works for lists of references to specialized books and essays.

Narrow Your Topic and Establish a Working Thesis

Before exploring outside sources, you should find out what you already know or think about your topic, a job that can be accomplished well only in writing. You might wish to investigate your own attitude toward your topic by using one or more of the prewriting strategies described in Chapter 5. You might also be surprised by what you know—or don't know—about the subject. This kind of self-questioning can help you discover a profitable direction for your research.

For a research paper in a course in American government, Charlotte Goble was given the topic category of grassroots attempts to legislate morality in American society. She chose the specific topic of textbook censorship. Here is the path she took as she looked for ways to limit the topic effectively and find a thesis.

GENERAL TOPIC   Textbook censorship
POTENTIAL TOPICS   How a local censorship campaign gets started
                   Funding censorship campaigns
                   Reasons behind textbook censorship
                   Results of censorship campaigns
WORKING THESIS   It is disconcertingly easy in our part of the state to launch a
                   textbook censorship campaign

Specific methods for discovering a thesis are discussed in Chapter 5. It is unlikely that you will come up with a satisfactory thesis at the beginning of your project. You need a way to guide yourself through the early stages of research as you work toward discovering a main idea that is both useful and manageable. Having in mind a *working thesis*—a preliminary statement of your purpose—can help you select the material that is of greatest interest to you as you examine potential sources. The working thesis will probably evolve as your research progresses, and you should be ready to accept such change. You must not fix on a thesis too early in the process, or you may miss opportunities to refine it.

Develop a Working Bibliography

As you begin your research, you will look for published sources—essays, books, or interviews with experts—that may help you. This list of potentially useful sources is your *working bibliography*. There are many ways to develop this bibliography. The cataloging system in your library will give you sources, as will the published bibliographies in your field. (Some of these bibliographies are listed below.) The general references in which you did your background reading may also list such works, and each specialized book or essay you find will have a bibliography that its writer used, which may be helpful to you.

It is from your working bibliography that you will select the items for the bibliography that will appear in the final draft of your paper. Early in your research, you will not know which of the sources will help you and which will not, but it is important to keep an accurate description of each entry in your working bibliography so that you will be able to tell clearly which items you have investigated and which you will need to consult again. Establishing the working bibliography also allows you to practice using the bibliographical format you are required to follow in your final draft. As you make your list of potential sources, be sure to include all the information about each one, in the proper format, using the proper punctuation. (Chapter 8 describes in detail the bibliographical formats most often required for political science papers.)

Write for Needed Information

In the course of your research, you may need to consult a source that is not immediately available to you. Working on the antidrug campaign paper, for example, you might find that a packet of potentially useful information may be obtained from a government agency or public interest group in Washington, DC. Or you may discover that a needed book is not owned by your university library or by any other local library, or that a successful antidrug program has been implemented in the school system of a city of comparable size in another state. In such situations, it may be tempting to disregard potential sources because of the difficulty of consulting them. If you ignore this material, however, you are not doing your job.

It is vital that you take steps to acquire the needed data. In the first case mentioned above, you can simply write to the Washington, DC, agency or interest group; in the second, you may use your library's interlibrary loan procedure to obtain the book; in the third, you can track down the council that manages the antidrug campaign by e-mail, phone, or Internet, and ask for information. Remember that many businesses and government agencies want to share their information with interested citizens; some have employees or entire departments whose job is to facilitate communication with the public. Be as specific as possible when asking for such information. It is a good idea to outline your own project briefly—in no more than a few sentences—to help the respondent determine the types of information that will be useful to you.

Never let the immediate unavailability of a source stop you from trying to consult it. And be sure to begin the job of locating and acquiring such long-distance material as soon as possible, to allow for the various delays that often occur.

Evaluate Written Sources

Fewer research experiences are more frustrating than trying to recall information found in a source that you can no longer identify. You must establish an efficient method of examining and evaluating the sources in your working bibliography. Suggestions for compiling an accurate record of your written sources are described below.

Determine Quickly the Potential Usefulness of a Source

For books, you can read the front material (the introduction, foreword, and preface), looking for the author's thesis; you can also examine chapter headings, dust jackets, and indexes. A journal article should announce its intention in its introduction, which in most cases will be a page or less in length. This sort of preliminary examination should tell you whether a more intensive examination is worthwhile. *Whatever you decide about the source, photocopy its title page,* making sure to include all important publication information (including title, date, author, volume number, and page numbers). Write on the photocopied page any necessary information that is not printed there. Without such a record, later in your research, you might forget that you have consulted a particular text and find yourself repeating your work.

When you have determined that a potential source is worth closer inspection, explore it carefully. If it is a book, determine whether you should invest the time needed to read it in its entirety. Whatever the source, make sure you understand not only its overall thesis but also each part of the argument that the writer sets up to illustrate or prove the thesis. You need to get a feel for the writer's argument—how the subtopics form (or do not form) a logical defense of the main point. What do you think of the writer's logic and the examples used? You may need more than one reading to arrive at an accurate appraisal.

As you read, try to get a feel for the larger argument in which the source takes its place. Its references to the works of other writers will show you where to look for additional material and indicate the general shape of scholarly opinion concerning your subject. If you can see the source you are reading as only one element of an ongoing dialogue, instead of the last word on the subject, then you can place its argument in perspective.

Use Photocopies

Periodicals and most reference works cannot be checked out of the library. Before the widespread availability of photocopy machines, students could use these materials only in the library, jotting down information on note cards. Although there are advantages to using the note card method (see below), photocopying saves you time in the library and allows you to take the original information home, where you can decide how to use it at your convenience.

If you do decide to copy source material, you should do the following:

- Be sure to follow all copyright laws.
- Have the exact change for the photocopy machines. Do not trust the change machines at the library. They are sometimes battle-scarred and cantankerous.
- Record all necessary bibliographical information on the photocopy. If you forget to do this, you might find yourself having to make an extra trip to the library just to get a date of publication or page numbers.

Remember that photocopying a source is not the same as examining it. You will still have to spend time going over the material, assimilating it to use it accurately. It is not enough merely to have the information close at hand or even to have read it once or twice. You must understand it thoroughly. Be sure to give yourself time for this kind of evaluation.

The Note Card—A Thing of the Past?   In many ways, note cards are an old-fashioned method of recording source material; for unpracticed researchers, they may seem unwieldy and unnecessary because the information jotted on them—one fact per card—will eventually have to be transmitted again, in the research paper. However, before you decide to abolish the note card system once and for all, consider its advantages:

1. Using note cards is a way of forcing yourself to think productively as you read. In translating the language of the source into the language of your notes, you are assimilating the material more completely than you would by merely reading it.
2. Note cards give you a handy way to arrange and rearrange your facts, looking for the best possible organization for your paper. Not even a computer gives you the flexibility of a pack of cards as you try to order your paper.

Determine Whether Interviews or Surveys Are Needed

If your project calls for primary research, you may need to use a questionnaire to interview experts on your topic or to conduct a survey of opinions among a select group. Be sure to prepare yourself as thoroughly as possible for any primary research. Here are some tips.

Conducting an Interview

Establish a purpose for each interview, bearing in mind the requirements of your working thesis. In what ways might your interview benefit your paper? Write down your description of the interview's purpose. Estimate its length, and inform your subject. Arrive for your interview on time and dressed appropriately. Be courteous.

Before the interview, learn as much as possible about your topic by researching published sources. Use this research to design your questions. If possible, learn something about the backgrounds of the people you interview. This knowledge may help you establish rapport with your subjects and will also help you tailor your questions. Take with you to the interview a list of prepared questions. However, be ready during the interview to depart from your list in order to follow any potentially useful direction that the questioning may take.

Take notes. Make sure you have extra pens. Do not use a tape recorder because it will inhibit most interviewees. If you must use tape, *ask for permission from your subject* before beginning the interview. Follow up your interview with a thank-you letter and, if feasible, a copy of the paper in which the interview is used.

Designing and Conducting a Survey

If your research requires a survey, see Chapter 20 for instructions on designing and conducting surveys, polls, and questionnaires.

Draft a Thesis and Outline

No matter how thoroughly you may hunt for data or how fast you read, you will not be able to find and assimilate every source pertaining to your subject, especially if it is popular or controversial, and you should not unduly prolong your research. You must bring this phase of the project to an end—with the option of resuming it, if the need arises—and begin to shape both the material you have gathered and your thoughts about it into a paper. During the research phase of your project, you have been thinking about your working thesis, testing it against the material you have discovered, and considering ways to improve it. Eventually, you must formulate a thesis that sets out an interesting and useful task, one that can be satisfactorily managed within the limits of your assignment and that effectively employs much, if not all, of the material you have gathered.

Once you have formulated your thesis, it is a good idea to make an outline of the paper. In helping you to determine a structure for your writing, the outline is also testing the thesis, prompting you to discover the kinds of work your paper will need to complete the task set out by the main idea. Chapter 5 discusses the structural requirements of the formal and the informal outline. (If you have used note cards, you may want to start outlining by organizing your cards according to the headings you have given them and looking for logical connections among the different groups of cards. Experimenting with structure in this way may lead you to discoveries that will further improve your thesis.)

No thesis or outline is written in stone. There is still time to improve the structure or purpose of your paper even after you have begun to write your first draft or, for that matter, your final draft. Some writers actually prefer to write a first draft before outlining, and then study the draft's structure to determine what revisions need to be made. *Stay flexible*, always looking for a better connection—a sharper wording of your thesis. All the time you are writing, the testing of your ideas continues.

Write a First Draft

Despite all the preliminary work you have done on your paper, you may feel a reluctance to begin your first draft. Integrating all your material and your ideas into a smoothly flowing argument is indeed a complicated task. It may help to think of your first attempt as only a rough draft, which can be changed as necessary. Another strategy for reducing reluctance to start is to begin with the part of the draft about which you feel most confident, instead of with the introduction. You may write sections of the draft in any order, piecing the parts together later. But however you decide to start writing—START.

Obtain Feedback

It is not enough that you understand your argument; others have to understand it, too. If your instructor is willing to look at your rough draft, you should take advantage of the opportunity and pay careful attention to any suggestions for improvement. Other readers may also be of help, although having a friend or a relative read your draft may not be as helpful as having it read by someone who is knowledgeable in your field. In any event, be sure to evaluate any suggestions carefully. Remember, the final responsibility for the paper rests with you.

9.3 HOW TO CONDUCT A LITERATURE REVIEW

Your goal in writing a research paper is to provide an opportunity for your readers to increase their understanding of the subject you are addressing. They will want the most current and precise information available. Whether you are writing a traditional library research paper, conducting an experiment, or preparing an analysis of a policy enforced by a government agency, you must know what has already been learned in order to give your readers comprehensive and up-to-date information or to add something new to what they already know about the subject. If your topic is welfare administration in Tennessee, for example, you will want to find out precisely what national, state, and local government policies currently affect welfare administration in Tennessee, and the important details of how and why these policies came to be adopted. When you seek this information, you will be conducting a *literature review*, a thoughtful collection and analysis of available information on the topic you have selected for study. It tells you, before you begin your paper, experiment, or analysis, what is already known about the subject.

Why do you need to conduct a literature review? It would be embarrassing to spend a lot of time and effort preparing a study, only to find that the information you are seeking has already been discovered by someone else. Also, a properly conducted literature review will tell you many things about a particular subject. It will tell you the extent of current knowledge, sources of data for your research, examples of what is *not* known (which in turn generate ideas for formulating hypotheses), methods that have been previously used for research, and clear definitions of concepts relevant to your own research.

Let us consider an example. Suppose that you have decided to research the following question: "How are voter attitudes affected by negative advertising?" First, you will need to establish a clear definition of "negative advertising"; then you will need to find a way to measure attitudes of voters; finally, you will need to use or develop a method of discerning how attitudes are affected by advertising. Using research techniques explained in this and other chapters of this manual, you will begin your research by looking for studies that address your research question or similar questions in the library, on the Internet, and through other resources. You will discover that many studies have been written on voters' attitudes and the effects of advertising on them. As you read these studies, certain patterns will appear. Some research methods will seem to have produced better results than others. Some studies will be quoted in others many times—some confirming and others refuting what previous studies have done. You will constantly be making choices as you examine these studies, reading very carefully those that are highly relevant to your purposes, and skimming those that are of only marginal interest. As you read, constantly ask yourself the following questions:

- How much is known about this subject?
- What is the best available information, and why is it better than other information?
- What research methods have been used successfully in relevant studies?
- What are the possible sources of data for further investigation of this topic?
- What important information is still not known, in spite of all previous research?
- Of the methods that have been used for research, which are the most effective for making new discoveries? Are new methods needed?
- How can the concepts being researched be more precisely defined?

You will find that this process, like the research process as a whole, is recursive. Insights related to one of the above questions will spark new investigations into others, and these investigations will then bring up a new set of questions, and so on.

Your instructor may request that you include a literature review as a section of the paper that you are writing. Your written literature review may be from one to several pages in length, but it should always tell the reader the following information:

1. Which previously compiled or published studies, articles, or other documents provide the best available information on the selected topic;
2. What these studies conclude about the topic;
3. What the apparent methodological strengths and weaknesses of these studies are;
4. What remains to be discovered about the topic;
5. What appear to be, according to these studies, the most effective methods for developing new information on the topic.

Your literature review should consist of a written narrative that answers—not necessarily consecutively—the above questions. The success of your own research project depends in large part on the extent to which you have carefully and thoughtfully answered these questions.

CHAPTER

10

LIBRARY INFORMATION RESOURCES

You will find a vast amount of information about writing, politics, and government in your college library. There is, in fact, so much information that discovering where to start looking can be a substantial task in itself. This section lists some important guides to information about politics and government that may help you launch your research project.

10.1   REFERENCE BOOKS

Reference Books: American Government and Politics

Barone, Michael, and Grant Ujifusa. *The Almanac of American Politics.* Washington, DC: National Journal. Annual. This compendium of information on national and state governments and officeholders includes essays, organized alphabetically by state, on U.S. governors, senators, and representatives. Charts summarize yearly voting records of each official. An index is included.

Budget of the United States Government. Washington, DC: Government Printing Office. Annual. The yearly government printing of the budget organizes its discussion of federal spending by specific current issues, then details the budgets of the specific government agencies. There is an index.

Congressional Quarterly Almanac. Washington, DC: Congressional Quarterly. Annual. This overview of legislation for the year's session of Congress is organized by subject headings, for example, "Economics and Finance" and "Government/ Commerce." There are three indexes: a bill number index, a roll-call vote index, and a general index.

Gimlin, Hoyt, ed. *Historic Documents.* Washington, DC: Congressional Quarterly. Annual. This series of yearly volumes publishes a selection of the current year's government documents. Chosen to reflect the editor's assessment of important events, the documents are organized chronologically, and the volumes are indexed every five years.

Graham, Judith, ed. *Current Biography Yearbook*. New York: H. W. Wilson. Annual. The essays in this series, some of them more than a page in length, sketch biographies of distinguished individuals from a variety of fields. Each entry includes a list of references. Contents are indexed by profession.

Inventory of Information Sources and Services Available to the U.S. House of Representatives, 1977. Westport, CT: Greenwood. This volume lists the tremendous number of information sources, both public and private, used by representatives. There is a general index.

Kay, Ernest. *Dictionary of International Biography*. Cambridge, MA: Melrose Press. Annual. This volume publishes brief biographical citations of individuals of interest in several fields. There is no index.

Mooney, Louis, ed. *The Annual Obituary*. Detroit: St. James Press. Annual. This series prints brief essays on notable individuals who died during the year. Each entry includes references. The volumes are indexed by profession.

Morris, Dan, and Inez Morris, 1974. *Who Was Who in American Politics*. New York: Hawthorn Books. A one-volume reference identifying approximately 4,200 national political figures either inactive in politics or deceased. Brief biographical descriptions list offices held. There is no index.

The National Cyclopedia of American Biography. New York: James T. White. Annual to 1978. This series of volumes, the first of which was issued in 1888, offers biographical essays on notable Americans, in a variety of fields, who were alive at the time of publication. An index of names is included.

Plano, Jack C., and Milton Greenburg, 2001. *The American Political Dictionary*. 11th ed. Belmont, CA: Wadsworth. This dictionary offers concise definitions of more than 4,000 terms of interest in politics and political science. Important terms are given more in-depth treatment. There is an index.

Public Papers of the Presidents. Washington, DC: Government Printing Office. This government series publishes the papers and speeches of every U.S. president since Herbert Hoover, except for Franklin D. Roosevelt, whose papers were published privately. There is a separate set of volumes for each president.

Schwarzkopf, LeRoy, comp. *Government Reference Books: A Biennial Guide to U.S. Government Publications*. Englewood, CO: Libraries Unlimited. Biennial. This listing of government reference books is part of a series that began in 1968–69. The entry for each government publication includes address, publication information, and a brief description of the contents. The entries are arranged by topic.

Troshynski-Thomas, Karen, and Deborah M. Burek, eds. *Gale Directory of Publications and Broadcast Media*. Detroit: Gale Research. (Formerly the Ayer Dictionary of Publications.) Annual. Volumes 1 and 2 of each year's edition list and describe briefly periodicals published in the United States and Canada, as well as radio and television stations and media cable systems. Entries are arranged by state and town. There is also a brief tally of information for each state, giving population and total number of newspapers and television stations. Volume 3 includes several indexes, tables, and maps.

United States Code. Washington, DC: Government Printing Office. This massive, multivolume publication, updated every six to eight years, prints all of the country's laws that are currently in force. Separate volumes index the contents.

Who Was Who in America, with World Notables, 2002. 15 vols. New Providence, NJ: Marquis Who's Who. This series publishes brief biographies of national and international figures who were no longer living at the time of publication. A separate volume contains a name index.

Who's Who in America. New Providence, NJ: Marquis Who's Who. Annual. This yearly series contains brief biographies of noteworthy living Americans in a variety of fields, listing achievements and home and office addresses. Contains geographic and professional indexes.

Who's Who in American Politics. 2 vols. New Providence, NJ: Bowker. Biennial. This series offers brief biographical summaries of Americans currently active in national, state, and local government. Included are sections representing U.S. holdings: Guam, Puerto Rico, and the Virgin Islands. Information given for each individual includes party affiliation, offices held, publications, memberships in various organizations, and religion. There is a name index.

Who's Who of American Women. New Providence, NJ: Marquis Who's Who. Biennial. This biographical dictionary surveys notable American women. There is no index.

Reference Books: International Politics and the World

Amnesty International. *Report on Human Rights Around the World.* Alameda, CA: Hunter House. Annual. This volume offers reports on the status of human rights in countries around the world. The entries, organized alphabetically by name of country, include essays, maps, and illustrations dealing with such topics as the use of the death penalty, voting rights and restrictions, and the treatment of minorities. There is no index.

Banks, Arthur S., ed. *Political Handbook of the World.* Binghamton, NY: CSA Publications. The essays in this volume, which is revised every one or two years, summarize the political history and current political situation of a variety of countries, arranged alphabetically. The essays profile political parties, list current government officials by name, and discuss issues such as local media. Also included is a chronology of important political events for the year and U.N. conferences. There is a general index.

Bowen, Thomas F., and Kelly S. Bowen, eds. *Countries of the World and Their Leaders Yearbook.* 2 vols. Detroit: Gale Research. Annual. This twenty-year-old series prints a variety of information, taken from U.S. State Department reports, relating to selected countries. Each entry includes tables and an essay profiling the country's history, ethnic makeup, and current political condition.

Brune, Lester H., 2002. *Chronological History of United States Foreign Relations.* 2 vols. New York: Routledge. This set of volumes is an extensive time line of events, each briefly summarized, in the history of American foreign policy. Also discussed are international political events that affected U.S. policy. For example, an entry for September 14, 1812, notes the French occupation of Moscow. Volume 2 includes a bibliography of references and a general index.

Central Intelligence Agency. *The World Factbook.* Washington, DC: Central Intelligence Agency. Annual. Published primarily for the use of government officials, this CIA compendium gives various kinds of information about different countries. Broad categories, represented by charts and maps as well as by written summaries, include agricultural development, import information, inflation profiles, and population growth. Entries are arranged alphabetically by name of country.

Clements, John. *Clements' Encyclopedia of World Governments.* Dallas: Political Research. Annual. The essays in this series offer analyses of historical events, current government programs, and economic and foreign affairs, among other topics. Each volume includes a chronological listing of important political events occurring during the years surveyed by the volume. There are appendixes and a geographical index.

Demographic Yearbook. New York: United Nations. Annual. This series publishes international demographic statistics from the United Nations. A dual-language text, the volume is printed in French and English. There is a subject index.

The Europa World Year Book. 2 vols. London: Europa. Annual. This publication examines the current status of political, economic, and commercial institutions of different countries. Contents are alphabetized by country, and the entries include charts and tables listing vital statistics for each country surveyed.

Flanders, Stephen A., and Carl N. Flanders, 1993. *Dictionary of American Foreign Affairs.* New York: Macmillan. The entries in this volume cover terms, events, documents, and individuals involved with U.S. foreign policy from 1776 to 1993. Appendix A is a useful time line of American foreign affairs. There is a bibliography of references, but no index.

Hunter, Brian, ed. *The Statesman's Yearbook.* New York: St. Martin's. Annual. There are two main divisions: one discussing international organizations, and the other profiling countries around the world, summarizing their history and present economic, technical, educational, and cultural status. Each entry includes a bibliography of references. There are three indexes: place and international organizations; products; and names of individuals.

The International Who's Who. London: Europa. Annual. This series offers paragraph-long biographies of notable individuals from different nations. The volumes are not indexed.

Kurian, George Thomas, 2002. *Encyclopedia of the World's Nations.* New York: Facts on File. A three-volume set incorporating volumes entitled *Encyclopedia of the First World, Encyclopedia of the Second World,* and *Encyclopedia of the Third World.* For each country surveyed, Kurian compiles data on various factors, including energy, labor, education, law enforcement, history, government, human rights, and foreign policy. The illustrated set includes appendixes, a bibliography of references, and a general index.

Lawson, Edward, and Mary Lou Bertucci, 1996. *Encyclopedia of Human Rights.* New York: Taylor & Francis. Various topics concerning international human rights activities from 1945 to 1990 are discussed, and significant government documents are reprinted, such as the text of the *Convention Relating to the Status of Refugees* (1951). The appendixes include a chronological list of international human rights documents and a list of worldwide human rights institutions. There is a subject index.

Mackie, Thomas T., and Richard Rose. *The International Almanac of Electoral History,* 1991. 3rd ed. Washington, DC: Congressional Quarterly. A revision of the 2nd ed. (1982). This volume publishes information, represented in both statistical charts and written analyses, on election results in Western nations from the late nineteenth century to the present. The information is arranged alphabetically by country. There is no index.

Staar, Richard F., ed. *Yearbook on International Communist Affairs.* Stanford, CA: Hoover Institution. Annual through 1991. Communism as it developed in both communist and noncommunist countries is surveyed in this publication. Countries are divided into broad geographical regions and then dealt with alphabetically. There is a name index and a subject index.

The World Almanac and Book of Facts. Mahwah, NJ: World Almanac/Funk & Wagnalls. Annual. This almanac publishes a wide variety of information on the United States and world affairs. Many tables and charts are included. There is an index.

World Debt Tables: External Debt of Developing Countries. Washington, DC: World Bank. Annual. The tables in this volume, summarizing data for the World Bank, break down and analyze debts owed by the developing nations. There is no index.

Other Reference Books

The Index and Abstract Directory: An International Guide to Services and Serials Coverage, 1993. 3rd ed. 2 vols. Birmingham, AL: Ebsco. The directory gives information on more than 35,000 serial publications in Ebsco's publishing database. Entries are arranged alphabetically by subject. Included are listings for national and international political science periodicals. There are two indexes: one for titles and the other for subjects.

Montney, Charles, ed. *Directories in Print.* Detroit: Gale Research. Annual. According to the introduction to the two-volume 1994 edition, Volume 1 "describes 15,900 directories, rosters, guides, and other print and nonprint address lists published in the United States and worldwide" (vii). Each entry includes address, fax number, price of the directory, and a description of its contents. Arrangement is by subject. Chapter 19 covers "Law, Military, and Government" directories. Volume 2 contains subject and title/keyword indexes.

Olson, Stan. *The Foundation Directory.* New York: The Foundation Center. Annual. This publication lists and describes over 6,300 foundations with at least $2 million in assets or $200,000 in annual giving. Listed alphabetically by state, each entry includes financial information, names of donors, and brief descriptions of the purpose and activities of the foundation, as well as a list of officers. Indexed.

Wesserman, Paul, ed. *Consumer Sourcebook.* 2 vols. Detroit: Gale Research. Biennial. This guide to information sources for consumers is arranged according to the types of organizations profiled. Subheadings include "Government Organizations," "Information Centers," "Associations," and "Media Services." Contents are indexed by name of organization, subject, and publications put out by the various organizations.

Wiener, Philip P., ed., 1980. *Dictionary of the History of Ideas.* 5 vols. New York: Scribner's. Originally published in 1973–74. The essays in these volumes discuss ideas that have helped to shape and continue to shape human culture. The essays are arranged alphabetically by topic, within a series of broad subheadings. The subheading on politics, for example, includes sixty essays on such topics as "Authority," "Democracy," "Legal Concept of Freedom," "Liberalism," and "Social Attitudes Towards Women." Volume 5 consists of a subject and name index. Digitized and placed on the web in 2003 by the University of Virginia and maintained by its Electronic Text Center. http://etext.lib.virginia.edu/DicHist/dict.html.

Woy, James, ed. *Encyclopedia of Business Information Sources.* Detroit: Gale Research. Annual. This guide to information on more than 1,100 business topics is arranged by subject and surveys in both print and electronic sources, such as online databases. Headings include "Customs House," "Government Publications," "Laws," and "United States Congress." There is no index.

Government and Politics Periodicals

Clements' International Report. Dallas, TX: Political Research. This monthly newsletter comprises essays on current international political and historical concerns. There is a biannual subject index.

Congressional Digest. Washington, DC: Government Printing Office. A magazine that selects topics for debate and presents arguments on different sides of the issues.

Congressional Quarterly Weekly Report. Washington, DC: Government Printing Office. A weekly magazine that describes all the major activities of the U.S. House and Senate.

Congressional Record. Washington, DC: Government Printing Office. The official, constitutionally mandated publication of the activities and official documents of Congress.

Federal Register. Washington, DC: Government Printing Office. Daily issues of the Federal Register print the regulations and legal notices issued by federal agencies.

GPO Monthly Catalog of United States Government Publications. Washington, DC: Government Printing Office. This publication includes citations from the annual Periodicals Supplement and the U.S. Congressional Serial Set Supplement. Topics covered include finance, business, and demographics.

Library of Congress. *Monthly Checklist of State Publications.* Washington, DC: Government Printing Office. This checklist, organized alphabetically by state, lists state documents received by the Library of Congress over the preceding month. There is a subject index.

Office of the Federal Register/National Archives and Records Administration. *Code of Federal Regulations.* Washington, DC: Government Printing Office. Annual. As explained in the brief introduction to each issue, this mammoth set of volumes, updated yearly, constitutes "a codification of the general and permanent rules published in the Federal Register by the Executive departments and agencies of the Federal Government." The code is divided into fifty "titles," which are, in turn, further subdivided.

PACs & Lobbies. This semimonthly newsletter reports on federal developments affecting campaign finance and lobbying activities.

U.S. Code Congressional and Administrative News. St. Paul, MN: West. Annual. This series of volumes reprints selected laws made during the current session of Congress. A subject index is included.

The United States Law Week: A National Survey of Current Law. Washington, DC: Bureau of National Affairs. This weekly newsletter summarizes important court decisions and prints articles on current legal topics.

World of Politics: Taylor's Encyclopedia of Government Officials, Federal and State. Dallas, TX: Political Research. This monthly newsletter publishes articles discussing responses from the various branches of government to current issues. The periodical is indexed three times a year.

10.2   PERIODICAL INDEXES

Newspaper Indexes

The following major newspapers have indexes available either in print or on microfilm:

The Chicago Tribune	The New York Times
The Houston Post	The Times of London
The Los Angeles Times	The Wall Street Journal
The National Observer	The Washington Post
The New Orleans Times-Picayune	

Periodical Indexes

America: History and Life (article abstracts and citations of reviews and dissertations on life in the United States and Canada)

The American Humanities Index

Bibliographic Index

Biography Index

Book Review Index

Book Reviews in Historical Periodicals

Combined Retrospective (an index of the *Journals in Political Science,* 1886–1974; 6 vols.)

Historical Abstracts

Humanities Index

An Index to Book Reviews in the Humanities

Index to U.S. Government Periodicals

International Political Science Abstracts

The New York Times Biographical Service (a monthly compilation of obituaries
photocopied from the *New York Times*, arranged chronologically, with an
index on the front cover of each issue)

PAIS International in Print (subject index to international periodical articles in the social and political sciences)

Public Affairs Information Service: PAIS

Reader's Guide to Periodical Literature

Social Sciences Index

Sociological Abstracts

Ulrich's International Periodicals Directory, 1993–94 (5 vols.)

United States Political Science Documents

Urban Affairs Abstracts

Weekly Compilation of Presidential Documents (weekly publication including
the president's "remarks, news conferences, messages, statements"—all
public presidential utterances for that week).

10.3   STATISTICS

Government Finance Statistics Yearbook. Washington, DC: International
Monetary Fund. Annual. This reference volume publishes tables that document
revenues and spending by governments around the world. There is no index.

Stanley, Harold W., and Richard G. Niemi. *Vital Statistics on American Politics.*
Washington, DC: Congressional Quarterly Press. The charts and tables in this
regularly updated reference guide for political statistics cover a wide range of
topics related to American politics, including the media (newspaper endorse-
ments of presidential candidates from 1932 are graphed), interest groups, and
the geographical and ethnic makeup of political bodies. There is an index.

Statistical Reference Index Annual: Abstracts. Bethesda, MD: Congressional
Information Service. Annual. This volume is a guide to American statistical publications from private organizations and state government sources. Contents are
organized by the type of organization publishing the reports. Each publication
listed is briefly described in an abstract. An accompanying volume includes four
separate indexes: subject and name, category, issuing sources, and title index.

Statistical Yearbook. New York: United Nations. Annual. Published in French
and English, this yearly volume summarizes data from several U.N. reports in
order to provide an analysis of the world's socioeconomic development over a
twelve-month period. Contents are arranged by topic. The book is not indexed.

Statistical Yearbook. Paris: UNESCO. Annual. The statistical charts in this
yearly publication cover education, science, and aspects of cultural life for 200
member nations of UNESCO. Material is generated from UNESCO questionnaires answered by a wide variety of respondents. The text is printed in three languages. There is no index.

U.S. Bureau of the Census. *Statistical Abstract of the United States.* Washington,
DC: Department of Commerce. Annual. This volume, part of a series published

since 1878, summarizes statistics on the country's social, political, and economic organization. There is an index.

Vital Statistics of the United States. 2 vols. Hyattsville, MD: U.S. Department of Health and Human Services. Annual. Each of the two volumes of this yearly series publishes statistics under a different heading. Volume 1 covers natality: tables of the year's birth statistics at the national and local levels and for U.S. holdings. Volume 2 covers mortality: death statistics.

Yearbook of Labour Statistics. Geneva: International Labour Office. Annual. This publication offers statistical tables on the economic development of countries around the world. There is an index of countries.

Statistical and political abstracts are also published by different public and private organizations for each state.

10.4   GOVERNMENT AGENCIES

For most papers you will write in other subjects, such as biology, history, or a foreign language, the library is the place where you will find most if not all of the information needed. As a student of political science, you will most certainly find much valuable information on the library shelves. However, topics in political science afford an unusual opportunity to get information from other sources because many political science topics require recent information about state and local governments, the U.S. government, and governments of other nations. When topics such as these are assigned or selected, government agencies, research centers, and public interest groups often have more recent and more detailed information than is available in most college and university libraries. In fact, in most cases, for whatever topic you select, someone in a public agency or private organization has probably already conducted significant research on the issue. If you can find the right person, you may be able to secure much more information in much less time than you can by looking in your local library.

Did you know, for example, that the members of the U.S. Senate and House of Representatives constantly use the services of the Congressional Research Service (CRS) and that, upon request to your representative or senator, CRS materials on the topic of your choice may be sent to you? Furthermore, every local, state, and national government agency has employees who are hired primarily to gather information to help their managers make decisions. Much of the research done by these employees is available upon request.

National Government Agencies

Congressional Yellow Book: Who's Who in Congress, Including Committees and Key Staff. Washington, DC: Monitor Leadership Directories. This quarterly publication, which is bound yearly, identifies senators and representatives by state and district, respectively. It lists committee assignments for each member of Congress and gives addresses and phone numbers of congressional committees and staff. State maps show the districts of members of Congress. There is an index of staff.

   The Government Directory of Addresses and Telephone Numbers. Detroit: Omnigraphics. Annual. Entries give names, addresses, and phone numbers for national, state, county, and municipal government officials.

   Lauber, Daniel. *Government Job Finder.* River Forest, IL: Planning/Communications. Lauber's biennial listing offers tips on how to find a job in national, state, or local government. A list of directories of various agencies is included. There is an index.

   Office of the Federal Register/National Archives and Records Administration. *The United States Government Manual.* Washington, DC: Government Printing Office. Annual. A special edition of the *Federal Register*, the volume gives brief descriptions of the agencies of all three branches of the government and peripheral agencies and organizations. The annotations summarize each agency's history and describe its function and activities.

   Office of Management and Budget. *Catalog of Federal Domestic Assistance.* Washington, DC: Government Printing Office. Annual. Government programs offering social and economic assistance to citizens are listed and described briefly in this guide. There is an index.

   Orvedahl, Jerry A., ed. *Washington Information Directory.* Washington, DC: Congressional Quarterly. This directory, published every two years, lists and describes various kinds of organizations located in Washington, DC. Contents of the book are divided into eighteen chapters, with such titles as "National Security," "Law and Justice," "Advocacy and Public Services," and "Education and Culture." There are separate subject and name indexes, and address lists for foreign embassies and U.S. ambassadors.

   Robinson, Judith Schiek, 1998. *Tapping the Government Grapevine: The User-Friendly Guide to U.S. Government Information Sources.* 3rd ed. Phoenix: Oryx. Robinson's manual offers practical help on finding information published by the government, including discussions of electronic media, such as CD-ROMs, databases, and electronic bulletin boards. There are chapters on how to access information from each branch of the government. An index is included.

International Agencies

   Yearbook of the United Nations. Dordrecht: Martinus Nijhoff. Annual. This publication contains essays describing U.N. participation in various world events.

10.5   PRIVATE RESEARCH ORGANIZATIONS

   Baker, Deborah J., ed., 2004. *National Directory of Nonprofit Organizations.* 17th ed. 2 vols. Rockville, MD: The Taft Group. This guide gives brief listings of over 167,000 nonprofit organizations in the United States, citing addresses, phone numbers, and IRS filing status. Volume 1 lists organizations with annual revenues of $100,000 or over; Volume 2 lists organizations with revenues of $25,000 to $99,000. The contents of both volumes are organized alphabetically by title. Included are an activity index and a geographic index.

Daniels, Peggy Kneffel, and Carol A. Schwartz, eds. *Encyclopedia of Associations.* Detroit: Gale Research. Annual. This guide lists entries for approximately 23,000 national and international organizations. Contents are organized into chapters by subject. Typical chapter titles are "Environmental and Agricultural Organizations" and "Legal, Governmental, Public Administration, and Military Organizations." Each entry includes a brief description of the organization's function and the publications available. There are several indexes.

Dresser, Peter D., and Karen Hill, eds. *Research Centers Directory.* Detroit: Gale Research. Annual. More than 11,700 university-related and other nonprofit research organizations are listed and briefly profiled. The entries are listed in sections by topics. Includes four subsections under the general heading "Private and Public Policy and Affairs." There is a subject index and a master index, as well as a supplemental volume.

Maxfield, Doris Morris, ed., 1993. *Charitable Organizations of the U.S.: A Descriptive and Financial Information Guide.* 2nd ed. Detroit: Gale Research. Approximately 800 major public charities are profiled in this guide. Information given includes summaries of each organization's history and purpose, its activities and programs, and financial data. There are three indexes: subject, geographic, and personnel.

Wilson, Robert, ed. *American Lobbyists Directory.* Detroit: Gale Research. More than 65,000 registered federal and state lobbyists are listed in this annual guide, along with the businesses they represent. Included are indexes for lobbyists, their organizations, and general subjects and specialties.

Zuckerman, Edward. *Almanac of Federal PACs.* Washington, DC: Amward. Annual. This directory profiles campaign contributions of every political action committee (PAC) that gave $50,000 or more to candidates for election to the U.S. Senate or House of Representatives. PACs are arranged alphabetically within chapters devoted to different target groups. Each entry includes a brief description of the goals and yearly activities of the PAC. There is a name index.

10.6   LIST OF POLITICAL SCIENCE PERIODICALS

Administration and Society

Administrative Science Quarterly

African Affairs

Africa Quarterly

Alternatives: A Journal for World Policy

American Behavioral Scientist

American Journal of International Law

American Journal of Political Science

American Political Science Review

American Politics Quarterly

Annals of the American Academy of Political and Social Science

Armed Forces and Society

Asian Affairs

Asian Quarterly

Asian Survey
Atlantic Community
  Quarterly
Australian Journal of Politics
  and History
Australian Journal of Public
  Administration
Behavioral Science
Behavior Science Research
Black Politician
British Journal of
  International Studies
British Journal of Law and
  Society
British Journal of Political
  Science
Bureaucrat
Campaign and Elections
Canadian Journal of
  Behavioral Science
Canadian Journal of Political
  Science
Canadian Public
  Administration
Canadian Public Policy
China Quarterly
Communist Affairs
Comparative Political
  Studies
Comparative Politics
Comparative Strategy
Comparative Studies in
  Society and History
Conflict
Conflict Bulletin
Conflict Management and
  Peace Science
Conflict Studies
Congress and the Presidency
Contemporary China
Cooperation and Conflict
Daedalus
Democracy
Development and Change
Diplomatic History
Dissent

East European Quarterly
Electoral Studies
Environmental Policy and
  Law
European Journal of Political
  Research
European Journal of Political
  Science
European Studies Review
Experimental Study of
  Politics
Foreign Affairs
Foreign Policy
General Systems
German Foreign Policy
German Political Studies
Global Political Assessment
Governance: An
  International Journal of
  Policy and Administration
Government & Opposition
Government Finance
Growth and Change
Harvard Journal on
  Legislation
History and Theory
History of Political
  Thought
Human Organization
Human Relations
Human Rights Review
Indian Journal of Political
  Science
Indian Journal of Public
  Administration
Indian Political Science
  Review
International Affairs
International Development
  Review
International Interactions
International Journal of
  Political Education
International Journal of
  Public Administration
International Organization

International Political
  Science Review (Revue
  Internationale de Science
  Politique)
International Relations
International Review of
  Social History
International Security
International Studies
International Studies
  Quarterly
Interpretation: Journal of
  Political Philosophy
Jerusalem Journal of
  International Relations
Journal of African Studies
Journal of Applied Behavioral
  Science
Journal of Asian Studies
Journal of Common Market
  Studies
Journal of Commonwealth
  and Comparative Politics
Journal of Conflict Resolution
Journal of Constitutional and
  Parliamentary Studies
Journal of Contemporary
  History
Journal of Developing Areas
Journal of Development
  Studies
Journal of European
  Integration
Journal of Health Politics,
  Policy, and Law
Journal of International
  Affairs
Journal of Japanese Studies
Journal of Law & Politics
Journal of Libertarian
  Studies
Journal of Modern African
  Studies
Journal of Modern History
Journal of Peace Research
Journal of Peace Science

*Journal of Policy Analysis
    and Management*
Journal of Policy Modeling
*Journal of Political and
    Military Sociology*
Journal of Political Economy
Journal of Political Science
Journal of Politics
Journal of Public Policy
Journal of Social History
Journal of Social Issues
*Journal of Social, Political,
    and Economic Studies*
Journal of Strategic Studies
Journal of the History of Ideas
Journal of Theoretical Politics
Journal of Urban Analysis
*Law and Contemporary
    Problems*
Law and Policy Quarterly
Law & Society Review
Legislative Studies Quarterly
Mathematical Social Sciences
Micropolitics
Middle Eastern Studies
Middle East Journal
Millennium
Modern China
*Multivariate Behavioral
    Research*
New Political Science
*Orbis: A Journal of World
    Affairs*
Pacific Affairs
Parliamentarian
Parliamentary Affairs
*Parliaments, Estates, and
    Representation*
Peace and Change
Peace Research
*Perspectives on Political
    Science*
Philosophy & Public Affairs
*Philosophy of the Social
    Sciences*
Planning and Administration

Policy Analysis
Policy and Politics
Policy Review
Policy Sciences
Policy Studies Journal
Policy Studies Review
Political Anthropology
Political Behavior
*Political Communication and
    Persuasion*
Political Geography Quarterly
Political Psychology
Political Quarterly
Political Science
Political Science Quarterly
Political Science Review
Political Science Reviewer
Political Studies
Political Theory
Politics
Politics & Society
Polity
Presidential Studies Quarterly
*Public Administration
    (Australia)*
*Public Administration
    (United States)*
Public Administration Review
Public Choice
Public Finance
Public Finance Quarterly
Public Interest
Public Law
Public Opinion Quarterly
Public Policy
*Publius: The Journal of
    Federalism*
*Quarterly Journal of
    Administration*
Res Publica
*Review of International
    Studies (formerly British
    Journal of International
    Studies)*
*Review of Law and Social
    Change*

Review of Politics
Revolutionary World
Round Table
Russian Review
*Scandinavian Political
    Studies*
Science and Public Affairs
Science and Public Policy
Science and Society
Simulation and Games
Slavic Review
*Slavonic and East European
    Review*
Social Forces
Social Indicators Research
Socialism and Democracy
Social Policy
Social Praxis
Social Research
Social Science Journal
Social Science Quarterly
Social Science Research
Social Theory and Practice
*Sociological Analysis and
    Theory*
*Sociological Methods and
    Research*
Sociology and Social Research
*Southeastern Political Science
    Review*
Soviet Review
Soviet Studies
Soviet Union
Strategic Review
*Studies in Comparative
    Communism*
*Studies in Comparative
    International Development*
Survey
Talking Politics
*Technological Forecasting and
    Social Change*
Terrorism
Theory and Decision
Theory and Society
Third World

Urban Affairs Quarterly
Urban Studies
War & Society
Washington Quarterly: A
   Review of Strategic and
   International Studies

Western Political Quarterly
West European Politics
Wilson Quarterly
Women & Politics: A
   Quarterly Journal of
   Research and Policy Studies

World Development
World Policy Journal
World Politics
Youth and Society

11

INTERNET RESOURCES

11.1 WRITING RESOURCES ON THE INTERNET

The preceding chapters of this book have given you much information about research and writing, but the Internet offers even more. A particularly good place to start your Internet search is your own college's Online Writing Lab (OWL). Purdue University's OWL, for example, may be found at http://owl. english.purdue.edu/. The Purdue OWL home page features many sources of help for people *in the Purdue community,* such as the following:

- One-on-one *tutorials*
- In-lab and in-class *workshops*
- *Study materials* for English as a second language
- Conversation groups for English practice
- A grammar hotline
- A collection of reference materials
- Computers and a printer
- Quiet space to study.

Purdue's OWL also, however, offers the following resources for *everyone:*

- The Writing Lab Newsletter (including online archives of back issues)
- Resources for teachers on using the Writing Lab and OWL, including using OWL in the new English 106/108 course
- Writing across the curriculum resources.

Your local OWL will also direct you to many more Internet writing resources.

11.2   POLITICS AND GOVERNMENT RESOURCES ON THE INTERNET

Even large catalogs can no longer hold all the potential Internet resources for politics, government, and political science. Fortunately, many Internet sites specialize in creating lists of links to excellent resources. The purpose of this chapter is to help you locate a few good sites that will in turn lead you to thousands of sources of information for your government and politics research projects.

Internet sources of information about government and politics may be organized into three major groups:

1. government agencies
2. universities, private interest groups, and research organizations; and
3. news agencies.

Government Agencies

An excellent place to start searching for information about American government agencies is USA.gov (http://www.usa.gov/index.shtml). The subtitle for this site is "Government Made Easy," and only a few minutes of experimentation will demonstrate the ease with which it provides not only dozens of direct links to representatives, senators, legislation, committees, and historical documents but also links to the executive and judicial branches and state and local government agencies.

For example, choosing the link for "federal government" on the left-hand side of the USA.gov home page takes you to a page with links for all three governmental branches. Choosing the link labeled "Executive Branch" brings up a page with links to agencies in the executive branch of the federal government. As of this writing, the list of Executive Branch links begins with the "Executive Office of the President," immediately under which are listed the following links:

- The President
- The Vice President
- The White House Home Page
- Offices within the Executive Office of the President
- The President's Cabinet

Following these links are a series under the heading "Executive Departments," consisted of the following links:

- Department of Agriculture (USDA)
- Department of Commerce (DOC)
- Department of Defense (DOD)
- Department of Education (ED)
- Department of Energy (DOE)
- Department of Health and Human Services (HHS)
- Department of Homeland Security (DHS)
- Department of Housing and Urban Development (HUD)
- Department of the Interior (DOI)
- Department of Justice (DOJ)
- Department of Labor (DOL)
- Department of State (DOS)
- Department of the Treasury
- Department of Transportation (DOT)
- Department of Veterans Affairs (VA)

Each of these departmental links in turn provides a list of links to organizations within the department. Among the links listed under the "Department of Homeland Security (DHS)," for instance, are links to such department components as U.S. Citizenship and Immigration Services and U.S. Customs and Border Protection.

The next major section of the page, "Independent Agencies and Government Corporations," offers a link to a page listing links to sixty-four government organizations, including the Central Intelligence Agency (CIA), the Federal Trade Commission (FTC), and the National Endowment for the Arts. Following "Independent Agencies" are the headings "Boards, Commissions, and Committees" and "Quasi-Official Agencies." The last item on the page is a link offering to help you "Learn More About the Executive Branch."

Each of these USA.gov links allows you to find easily the home page for its specific department, agency, commission, or bureau, which will, in turn guide you to further information.

Of course, the above sites are only the tip of the government Web site iceberg. At the end of this chapter, we have listed list some useful Internet resources for information about political science.

If you return to USA.gov and select the link named "Judicial Branch," you find yourself confronting links that provide a wide array of information about the Supreme Court, lower courts, special courts, and such court support organizations as the Federal Judicial Center and the U.S. Sentencing Commission. And as you might expect, selecting the link for the "Legislative Branch" on the USA.gov page devoted to the federal government will give you access to a wide range of sites concerning the U.S. Senate, the U.S. House of Representatives, and an array of agencies that support Congress.

Universities, Private Interest Groups, and Research Organizations

Another major category of information sources about politics and government includes universities, private interest groups, and research organizations. Many college political science departments provide Internet sites that feature links to thousands of politics and government sites. The Lehman Social Sciences Library site at Columbia University is a good example (http://www.columbia.edu/cu/lweb/indiv/lehman/guides/uspolitics.html).

Public interest groups also provide a great deal of information on political issues. However, as you search these sites, you must be aware that these groups are in existence to promote a cause and may or may not provide a balanced view of any particular issue. The following list is but a very small list of examples of the hundreds of public interest groups in the United States:

American Association of Retired Persons (AARP)
Amnesty International
Christian Coalition
Environmental Defense Fund
Greenpeace International
National Association of Arab Americans

National Gay and Lesbian Task Force
National Organization for Women (NOW)
National Rifle Association (NRA)
National Right to Life
Planned Parenthood
Sierra Club
Vietnam Veterans of America.

In addition to the above-listed public interest groups, there are many "think tanks," or private research organizations, that provide high-quality political, economic, and social analyses. Links to some of these organizations may be found by selecting the "Think Tanks" link at the Kennedy School of Government OPIN site described previously.

News Agencies

The third major category of Internet resources for government and politics includes hundreds of news organizations around the world. CNN, *U.S. News and World Report*, and dozens of other major journalistic ventures provide enormous amounts of information. For example, the *New York Times*, in addition to all its regular news coverage, features a page entitled "Politics Navigator," by Rich Meislin (www.nytimes.com/ref/politics/POLI_NAVI.html). This page contains dozens of links to good sources of information about national, international, state, and local political events, trends, and resources.

11.3   POLITICAL SCIENCE RESOURCES ON THE INTERNET

The first site to visit for political science resources is the home page of the American Political Science Association (APSA), the largest organization of professional political scientists in the world. It is found at http://www.apsanet.org/. The links on this page lead to dozens of departments, organizations, conferences, journals, and other sources of information about the discipline of political science.

11.4   ASSESSING THE QUALITY OF INTERNET RESOURCES

How do you know if the material you have found in a particular magazine article, Web site, or book is trustworthy? Just because the material has been published does not necessarily make it accurate or fair. Before you consider using any source material, answer the following questions about it:

• *Who is its author?* Is he or she an acknowledged expert in the field? Can you find out anything about the author's credentials? From your reading of the text, what do you feel is the author's personal attitude or bias toward the topic? Say you are researching the practical possibilities of banning smoking in all municipal buildings in your city. Whose data on second-hand smoke would you have more confidence in, data from a study funded by the tobacco industry or data from a study funded by an independent consumer group?

- *Who is the publisher?* Readers generally consider university presses more academically sound than popular presses. University presses usually submit the material they publish to rigorous scrutiny by experts in the field. Popular presses do not always do this. And because profit is a more demanding goal for popular presses than for university presses, which are subsidized by their universities, material published by popular presses may sometimes sacrifice evenhandedness for the sensationalism that sells.

- *Does the source you are evaluating contain a bibliography?* If not, how will you know if the author's assertions are based on solid scholarship?

- *How old is the source?* Always check the date of publication. An extensive work on the relationship of the United States to Russia published before 1989 may well have lost much of its usefulness in the intervening decade and a half.

- *For whom is the source written?* Scholars usually write for a specific audience. A book on presidential elections of the nineteenth century written for high-school history students may simplify its material in a way that would make it unsuitable for the senatorial staff your article is going to brief. Most texts give away their target audience in the first few paragraphs, and you need to be sensitive to your source author's understanding of his or her audience.

It is extremely important that you ask these questions of Internet sources as well as print sources. The growth of the Internet has allowed anyone with a computer and a cause to establish a Web site on virtually any subject imaginable. How do you know whether the Web site you are evaluating reflects evenhanded, knowledgeable scholarship or enthusiastic, poorly researched partisan opinion? One extra tip, in addition to the ones listed above, is to check the three-character extension to the Web site's URL (its Uniform Resource Locator, commonly known as its Web address). A "com" extension normally refers to a commercial (for profit) organization. An "org" extension (normally) refers to a not-for-profit organization. The extension "gov" refers to U.S. government agencies. Other countries have their own extensions: www.lemonde.fr., for example, is France's *Le Monde* Newspaper.

Finally, reflect on the potentially varying degrees of Web site reliability that might be indicated by the following site extensions:

.com = commercial
.edu = educational
.mil = military
.org = nonprofit organization
.gov = U.S. government
.net = network

CHAPTER

12

BOOK REVIEWS AND ARTICLE CRITIQUES

12.1   BOOK REVIEWS

Successful book reviews answer three questions:

- What did the writer of the book try to communicate?
- How clearly and convincingly did he or she get this message across to the reader?
- Was the message worth reading?

Capable book reviewers of several centuries have answered these three questions well. People who read a book review want to know if a particular book is worth reading, for their own particular purposes, before buying or reading it. These potential readers want to know the book's subject and its strengths and weaknesses, and they want to gain this information as easily and quickly as possible. Your goal in writing a book review, therefore, is to help people efficiently decide whether to buy or read a book. Your immediate objectives may be to please your instructor and get a good grade, but these objectives are most likely to be met if you focus on a book review's audience: people who want help in selecting books to buy or read. In the process of writing a book review that reaches this primary goal, you will also:

- learn about the book you are reviewing
- learn about professional standards for book reviews in political science
- learn the essential steps of book reviewing that apply to any academic discipline

This final objective, learning to review a book properly, has more applications than you may at first imagine. First, it helps you to focus quickly on the essential elements of a book, and to draw from a book its informational value for yourself and others. Some of the most successful people in government, business, and the professions speed-read several books a week, more for the knowledge they contain than for enjoyment. These readers then apply this knowledge to substantial advantage in their professions. It is normally not wise to speed-read a book you are reviewing because you are unlikely to gain enough information to evaluate it fairly from such a fast reading. Writing book reviews, however, helps you become proficient in quickly sorting out valuable information from material that is not. The ability to make such discriminations is a fundamental ingredient in management and professional success.

In addition, writing book reviews for publication allows you to participate in the discussions of the broader intellectual and professional community of which you are a part. People in law, medicine, teaching, engineering, administration, and other fields are frequently asked to write book reviews to help others assess newly released publications.

Before beginning your book review, read the following sample. It is Gregory M. Scott's review of *Political Islam: Revolution, Radicalism, or Reform?*, edited by John L. Esposito. The review appeared in volume 26 of the *Southeastern Political Science Review* (June 1998) and is reprinted here by permission:

> Behold an epitaph for the specter of monolithically autocratic Islam. In its survey of Islamic political movements from Pakistan to Algeria, *Political Islam: Revolution, Radicalism, or Reform?* effectively lays to rest the popular notion that political expressions of Islam are inherently violent and authoritarian. For this accomplishment alone John L. Esposito and company's scholarly anthology merits the attention of serious students of religion and politics, and justifies the book's own claim to making a "seminal contribution." Although it fails to identify how Islam as religious faith and cultural tradition lends Muslim politics a distinctively Islamic flavor, this volume clearly answers the question posed by its title: yes, political Islam encompasses not only revolution and radicalism, but moderation and reform as well.
>
> Although two of the eleven contributors are historians, *Political Islam* exhibits both the strengths and weaknesses of contemporary political science with respect to religion. It identifies connections between economics and politics, and between culture and politics, much better than it deciphers the nuances of the relationships between politics and religious belief. After a general introduction, the first three articles explore political Islam as illegal opposition, first with a summary of major movements and then with studies of Algeria and the Gulf states. In her chapter titled "Fulfilling Prophecies: State Policy and Islamist Radicalism," Lisa Anderson sets a methodological guideline for the entire volume when she writes:
>
>> Rather than look to the substance of Islam or the content of putatively Islamic political doctrines for a willingness to embrace violent means to desired ends, we might explore a different perspective and examine the political circumstances, or institutional environment, that breeds political radicalism, extremism, or violence independent of the content of the doctrine (18).
>
> Therefore, rather than assessing how Islam as religion affects Muslim politics, all the subsequent chapters proceed to examine politics, economics, and culture in a variety of Muslim nations. This means that the title of the book is slightly misleading: it discusses Muslim politics rather than political Islam. Esposito provides the book's conclusion about the effects of Islamic belief on the

political process when he maintains that "the appeal to religion is a two-edged sword. . . . It can provide or enhance self-legitimation, but it can also be used as a yardstick for judgment by opposition forces and delegitimation" (70).

The second part of the volume features analyses of the varieties of political processes in Iran, Sudan, Egypt, and Pakistan. These chapters clearly demonstrate not only that Islamic groups may be found in varied positions on normal economic and ideological spectrums, but that Islam is not necessarily opposed to moderate, pluralist politics. The third section of the anthology examines the international relations of Hamas, Afghani Islamists, and Islamic groups involved in the Middle East peace process. These chapters are especially important for American students because they present impressive documentation for the conclusions that the motives and demands of many Islamic groups are considerably more moderate and reasonable than much Western political commentary would suggest.

The volume is essentially well written. All the articles with the exception of chapter two avoid unnecessarily dense political science jargon. As a collection of methodologically sound and analytically astute treatments of Muslim politics, *Political Islam: Revolution, Radicalism, or Reform?* is certainly appropriate for adoption as a supplemental text for courses in religion and politics. By way of noting what it does not cover, readers may consider that although it is sufficient for its purposes as it stands, the volume could be a primary text in a course on Islamic politics if it included four additional chapters:

1. an historical overview of the origins and varieties of Islam as religion
2. a summary of the global Islamic political–ideological spectrum (from liberal to fundamentalist)
3. an overview of the varieties of global Islamic cultures
4. an attempt to describe in what manner, if any, Islam, in all its varieties, gives politics a different flavor from the politics of other major religions.

Elements of a Book Review

Book reviews in political science contain the same essential elements of all book reviews. Because political science is nonfiction, book reviews within the discipline focus less on a work's writing style and more on its content and method than do reviews of fiction. Your book review should generally contain four basic elements, although not always in this order:

1. Enticement
2. Examination
3. Elucidation
4. Evaluation

Enticement

Your first sentence should entice people to read your review. A crisp summary of what the book is about entices your readers because it lets them know that you can quickly and clearly come to the point. They know that their time and efforts will not be wasted in an attempt to wade through your vague prose in hopes of finding out something about the book. Notice Scott's opening line: "Behold an epitaph for the specter of monolithically autocratic Islam." It is a bit overburdened with large words, but it is engaging and precisely sums up the essence of the review. Your opening statement can be engaging and "catchy," but be sure that it provides an accurate portrayal of the book in one crisp statement.

Examination

Your book review should allow the reader to join you in examining the book. Tell the reader what the book is about. One of the greatest strengths of Scott's review is that his first paragraph immediately tells you exactly what he thinks the book accomplishes.

When you review a book, write about what is actually in the book, not what you think is probably there or ought to be there. Do not explain how you would have written the book, but instead how the author wrote it. Describe the book in clear, objective terms. Tell enough about the content to identify the author's major points.

Elucidation

Elucidate, or clarify, the book's value and contribution to political science by defining (1) what the author is attempting to do and (2) how the author's work fits within current similar efforts in the discipline of political science or scholarly inquiry in general. Notice how Scott immediately describes what Esposito is trying to do: "This volume clearly answers the question posed by its title." Scott precedes this definition of the author's purpose by placing his work within the context of current similar writing in political science by stating that "for this accomplishment alone John L. Esposito and company's scholarly anthology merits the attention of serious students of religion and politics, and justifies the book's own claim to making a 'seminal contribution.'"

The elucidation portion of book reviews often provides additional information about the author. Scott has not included such information about Esposito in his review, but it would be helpful to know, for example, if Esposito has written other books on the subject, has developed a reputation for exceptional expertise on a certain issue, or is known to have a particular ideological bias. How would your understanding of this book be changed, for example, if you knew that its author were a leader of Hamas or the PLO? Include information in your book review about the author that helps the reader understand how this book fits within the broader concerns of political science.

Evaluation

Once you explain what the book is attempting to do, you should tell the reader the extent to which this goal has been met. To evaluate a book effectively, you will need to establish evaluation criteria and then compare the book's content to those criteria. You do not need to define your criteria specifically in your review, but they should be evident to the reader. Your criteria will vary according to the book you are reviewing, and you may discuss them in any order that is helpful to the reader. Consider, however, including the following among the criteria that you establish for your book review:

- How important is the subject to the study of politics and government?
- How complete and thorough is the author's coverage of the subject?

- How carefully is the author's analysis conducted?
- What are the strengths and limitations of the author's methodology?
- What is the quality of the writing? Is it clear, precise, and interesting?
- How does this book compare with others on the subject?
- What contribution does this book make to political science?
- Who will enjoy or benefit from this book?

When giving your evaluations according to these criteria, be specific. If you write, "This is a good book; I liked it very much," you tell nothing of interest or value to the reader. Notice, however, how Scott's review helps to clearly define the content and the limitations of the book by contrasting the volume with what he describes as an ideal primary text for a course in Islamic politics: "By way of noting what it does not cover, readers may consider that although it is sufficient for its purposes as it stands, the volume could be a primary text in a course on Islamic politics if it included four additional chapters."

Qualities of Effective Political Science Book Reviews

Effective political science book reviews

- Serve the reader
- Are fair
- Are concise and specific, not vague and general

Write your review with the potential reader, not yourself or the book's author, in mind. The person who may read the book is, in a manner of speaking, your client.

Your reader wants a fair review of the book. Do not be overly generous to a book of poor quality, but do not be too critical of an honest effort to tackle a very complex or difficult problem. If you have a bias that may affect your review, let your reader know this, but do so briefly. Do not shift the focus from the book's ideas to your own. Do not attack a work because of the author's politics. Do not chide the author for not having written a book different from the one he or she has written.

The reader of your book review is not interested in your thoughts about politics or other subjects. Try to appreciate the author's efforts and goals, and sympathize with the author, but remain sufficiently detached to identify errors. Try to show the book's strengths and weaknesses as clearly as possible.

Write a review that is interesting, appealing, and even charming, but not at the expense of accuracy or of the book being reviewed. Be erudite but not prolix. (To be *erudite* is to display extensive knowledge. To be *prolix* is to be wordy and vague.) Your goal is to display substantial knowledge of the book's content, strengths, and weaknesses in as few words as possible.

Preliminaries: Before Writing a Book Review

Before sitting down to write your review, make sure you do the following:

- *Get further directions from your instructor.* Ask if there are specific directions beyond those in this manual for the number of pages or the content of the review.

- *Read the book.* Reviewers who skim or merely read a book's jacket do a great disservice to the author. Read the book thoroughly.
- *Respond to the book.* As you read, make notes on your responses to the book. Organize them into the categories of enticement, examination, elucidation, and evaluation.
- *Get to know the subject.* Use your library to find a summary of works on the issue. Such a summary may be found in a review, in a journal, or in a recent textbook on the subject.
- *Familiarize yourself with other books by the author.* If the author has written other works, learn enough about them to be able to describe them briefly to your readers.
- *Read reviews of other political science books.* Many political science journals have book review sections, usually at the end of an issue. Go to the library and browse through some of the reviews in several journals. Not only will you get to know what is expected from a political science book review, but you will also find many interesting ideas on how books are approached and evaluated.

Format and Content

The directions for writing papers provided in Chapters 5 through 7 apply to book reviews as well. Some further instructions specific to book reviews are needed, however. First, list on the title page, along with the standard information required for political science papers, data on the book being reviewed: title, author, place and name of publisher, date, and number of pages. As the sample that follows shows, the title of the book should be in italics or underlined, but not both:

Shoveling Smoke

A Clay Parker Crime Novel

by

Austin Davis

San Francisco: Chronicle Books

2003. 256 pages.

reviewed by

Constance Squires

POL 213

Dr. Christopher Givan

Central Mideastern University

January 1, 2006

Reflective or Analytical Book Reviews

Instructors in the humanities and social sciences normally assign two types of book reviews: the *reflective* and the *analytical. Ask your instructor which type of book review you are to write.* The purpose of a reflective book review is for the student reviewer to exercise creative analytical judgment without being influenced by the reviews of others. Reflective book reviews contain all the elements covered in this chapter—enticement, examination, elucidation, and evaluation—but they do not include the views of others who have also read the book.

Analytical book reviews contain all the information provided by reflective reviews but add an analysis of the comments of other reviewers. The purpose is, thus, to review not only the book itself but also its reception in the professional community.

To write an analytical book review, insert a review analysis section immediately after your summary of the book. To prepare this section, use the *Book Review Digest* and *Book Review Index* in the library to locate other reviews of the book that have been published in journals and other periodicals. As you read these reviews:

1. List the criticisms of the book's strengths and weaknesses that are made in the reviews.
2. Develop a concise summary of these criticisms, indicate the overall positive or negative tone of the reviews, and mention some of the most commonly found comments.
3. Evaluate the criticisms found in these reviews. Are they basically accurate in their assessment of the book?
4. Write a review analysis of two pages or less that states and evaluates steps 2 and 3 above, and place it in your book review immediately after your summary of the book.

Length of a Book Review

Unless your instructor gives you other directions, a reflective book review should be three to five typed pages long, and an analytical book review should be five to seven pages long. In either case, a brief, specific, and concise book review is almost always preferred over one of greater length.

12.2   ARTICLE CRITIQUES

An *article critique* is a paper that evaluates an article published in an academic journal. A good critique tells the reader what point the article is trying to make and how convincingly it makes that point. Writing an article critique achieves three purposes. First, it provides you with an understanding of the information contained in a scholarly article and a familiarity with other information written on the same topic. Second, it provides you with an opportunity to apply and develop your critical thinking skills as you attempt to critically evaluate a political scientist's work. Third, it helps you to improve your own writing skills as you attempt to describe the selected article's strengths and weaknesses so that your readers can clearly understand them.

The first step in writing an article critique is to select an appropriate article. Unless your instructor specifies otherwise, select an article from a scholarly journal (such as the *American Political Science Review, Journal of Politics,* or *Southeastern Political Science Review*) and not a popular or journalistic publication (such as *Time* or the *National Review*). Chapter 10 of this manual includes a substantial list of academic political science journals, but your instructor may also accept appropriate articles from academic journals in other disciplines, such as history, economics, or sociology.

Choosing an Article

Three other considerations should guide your choice of an article. First, browse article titles until you find a topic that interests you. Writing a critique will be much more satisfying if you have an interest in the topic. Hundreds of interesting journal articles are published every year. The following articles, for example, appeared in the Spring 2004 (6:1) issue of the *Hedgehog Review:*

"Religion and Violence"

Introduction	The Puzzle of Religion and Violence
René Girard	Violence and Religion: Cause or Effect?
Mark Juergensmeyer	Is Religion the Problem?
William T. Cavanaugh	Sins of Omission: What "Religion and Violence" Arguments Ignore
Slavica Jakelic	Religion, Collective Identity, and Violence in Bosnia and Herzegovina
Khaled Abou El Fadl	Speaking, Killing, and Loving in God's Name
Thomas Cushman	A Conversation on Religion and Violence with Veena Das
Jennifer L. Geddes	Peacemaking among the abrahamic Faiths: An Interview with Peter Ochs
Justin S. Holcomb	A Review of Anna Lännström's *Promise and Peril*
Charles K. Bellinger	Religion and Violence: A Bibliography

The second consideration in selecting an article is your current level of knowledge. Many political science studies, for example, employ sophisticated statistical techniques. You may be better prepared to evaluate them if you have studied statistics.

The third consideration is to select a current article, one written within the last twelve months. Most material in political science is quickly superseded by new studies. Selecting a recent study will help ensure that you will be engaged in an up-to-date discussion of your topic.

Writing the Critique

Once you have selected and carefully read your article, you may begin to write your critique, which will cover five areas:

1. Thesis
2. Methods
3. Evidence of thesis support
4. Contribution to the literature
5. Recommendation

Thesis

Your first task is to find and clearly state the thesis of the article. The thesis is the main point the article is trying to make. In a 1997 article entitled "Unequal Participation: Democracy's Unresolved Dilemma," APSA President Arend Lijphart, Research Professor of Political Science at the University of California, San Diego, states his thesis very clearly:

> Low voter turnout is a serious democratic problem for five reasons: (1) It means unequal turnout that is systematically biased against less well-to-do citizens. (2) Unequal turnout spells unequal political influence. (3) U.S. voter turnout is especially low, but, measured as percent of voting-age population, it is also relatively low in most other countries. (4) Turnout in midterm, regional, local, and supranational elections—less salient but by no means unimportant elections—tends to be especially poor. (5) Turnout appears to be declining everywhere.

Many authors, however, do not present their theses this clearly. After you have read the article, ask yourself whether you had to hunt for the thesis. Comment about the clarity of the author's thesis presentation and state the author's thesis in your critique. Before proceeding with the remaining elements of your critique, consider the importance of the topic. Has the author written something that is important for us as citizens or political scientists to read?

Methods

In your critique, carefully answer the following questions:

1. What methods did the author use to investigate the topic? In other words, how did the author go about supporting the thesis?
2. Were the appropriate methods used?
3. Did the author's approach to supporting the thesis make sense?

4. Did the author employ the selected methods correctly?

5. Did you discover any errors in the way he or she conducted the research?

Evidence of Thesis Support

In your critique, answer the following questions:

1. What evidence did the author present in support of the thesis?

2. What are the strengths of the evidence presented?

3. What are the weaknesses of the evidence?

4. On balance, how well did the author support the thesis?

Contribution to the Literature

This step will probably require you to undertake some research of your own. Using the research resources discussed in Chapters 10 and 11 of this manual, identify articles and books published on the subject of your selected article within the past five years. Browse the titles and read perhaps half a dozen of the publications that appear to provide the best discussion of the topic. In your critique, list the most important other articles or books that have been published on your topic and then, in view of these publications, evaluate the contribution that your selected article makes to a better understanding of the subject.

Recommendation

In this section of your critique, summarize your evaluation of the article. Tell your readers several things: Who will benefit from reading this article? What will the benefit be? How important and extensive is that benefit? Clearly state your evaluation of the article in the form of a thesis for your own critique. Your thesis might be something like the following:

> Arend Lijphart's article entitled "Unequal Participation: Democracy's Unresolved Dilemma" is the most concise and comprehensive discussion of the problem of unequal participation published in recent years. Political scientists should conscientiously confront Lijphart's warning because he conclusively demonstrates that unequal participation presents an imminent threat to American democracy.

When writing this assignment, follow the directions for paper formats in Chapter 7 of this manual. Ask your instructor for directions concerning the length of the critique, but in the absence of further guidelines, your paper should not exceed five pages (typed, double-spaced).

CHAPTER
13

WRITING TO COMMUNICATE AND ACT

13.1   LETTERS TO NEWSPAPER EDITORS

A letter to a newspaper editor is neither an exercise in creative writing nor a philosophical thought piece. Its audience is not the editor so much as the general public, for your goal in writing the letter is to get it published in the newspaper so that you can influence the opinions of others. Because your aim is publication, remember that most letters that are actually published are responses to a specific editorial, article, or letter that has already (and recently) appeared in the paper. Successful letters to the editor, therefore, are well written statements that

- point out and then correct inaccurate, false, or misleading information in a recently printed news item, editorial, or letter
- supplement, reinforce, refute, or clarify a recently printed statement with new information
- offer a new point of view on a current issue or a recently printed statement

How Do I Find a Topic?

On the shelves of the periodicals room of your college library you can find the last several issues of your local newspaper. Read through them, looking for articles or other items that particularly interest you. Can you find something that you feel passionate about? Pay special attention to letters to the editor. Note the types of letters that the newspaper is printing. Are they long or short? Are they well balanced, or do they tend to be incendiary? Find a specific news article, editorial, or letter to the editor that interests you personally and that you believe is of interest to people in your community. Examine the article carefully. What point is it trying to make? What are the article's strengths and weaknesses? Did the author of the article leave out something important? What do you have to say about the issue at hand? Do you have any new ideas? Identify one or two specific points that you would like to make about the issue in general and specifically about the published article you are writing about. Do not attempt to address every issue in the article you have selected, only one or two of the major ones.

How Do I Go About Writing the Letter?

Start by preparing an outline of the points you want to make in your letter (see Chapter 5). You should make no more than three major points, and one or two is better. You will, however, need to support your point(s) with persuasive argument, facts, and a clear explanation of the issue you are addressing. It is imperative to make your point clearly and immediately, and only then go on to defend it. It is a good practice, therefore, to have your thesis sentence (see Chapter 5, page 101) be the first sentence in the letter. Your thesis sentence is the main point you are trying to make. Either in or immediately after the thesis sentence, identify the article or editorial to which you are responding.

After your thesis sentence, present a concise, logical argument for the point you are making. Some other considerations are worthy of thought. Letters that sound too extreme are less likely to be effective than those that appear thoughtful and balanced. Be sure to write the letter so that it stands on its own, that is, the reader can understand it without having to read other materials. One more thing: Letters do not always have to be critical. It is often helpful to be as positive as possible, pointing out the competencies and successes of others.

The Importance of Correctness

Have you ever read something—an article, a billboard, or an ad in a paper—trying to convince you to take a particular action ("vote for me," "eat at Joe's") and found a glaring grammar error? "You're future is safe with Senator Smith." What does it do to your confidence in the argument being made to find that its writer is careless in this way? Most people find their attention going to the error, their focus deflected into rumination on the intelligence or education of the person who wrote or copied the offending text. It may not seem fair to you, but it is a fact: simple mistakes in your text can devastate your argument. In the case of a letter to the editor, a single typo or grammar error—"hat" instead of "has," "it's" instead of "its"—may be so off-putting to the editorial staff that your letter gets filed in the wastebasket rather than published. Proofread.

The format of your letter is important. You should use a standard business letter format. Most of them call for single spacing the text and the various addresses, double spacing only between paragraphs and between elements of the letter. In addition, look in the newspaper's editorial section and you will probably find specific directions and policies for submitting letters. Type your letter on good quality paper. Address the letter to the Editor of the newspaper. Include your name, address, phone number, and e-mail address. The newspaper may check to be sure you are who you claim to be. After you write the letter, send it immediately so it will be fresh and pertinent. Check the paper daily to see if it has been printed. After a week, if you have not had a reply, send a follow-up letter to check your letter's status.

Sample Letter to the Editor

September 10, 2005

Mildred K. Feswick
Editor
Freetown Daily News
P.O., Box 2367
Freetown, TX 05672

Dear Ms. Feswick:

Education is the cornerstone of our society and deserves much more public support than it is currently getting. In an editorial that appeared on page 10 of the Freetown Daily News on Thursday, September 8, you stated "The Federal government spends too much money on education." I hope you will reconsider your opinion.

First, consider the impressive and pervasive value of education. The acquisition of knowledge is beneficial not only for the personal satisfaction that comes from learning about yourself and your culture, but for the resulting intellectual contributions to society as well. Statistics show that educated people make better decisions and contribute more to society than uneducated people do. National statistics clearly demonstrate the effectiveness of an education. College graduates have an unemployment rate that is half that of high school graduates and the median income of a college graduate is $15,000 greater than the income of a high school graduate. Despite the effectiveness of these programs and the stunning statistics they produce, the government insists on cutting back on educational spending.

Parents are aware of the opportunities and insight a good education provides. In a recent poll, 98 percent of parents in America said they wanted their children to attend college. However, it is becoming increasingly difficult for parents to finance that education. Pell grants, which originally funded up to 75 percent of a student's education, now fund only up to 25 percent. Studies show that federal student aid programs have been extremely effective at educating people who otherwise could not have afforded college. Despite clear evidence that education is a good investment, it is not high on many legislators' lists of priorities. Funding for public schools and higher education is diminishing in the wake of excessive spending on other programs. For example, a report recently issued by the Justice Policy Institute, a research and advocacy organization in Washington, DC, reveals that California and Florida now spend more money on prisons than on higher education. The report also says the average cost to incarcerate a felon is from $22,000 to $25,000 per year, the same amount charged by selective liberal arts colleges. If we can pay large sums of money to keep people from being productive, we should be able to find the funds to help people lead more productive and fulfilling lives.

President Bush has spearheaded the effort to slash educational appropriations programs. Rather than providing sufficient funds for public schools, his "No Child Left Behind" program withdraws funds from schools that do not meet federal standards. This policy might be reasonable if schools had adequate funding to begin with, but they don't. Many of the nation's teachers pay for school supplies out of their own pockets.

Education is the key to our country's economic future. We have the world's strongest economy because our educational institutions lead the world in producing competent graduates. It is therefore easy to see that the statement "The federal government spends too much money on education" is refuted by a thoughtful analysis of the benefits of federal aid to education. The comparatively small amount of money set aside for education is a clear indication of our country's lack of concern for our future. Today education is more important than ever. Our potential will go unmet unless we invest in properly training our minds. Education is the catalyst of a successful future.

Sincerely,

Jeremy M. Scott
3251 Matlock Road #22
Mansfield, TX 76063

13.2   OP-ED ESSAYS

An *op-ed essay* is a statement of perspective on an issue or matter of concern to the community that normally appears on the page of the newspaper "op-ed" (opposite the editorial page). It is neither an editorial (written by the newspaper editor) nor a letter to the editor (most often responding to an article or editorial previously published). Instead, it is a carefully formulated and engagingly written attention-grabbing essay that is intended primarily to stimulate thinking on part of newspaper readers with the ultimate goal of influencing their opinions. Unlike letters to the editor, an op-ed essay is often both an exercise in creative writing and a philosophical thought piece. Like letters to the editor, an op-ed's audience is the general public. Successful (published) op-ed essays usually display some or all of the following characteristics:

- A radical, incendiary, or at least distinctive point of view
- A new angle on a common topic
- A consistent, coherent theme
- Facts and anecdotes
- Humor or satire

How Do I Find a Topic?

Begin your topic search in the same manner you look for a topic for a letter to the editor. On the shelves of the periodicals room of your college library you can find the last several issues of your local newspaper. Read through them, looking for articles or other items that particularly interest you. Can you find something that you feel passionate about? Pay special attention to the op-ed pieces you find. Notice their subjects, styles, and approaches to issues. Pay special attention to their length. Find an issue that interests you personally and that you believe is of interest to people in your community. Identify one or two specific points that you would like to make about the issue.

How Do I Go About Writing the Op-ed Essay?

As you would with a letter to the editor, start by preparing an outline of the points you want to make in your essay (see Chapter 5). You should make no more than three major points in your essay. You will need to support your point(s) with persuasive argument, facts, and a clear explanation of the issue you are addressing. It is imperative to clearly and immediately make your point, and only then go on to defend it. It is a good practice, therefore, to make your thesis sentence the first sentence in the essay (see Chapter 5, page 101). Your thesis sentence is the main point you are trying to make.

After your thesis sentence, present a concise, logical argument for your point. Some other considerations are worthy of thought. Although op-ed pieces are often more radical in viewpoint than letters to the editor, an essay that simply thrashes at people or presents an unending stream of sarcasm is unlikely to be effective—or published. You may be dramatic to engage the reader, but be sure also to make a well-reasoned and well-documented argument. Be sure to write the essay so that it stands on its own, that is, so that the reader can understand it without reading other materials. Do not forget to proofread and check for spelling and grammar errors. As with letters to the editor, careful proofreading is absolutely essential to the success of your op-ed piece.

The format of your essay is important. You should format the essay as you would a college term paper. In addition, look in the newspaper's editorial section and you will probably find specific directions and policies for submitting op-ed essays. Type your essay on good quality paper. Include a cover letter to the editor citing your name, address, phone number, and e-mail address. The newspaper may check to be sure you are who you claim to be. Check the paper daily to see if your essay has been printed. After a week, if you have not had a reply, send a follow-up letter to check your essay's status.

Sample Op-ed Essay

In her Christmas 2004 op-ed essay, *New York Times* columnist Maureen Dowd, the columnist conservatives love to hate, lambastes the Bush administration for its handling of the war in Iraq.

Christmas Eve of Destruction

By Maureen Dowd
The New York Times, December 23, 2004

In Iraq, as Yogi Berra would say, the future ain't what it used to be.

Now that the election's over, our leaders think it's safe to experiment with a little candor.

President Bush has finally acknowledged that the Iraqis can't hack it as far as securing their own country, which means, of course, that America has no exit strategy for its troops, who will soon number 150,000.

News organizations led with the story, even though the president was only saying something that everybody has known to be true for a year. The White House's policy on Iraq has gone from a total charade to a limited modified hangout. Mr. Bush is conceding the obvious, that the Iraqi security forces aren't perfect, so he doesn't have to concede the truth: that Iraq is now so dire no one knows how or when we can get out.

If this fiasco ever made sense to anybody, it doesn't any more.

John McCain, who lent his considerable credibility to Mr. Bush during the campaign and vouched for the president and his war, now concedes that he has no confidence in Donald Rumsfeld.

And Rummy admitted yesterday that his feelings got hurt when people accused him of being insensitive to the fact that he arrogantly sent his troops into a sinkhole of carnage—a vicious, persistent insurgency—without the proper armor, equipment, backup or preparation.

The subdued defense chief further admitted that despite all the American kids who gave their lives in Mosul on the cusp of Christmas, battling an enemy they can't see in a war fought over weapons that didn't exist, we're not heading toward the democratic halcyon Mr. Bush promised.

"I think looking for a peaceful Iraq after the elections would be a mistake," Mr. Rumsfeld said.

His disgraceful admission that his condolence letters to the families of soldiers killed in Iraq were signed by machine—"I have directed that in the future I sign each letter," he said in a Strangelovian statement—is redolent of the myopia that has led to the dystopia.

The Bushies are betting a lot on the January election, even though a Shiite-dominated government will further alienate the Sunnis—and even though Iraq may be run by an Iranian-influenced ayatollah. That would mean that Iraq would have a leadership legitimized by us to hate us.

International election observers say it's too dangerous to actually come in and monitor the vote in person; they're going to "assess" the vote from the safety of Amman, Jordan. Isn't that like refereeing a football game while sitting in a downtown bar?

The administration hopes that once the Iraqis understand they have their own government, that will be a turning point and they will realize their country is worth fighting for. But this is the latest in a long list of turning points that turn out to be cul-de-sacs.

From the capture of Saddam to the departure of Paul Bremer and the assault on Falluja, there have been many false horizons for peace.

The U.S. military can't even protect our troops when they're eating lunch in a supposedly secure space—even after the Mosul base commanders had been warned of a "Beirut-style" attack three weeks before—because the Iraqi security forces and support staff have been infiltrated by insurgency spies.

Each milestone, each thing that is supposed to enable us to get some traction and change the basic dynamic in Iraq, comes and goes without the security getting any better. The *Los Angeles Times* reported yesterday that a major U.S. contractor, Contrack International Inc., had dropped out of the multibillion-dollar effort to rebuild Iraq, "raising new worries about the country's growing violence and its effect on reconstruction."

The Bush crowd thought it could get in, get out, scare the Iranians and Syrians, and remove the bulk of our forces within several months.

But now we're in, and it's the allies, contractors and election watchdogs who want out.

Aside from his scintilla of candor, Mr. Bush is still not leveling with us. As he said at his press conference on Monday, "the enemies of freedom" know that "a democratic Iraq will be a decisive blow to their ambitions because free people will never choose to live in tyranny."

They may choose to live in a theocracy, though. Americans did.

13.3   LETTERS TO ELECTED REPRESENTATIVES

Elected representatives, especially members of the U.S. Senate and House of Representatives, receive scores of letters every day. Although you may write to wish your senator a happy birthday or complain about the senator's wardrobe, most letters to elected representatives are for two purposes: (1) to influence her or him to vote a certain way on an issue that is currently being considered before the legislature or (2) to request that some member of the representative's staff perform a specific service, such as providing information or helping solve a problem encountered with a government agency. You may write a letter on any matter you please, but the goal of this particular assignment is to help you write the former type, that is, a letter that requests a representative to vote a certain way on impending legislation.

Letters to representatives are most likely to be influential when they are persuasively written and when they represent the view of a constituent. Your letter, therefore, should be addressed to your own senator or representative, and you should view it primarily as an exercise in persuasion. Letters that influence the votes of legislators often have several characteristics. First, they are brief and concise. Elected officials are very busy and, because they take in an immense amount of information each day, have very little patience for long-winded epistles that fail to get to the point. Second, good letters clearly identify a single action that their authors want the representative to take, stating and justifying the need for the requested action. Finally, good letters that concern a bill currently before Congress letter provide a brief summary of what the bill does. This may seem unnecessary, but Congress considers hundreds of bills each year, and often several appear simultaneously to address the same issue. You will want to save the representative some time by explaining exactly what she or he will be voting for.

How Do I Find a Topic?

The best place to start is THOMAS (http://thomas.loc.gov/), the home page of the Library of Congress, which provides online search engines and texts for all current legislation. Think of a topic in which you have a personal interest. Are you majoring in nursing? You may want to examine current legislation related to health care. Are you a music lover? Is any legislation passing that affects the music industry or your access to music on the Internet? Is there an issue pending that affects your personal congressional district? Whatever your interest, identify one or two key works and enter them into the THOMAS legislation search engine. You will then be presented a list of legislation in which your search terms are mentioned. After you locate a bill currently being considered by Congress that interests you, use the THOMAS Congressional Record search engine, enter the name of the bill, and you will find a record of speeches that have been made in Congress for and against the measure in question. Next, decide whether you are for or against the legislation and write down an initial list of your reasons for supporting or opposing it.

How Do I Go About Writing the Letter?

First, address your letter properly. A table providing proper forms of address is printed at the end of this section of this chapter. Begin your letter by telling the representative exactly what you want him or her to do and which piece of legislation is affected. Be sure to include the following information, which you will find when you locate the bill in the online *Congressional Digest:*

- Name of the bill (e.g., Environmental Justice Act of 2003)
- Subtitle of the bill (e.g., "an act to require federal agencies to develop and implement policies and practices that promote environmental justice, and for other purposes")
- Bill's number (e.g., H. R. 2200)
- Current status of the bill (e.g., referred to the Subcommittee on Commercial and Administrative Law)

Next, address two of the legislator's primary concerns. For every bill that comes to the representative's attention, he or she must answer two questions: (1) "Is legislative action needed to deal with whatever problem or issue is at hand?" and (2) "If legislation is needed, is the specific legislation in question the best way to address the issue?" To answer these two questions you will need to make the following two arguments: (1) That the issue or problem warrants (or does not warrant) legislative action and (2) that the specific proposed legislation appropriately deals (or does not appropriately deal) with the issue or problem.

Provide at least a few facts and examples or anecdotes. Include any personal experience or involvement that you have in the issue or problem. You do not need to provide all the information the legislator will need to make a decision, but provide enough to get her or him interested in the issue enough to examine the matter further and give it serious thought. Format the letter as you do a standard business letter and, of course, proofread your final draft carefully.

Sample Letter to a Representative

October 5, 2008

The Honorable Stephanie Herseth
1504 Longworth House Office Building
Washington, DC, 20515

Dear Representative Herseth:

I am writing to ask you to vote for the Environmental Justice Act of 2008 (H. R. 2200, currently under consideration by the Subcommittee on Commercial and Administrative Law), an act "To require Federal agencies to develop and implement policies and practices that promote environmental justice, and for other purposes." Native Americans, Latinos, and Blacks have suffered too long under unhealthy environmental conditions on reservations and in substandard neighborhoods across the country. In my neighborhood the toxic waste from old mining operations has caused illness in more than twenty children.

Across the country Superfund sites and pockets of polluted air and water are affecting most the people with the fewest resources and the least political clout to deal with the problem. In Los Angeles, for example, more than 70 percent of African-Americans and half of Latinos reside in the most highly polluted areas while only a third of the local whites live in these areas. Again, workers in the meatpacking plants of South Omaha, Nebraska, are battling to restore the vitality of city parks and improve unsanitary conditions in the plants. Too often people in these communities face greater exposure to toxins and dangerous substances because waste dumps, industrial facilities, and chemical storage facilities take fewer precautions in low-income communities than they do in high-income communities. Sadly, the captains of industry view these communities as expendable, denying the human beings who live in them the dignity and respect that is their constitutional right as American citizens.

What can be done? The first step is to solve a problem in and among federal agencies. Recent environmental and health policy studies have determined that most federal agencies, including the Environmental Protection Agency, do not adequately understand that environmental justice is being continuously denied to American citizens. Furthermore, there is currently no mechanism in place to coordinate and therefore make effective the environmental justice efforts that are currently under way.

The Environmental Justice Act of 2008 does much to correct these problems. In addition to focusing federal agency attention on the environmental and human health conditions in minority, low-income, and Native American communities, this legislation takes several positive steps in the direction of securing environmental justice for Native Americans. It

- ensures that all federal agencies develop practices that promote environmental justice
- increases cooperation and coordination among federal agencies
- provides minority, low-income, and Native American communities greater access to public information and opportunity for participation in environmental decision-making
- mitigates the inequitable distribution of the burdens and benefits of federal programs having significant impact on human health and the environment, and
- holds federal agencies accountable for the effects of their projects and programs on all communities.

Your support in this urgent matter is much appreciated.

Sincerely,

P. Charles Longbranch III
18 Lake Charles Way
Passamadumcott, SD 57003

13.4   TABLE OF FORMS OF PROPER ADDRESS FORMATS

This table was adapted from Appendix 6 of the *Department of Defense Manual for Written Material* (March 2, 2004, Director of Administration and Management, Office of the Secretary of Defense). It provides proper address formats for a wide variety of elected and nonelected public officials at local, state, national, and international levels of government.

ADDRESSEE	ADDRESS ON LETTER AND ENVELOPE	SALUTATION AND CLOSE
The President	The President The White House 1600 Pennsylvania Avenue, NW Washington, DC 20500	Dear Mr./Madam President: Respectfully yours,

ADDRESSEE	ADDRESS ON LETTER AND ENVELOPE	SALUTATION AND CLOSE
Spouse of the President	Mr./Mrs. (full name) The White House 1600 Pennsylvania Avenue, NW Washington, DC 20500	Dear Mr./Mrs. (surname): Sincerely,
Director, Office of Management and Budget	The Honorable (full name) Director, Office of Management and Budget Washington, DC 20503	Dear Mr./Ms. (surname): Sincerely,
The Vice President	The Vice President 276 Eisenhower Executive Office Building Washington, DC 20501	Dear Mr./Madam Vice President: Sincerely,
The Chief Justice	The Chief Justice The Supreme Court Washington, DC 20543	Dear Chief Justice: Sincerely,
Associate Justice	The Honorable (full name) The Supreme Court Washington, DC 20543	Dear Justice (Surname): Sincerely,
Judge of a federal, state, or local court	The Honorable (full name) Judge of the (name of court) (address)	Dear Judge (surname): Sincerely,
Clerk of a court	Mr. (full name) Clerk of the (name of court) (address)	Dear Mr./Ms. (surname): Sincerely,
Senator (Washington office)	The Honorable (full name) United States Senate Washington, DC 20510-(+4 Code)	Dear Senator (surname): Sincerely,
Speaker of the House of Representatives	The Honorable (full name) Speaker of the House of Representatives U.S. House of Representatives Washington, DC 20515-(+4 Code)	Dear Mr./Madam Speaker: Sincerely,
Representative (Washington office)	The Honorable (full name) U.S. House of Representatives Washington, DC 20515-(+4 Code)	Dear Representative (surname): Sincerely,

(continued)

ADDRESSEE	ADDRESS ON LETTER AND ENVELOPE	SALUTATION AND CLOSE
Resident Commissioner	The Honorable (full name) Resident Commissioner from Puerto Rico U.S. House of Representatives Washington, DC 20515-(+4 Code)	Dear Mr./Ms. (surname): Sincerely,
Delegate	The Honorable (full name) Delegate from (location) U.S. House of Representatives Washington, DC 20515-(+4 Code)	Dear Mr./Ms. (surname): Sincerely,
Members of the Cabinet addressed as Secretary	The Honorable (full name) Secretary of (name of Department) Washington, DC (ZIP+4 Code)	Dear Mr./Madam Secretary: Sincerely,
Attorney General	The Honorable (full name) Attorney General Washington, DC 20530	Dear Mr. Attorney General: Sincerely,
Deputy Secretary of a department	The Honorable (full name) Deputy Secretary of (name of Department) Washington, DC (ZIP+4 Code)	Dear Mr./Ms. (surname): Sincerely,
Head of a federal agency, authority, or board	The Honorable (full name) (title) (agency) Washington, DC (ZIP+4 Code)	Dear Mr./Ms. (surname): Sincerely,
President of a commission or board	The Honorable (full name) President, (name of commission) Washington, DC (ZIP+4 Code)	Dear Mr./Ms. (surname): Sincerely,
Chairman of a commission or board	The Honorable (full name) Chairman, (name of commission) Washington, DC (ZIP+4 Code)	Dear Mr./Madam Chairman: Sincerely,
Postmaster General	The Honorable (full name) Postmaster General 475 L'Enfant Plaza West, SW Washington, DC 20260	Dear Mr./Madam Postmaster General: Sincerely,
American Ambassador	The Honorable (full name) American Ambassador (city) (city), (country)	Dear Mr./Madam Ambassador: Sincerely,
Foreign ambassador in the United States	His/Her Excellency (full name) Ambassador of (country) Washington, DC (ZIP+4 Code)	Dear Mr./Madam Ambassador: Sincerely,

ADDRESSEE	ADDRESS ON LETTER AND ENVELOPE	SALUTATION AND CLOSE
Secretary General of the United Nations	The Honorable (full name) Secretary General of the United Nations New York, NY 10017	Dear Mr./Madam Secretary General: Sincerely,
United States Representative to the United Nations	The Honorable (full name) United States Representative to the United Nations New York, NY 10017	Dear Mr./Ms. (surname): Sincerely,
State Governor	The Honorable (full name) Governor of (state) (city) (state) (ZIP Code)	Dear Governor (surname): Sincerely,
State Lieutenant Governor	The Honorable (full name) Lieutenant Governor of (state) (city), (state) (ZIP Code)	Dear Mr./Ms. (surname): Sincerely,
State Secretary of State	The Honorable (full name) Secretary of State of (state) (city), (state) (ZIP Code)	Dear Mr./Madam (surname): Sincerely,
Chief Justice of a State Supreme Court	The Honorable (full name) Chief Justice Supreme Court of the State of (state) (city), (state) (ZIP Code)	Dear Mr./Madam Chief Justice: Sincerely,
State Attorney General	The Honorable (full name) Attorney General State of (state) (city), (state) (ZIP Code)	Dear Mr./Madam Attorney General: Sincerely,
State Treasurer, Comptroller, or Auditor	The Honorable (full name) State Treasurer (Comptroller) (Auditor) State of (state) (city), (state) (ZIP Code)	Dear Mr./Ms. (surname): Sincerely,
President, State Senate	The Honorable (full name) President of the Senate of the State of (state) (city), (state) (ZIP Code)	Dear Mr./Ms. (surname): Sincerely,
State Senator	The Honorable (full name) (state) Senate (city), (state) (ZIP Code)	Dear Mr./Ms. (surname): Sincerely,

(continued)

ADDRESSEE	ADDRESS ON LETTER AND ENVELOPE	SALUTATION AND CLOSE
Speaker, State House of Representatives, Assembly or House of Delegates	The Honorable (full name) Speaker of the House of Representatives (Assembly) (House of Delegates) of the State of (state) (city), (state) (ZIP Code)	Dear Mr./Ms. (surname): Sincerely,
State Representative, Assemblyman, or Delegate	The Honorable (full name) (state) House of Representatives (Assembly) (House of Delegates) (city), (state) (ZIP Code)	Dear Mr./Ms. (surname): Sincerely,
Mayor	The Honorable (full name) Mayor of (city) (city), (state) (ZIP Code)	Dear Mayor (surname) Sincerely,
President of a Board of Commissioners	The Honorable (full name) President, Board of Commissioners of (city) (city), (state) (ZIP Code)	Dear Mr./Ms. (surname): Sincerely,

CHAPTER

14

CRITICAL THINKING EXERCISES

As you have probably already discovered, college, among other things it does, helps you increase your knowledge, develop your communications skills, and clarify your fundamental values. The following exercises provide a means of attaining these three objectives simultaneously. Writing these essays will help you learn to (1) observe critically, (2) grasp the political power of metaphor, (3) clarify your fundamental values, and (4) improve your ability to explain your thoughts to others.

14.1   AN INTRODUCTION TO THE OBSERVATION OF POLITICS

Using simple questionnaires, psychologists can easily demonstrate that few people recall with any detail or accuracy events that happened just moments before the questionnaires were distributed. Considerable evidence suggests that many of us go through our lives from one day to the next observing virtually nothing at all. Perhaps we can do better.

Successful scientists agree that precise, prolonged, detailed observation initiates discovery. Greek philosopher Aristotle (384–322 BCE), German physicist Albert Einstein (1879–1955), and Swiss psychologist Jean Piaget (1896–1980) permanently altered how we see the world. Surprisingly, they did so neither by accidentally stumbling upon hidden mystical phenomena nor by activating rational processes available only to geniuses. Instead, they all did it the simplest (and perhaps the hardest) way possible. They simply looked at what was directly in front of them—in front of each of us—in everyday life. They did so, however, with much more patience, intensity, and precision that we are normally willing to use.

Einstein is a clear example. He revolutionized his generation's concepts of time and matter, the very substance of the universe. He also taught us that the ordinary is the key to the extraordinary. As a young adult Einstein worked as a clerk at a patent office in Geneva, Switzerland. On the train to and from work, instead of reading the newspaper, Einstein stared out the window, gazing for many hours at the appearance of telegraph poles passing through the passenger car windows. For a period of two weeks he spent his evening hours at home staring at tea leaves as they floated to the bottom of his cup. Over and over, hour after hour, day after day, he stirred them, just to watch the movements they made as they fell to the bottom of the cup. Had we been able to observe Einstein during these moments, we would likely conclude that his mental capacities were abnormal or deficient. But the long hours he spent observing such common processes led him to insights that changed life as we know it.

Jean Piaget thought and acted like Einstein. A founding father of developmental psychology, a person who restructured our way of understanding how children work, play, interact, and become adults, Piaget formulated his theories after spending many months, one day at a time, sitting in a school yard with his notebooks, patiently writing down everything he saw and heard. Billions of mothers may have loved their children, but not one of them, as far as we know, saw their children as clearly as Piaget saw the subjects of his schoolyard observations.

Aristotle, who preceded Einstein and Piaget by more than two millennia, became known as the father of political science when he applied what is now known as the scientific method to the study of politics. His mentor Plato had studied politics by applying deductive reasoning to problems of justice and good government. Aristotle, to the contrary, in order to understand what good government is, decided to look not to pure rationality but instead to consider governments existing in the world around him. The very first words of Aristotle's monumental *Politics* are "Observation shows us. . . ." He successfully examined and categorized more than 350 of the city-states of the Mediterranean world of his day, and political scientists have been following his example ever since.

14.2   AN EXERCISE IN OBSERVATION: CAMPAIGN COMMERCIALS

Now it is your turn to observe politics. Using the directions that follow and employing the paper formats described in previous chapters in this book, write a ten-page (double-spaced) paper.

1. On the Internet locate this Web site: http://livingroomcandidate. movingimage.us/index.php. Here you will find a collection of televised presidential campaign commercials from 1952 to 2004.
2. Browsing through the offerings, view several commercials in different years in order to familiarize yourself with the variety of campaign ads offered.
3. Select six commercials, no more than two from any one candidate.
4. Make a set of notes for yourself (not to be submitted to the instructor) that answer at least the following questions for each of the six commercials:
   a. Which party has prepared the commercial?
   b. Who is portrayed in the commercial?

    c. What, exactly, does the commercial say?

    d. What "techniques," such as humor, sarcasm, irony, fear, education, or slander, does the commercial use to get its point across?

    e. What is the specific objective (beyond getting a particular candidate elected) of this particular commercial?

    f. What is the commercial attempting to imply about the candidates involved in that particular race?

    g. What is the commercial attempting to imply about an issue or issues involved in that particular race?

    h. To what extent is the message of the commercial "positive," that is, portraying someone or some idea in an optimistic or affirming way?

    i. To what extent is the message of the commercial "negative," that is, portraying someone or some idea in a disapproving or unenthusiastic way?

    j. How accurate is the commercial?

    k. How honest is the commercial?

    l. How effective is the commercial?

    m. What criteria have you used to assess the effectiveness of the commercial?

    n. What does this commercial tell you about the candidate who sponsored it?

    o. What does this commercial tell you about the candidate at whom the commercial is aimed?

    p. What does this commercial tell you about American politics?

5. Now, using your observations generated by answering the questions above, write a ten-page essay in which you evaluate and compare the commercials you have viewed. In the course of your essay,

- describe the six commercials (election year, sponsoring candidate, commercial content)
- compare the techniques used
- compare the effectiveness of the commercials
- explain what this exercise in observation has shown you about American politics

14.3 DIRECTIONS FOR WRITING AN ALLEGORY ANALYSIS

Webster's New Collegiate Dictionary defines *allegory* as "the expression by means of symbolic fictional figures and actions of truths or generalizations about human existence . . . an instance (as in a story or painting) of such expression . . . a symbolic representation." An allegory often appears in the form of a *parable* (*Webster:* a "short fictitious story that illustrates a moral attitude or a religious principle").

Most of us are introduced to allegories before we have the slightest understanding of what they mean. Our parents often begin reading us their favorite fables and children's stories—the "Three Little Pigs," "Goldilocks and the Three Bears," "Little Red Riding Hood"—long before we are able to read them or apply them to our lives.

Successful philosophers (intuitive observers all) appreciate allegory as a tool for helping the human mind grasp the meaning of what it has observed. Aristotle's mentor Plato, Harvard University political scientist John Rawls, and French philosopher Michel Foucault have provided powerful allegories, summarized below, that offer us the opportunity not only to understand the political world better but to clarify some of our own fundamental values as well.

Complete the following tasks in writing your political allegory analysis paper. First, read the political allegories and the "matters for consideration" following each allegory provided in the next three sections of this chapter (Sections 14.4, 14.5, and 14.6). Second, select one of the allegories as the focus of your analysis. Third, write a five- to seven-page essay about the selected allegory in which you

1. summarize the allegory
2. identify precisely the meaning the author is attempting to convey
3. explain the implications of the allegory
4. apply the symbolic meaning of the allegory to politics in the United States or the world today
5. utilize the "matters for consideration" provided after each allegory without limiting yourself exclusively to them

14.4   ALLEGORY 1: PLATO'S PHILOSOPHER KING

Plato (427–347 BCE), father of political philosophy, recorded his mentor Socrates' most influential ideas in the form of fictional dialogues, conversations that Socrates held with prominent Athenians of his day. Although many of the dialogues address political issues, Plato's most important treatise on politics is contained in *The Republic*, in which Socrates discusses justice and how it is to be achieved in society. In Book II of *The Republic*, Glaucon, one of Socrates' imaginary interlocutors, insists that to be just—that is, to follow commonly accepted standards of justice—is rational only if one is constrained to do so:

> They say that to do injustice is, by nature, good; to suffer injustice, evil; but that the evil is greater than the good. And so when men have both done and suffered injustice and have had experience of both, not being able to avoid the one and obtain the other, they think that they had better agree among themselves to have neither; hence there arise laws and mutual covenants; and that which is ordained by law is termed by them lawful and just. This they affirm to be the origin and nature of justice;—it is a mean or compromise, between the best of all, which is to do injustice and not be punished, and the worst of all, which is to suffer injustice without the power of retaliation; and justice, being at a middle point between the two, is tolerated not as a good, but as the lesser evil, and honoured by reason of the inability of men to do injustice. For no man who is worthy to be called a man would ever submit to such an agreement if he were able to resist; he would be mad if he did. Such is the received account, Socrates, of the nature and origin of justice.

Now that those who practise justice do so involuntarily and because they have not the power to be unjust will best appear if we imagine something of this kind: having given both to the just and the unjust power to do what they will, let us watch and see whither desire will lead them; then we shall discover in the very act the just and unjust man to be proceeding along the same road, following their interest, which all natures deem to be their good, and are only diverted into the path of justice by the force of law. The liberty which we are supposing may be most completely given to them in the form of such a power as is said to have been possessed by Gyges the ancestor of Croesus the Lydian. According to the tradition, Gyges was a shepherd in the service of the king of Lydia; there was a great storm, and an earthquake made an opening in the earth at the place where he was feeding his flock. Amazed at the sight, he descended into the opening, where, among other marvels, he beheld a hollow brazen horse, having doors, at which he stooping and looking in saw a dead body of stature, as appeared to him, more than human, and having nothing on but a gold ring; this he took from the finger of the dead and reascended. Now the shepherds met together, according to custom, that they might send their monthly report about the flocks to the king; into their assembly he came having the ring on his finger, and as he was sitting among them he chanced to turn the collet of the ring inside his hand, when instantly he became invisible to the rest of the company and they began to speak of him as if he were no longer present. He was astonished at this, and again touching the ring he turned the collet outwards and reappeared; he made several trials of the ring, and always with the same result—when he turned the collet inwards he became invisible, when outwards he reappeared. Whereupon he contrived to be chosen one of the messengers who were sent to the court; where as soon as he arrived he seduced the queen, and with her help conspired against the king and slew him, and took the king-dom. Suppose now that there were two such magic rings, and the just put on one of them and the unjust the other; no man can be imagined to be of such an iron nature that he would stand fast in justice. No man would keep his hands off what was not his own when he could safely take what he liked out of the market, or go into houses and lie with any one at his pleasure, or kill or release from prison whom he would, and in all respects be like a God among men. Then the actions of the just would be as the actions of the unjust; they would both come at last to the same point. And this we may truly affirm to be a great proof that a man is just, not willingly or because he thinks that justice is any good to him individually, but of neces-sity, for wherever any one thinks that he can safely be unjust, there he is unjust. For all men believe in their hearts that injustice is far more prof-itable to the individual than justice, and he who argues as I have been sup-posing, will say that they are right. If you could imagine any one obtaining this power of becoming invisible, and never doing any wrong or touching what was another's, he would be thought by the lookers-on to be a most wretched idiot, although they would praise him to one another's faces, and keep up appearances with one another from a fear that they too might suf-fer injustice. Enough of this. (Jowett http://classics.mit.edu/Plato/republic.3.ii.html)

Matters for Consideration

1. What would you do if you had Gyges' ring?
2. To what extent are people naturally unjust?
3. To what extent are people constrained from injustice only by fear of penalty?
4. If Glaucon is right, how should society be constructed?
5. If Glaucon is wrong, how should society be constructed?

14.5   ALLEGORY 2: RAWLS' VEIL OF IGNORANCE

The late Harvard University political scientist John Rawls (1921–2002) reinvigorated the ancient quest for justice and good government in his works, the most prominent of which is *A Theory of Justice.* In this book, Rawls proposes a particular set of definitions of justice, equality, and freedom. Of interest for this writing exercise is an allegory Rawls employs to answer the question Socrates pursued in *The Republic:* "What is justice?" Rawls replies: "Justice is fairness."

Rawls proposes, in part, that to understand how justice as fairness can be actualized in society we must imagine ourselves to be participant in an allegory that may be called the "veil of ignorance." First we assume an "original position of equality."

> In justice as fairness the original position of equality corresponds to the state of nature in the traditional theory of the social contract. This original position is not, of course, thought of as an actual historical state of affairs, much less as a primitive condition of culture. It is understood as a purely hypothetical situation characterized so as to lead to a certain conception of justice. Among the essential features of this situation is that no one knows his place in society, his class position or social status, nor does any one know his fortune in the distribution of natural assets and abilities, his intelligence, strength, and the like. I shall even assume that the parties do not know their conceptions of the good or their special psychological propensities. The principles of justice are chosen behind a veil of ignorance. (Rawls 1971)

Just to make sure we understand what Rawls is getting at here, let us paraphrase, very liberally, using a common religious metaphor that Rawls does not use. Imagine you are up in heaven standing in line waiting to be born. Like the other souls before and after you, you enter the next conceived fetus, wherever it occurs on earth. You have no idea whether you will be born in Massachusetts, the Ukraine, or the Congo. You have no idea whether your mother will be a Hollywood star or a drug-addicted prostitute. You have no idea whether your father will be a multimillionaire or a slave in Sudan. You have no idea if your IQ will be 150 or 50, whether you will have the physique of Arnold Schwarzenegger or the functional capacities of a quadriplegic, or if you will physically resemble

Tom Cruise or Quasimodo. While you are pondering the odds, the archangel Michael tells you and the other prenatal souls that you have been granted the chance to construct the constitution of the society in which you will live.

Matters for Consideration

1. What specific constitutional measures will you propose in order to construct a society that will protect your interest should you be someone who is physically or mentally disadvantaged?
2. What specific constitutional measures will you propose in order to construct a society that will protect your interest should you be someone who is financially disadvantaged?
3. What specific constitutional measures will you propose in order to construct a society that will protect your interest should you be someone who is physically or mentally superior?
4. What specific constitutional measures will you propose in order to construct a society that will protect your interest should you be someone who is financially advantaged?
5. What specific constitutional measures will you propose in order to construct a society that will protect the interests of everyone in the categories listed immediately above?

14.6 ALLEGORY 3: FOUCAULT'S PANOPTICON

French philosopher Michel Foucault (1926–1984) wrote several volumes of what he called genealogy. He was not interested in tracing family trees. Instead, he attempted to trace patterns of political power as they emerged in society. He was most interested in identifying how political power is created and wielded and how people perceive it and are affected by it. His studies led him to conclude that political power is much more pervasive than many people assume. To illustrate his principle he proposed an allegorical panopticon.

A real, tangible panopticon had been invented by the eighteenth-century British utilitarian philosopher Jeremy Bentham. Bentham wanted to reform the British penal system. As Foucault notes in *Discipline and Punish* (1995), in 1791 Bentham proposed a new, more humane, and more efficient prison design than was in use in the eighteenth and nineteenth centuries:

> Bentham's Panopticon is the architectural figure of this composition. We know the principle on which it was based: at the periphery, an annular building; at the centre, a tower; this tower is pierced with wide windows that open onto the inner side of the ring; the peripheric building is divided into cells, each of which extends the whole width of the building; they have two windows, one on the inside, corresponding to the windows of the tower; the other, on the outside,

allows the light to cross the cell from one end to the other. All that is needed, then, is to place a supervisor in a central tower and to shut up in each cell a madman, a patient, a condemned man, a worker or a schoolboy. By the effect of backlighting, one can observe from the tower, standing out precisely against the light, the small captive shadows in the cells of the periphery. They are like so many cages, so many small theatres, in which each actor is alone, perfectly individualized and constantly visible. The panoptic mechanism arranges spatial unities that make it possible to see constantly and to recognize immediately. In short, it reverses the principle of the dungeon; or rather of its three functions—to enclose, to deprive of light and to hide—it preserves only the first and eliminates the other two. Full lighting and the eye of a supervisor capture better than darkness, which ultimately protected. Visibility is a trap.

To begin with, this made it possible—as a negative effect—to avoid those compact, swarming, howling masses that were to be found in places of confinement, those painted by Goya or described by Howard. Each individual, in his place, is securely confined to a cell from which he is seen from the front by the supervisor; but the side walls prevent him from coming into contact with his companions. He is seen, but he does not see; he is the object of information, never a subject in communication. The arrangement of his room, opposite the central tower, imposes on him an axial visibility; but the divisions of the ring, those separated cells, imply a lateral invisibility. And this invisibility is a guarantee of order. If the inmates are convicts, there is no danger of a plot, an attempt at collective escape, the planning of new crimes for the future, bad reciprocal influences; if they are patients, there is no danger of contagion; if they are madmen there is no risk of their committing violence upon one another; if they are schoolchildren, there is no copying, no noise, no chatter, no waste of time; if they are workers, there are no disorders, no theft, no coalitions, none of those distractions that slow down the rate of work, make it less perfect or cause accidents. The crowd, a compact mass, a locus of multiple exchanges, individualities merging together, a collective effect, is abolished and replaced by a collection of separated individualities. From the point of view of the guardian, it is replaced by a multiplicity that can be numbered and supervised; from the point of view of the inmates, by a sequestered and observed solitude [Bentham, 60–64].

Hence the major effect of the Panopticon: to induce in the inmate a state of conscious and permanent visibility that assures the automatic functioning of power. So to arrange things that the surveillance is permanent in its effects, even if it is discontinuous in its action; that the perfection of power should tend to render its actual exercise unnecessary; that this architectural apparatus should be a machine for creating and sustaining a power relation independent of the person who exercises it; in short, that the inmates should be caught up in a power situation of which they are themselves the bearers. To achieve this, it is at once too much and too little that the prisoner should be constantly observed by an inspector: too little, for what matters is that he knows himself to be observed; too much, because he has no need in fact of being so. In view of this, Bentham laid down the principle that power should be visible and unverifiable. Visible: the inmate will constantly have before his eyes the tall outline of the central tower from which he is spied upon. Unverifiable: the inmate must never know whether he is being looked at at any one moment; but he must be sure that he may always be so. In order to make the presence or absence of the inspector unverifiable, so that the prisoners, in their cells, cannot even see a shadow, Bentham envisaged not only venetian blinds on the windows of the central observation hall, but, on the inside, partitions that intersected the hall at right angles and, in order to pass from one quarter to the other, not doors but zig-zag openings; for the slightest noise, a gleam of light, a brightness in a half-opened door would betray the presence of the guardian. The Panopticon is a machine for dissociating the see/being seen dyad: in the peripheric ring, one is totally seen, without ever seeing; in the central tower, one sees everything without ever being seen.

It is an important mechanism, for it automatizes and disindividualizes power. Power has its principle not so much in a person as in a certain concerted distribution of bodies, surfaces, lights, gazes; in an arrangement whose internal mechanisms produce the relation in which individuals are caught up. The ceremonies, the rituals, the marks by which the sovereign's surplus power was manifested are useless. There is a machinery that assures dissymmetry, disequilibrium, difference. Consequently, it does not matter who exercises power. Any individual, taken almost at random, can operate the machine: in the absence of the director, his family, his friends, his visitors, even his servants (Bentham, 45). Similarly, it does not matter what motive animates him: the curiosity of the indiscreet, the malice of a child, the thirst for knowledge of a philosopher who wishes to visit this museum of human nature, or the perversity of those who take pleasure in spying and punishing. The more numerous those anonymous and temporary observers are, the greater the risk for the inmate of being surprised and the greater his anxious awareness of being observed. The Panopticon is a marvellous machine which, whatever use one may wish to put it to, produces homogeneous effects of power.

A real subjection is born mechanically from a fictitious relation. So it is not necessary to use force to constrain the convict to good behaviour, the madman to calm, the worker to work, the schoolboy to application, the patient to the observation of the regulations. Bentham was surprised that panoptic institutions could be so light: there were no more bars, no more chains, no more heavy locks; all that was needed was that the separations should be clear and the openings well arranged. The heaviness of the old "houses of security," with their fortress-like architecture, could be replaced by the simple, economic geometry of a "house of certainty." The efficiency of power, its constraining force, have, in a sense, passed over to the other side—to the side of its surface of application. He who is subjected to a field of visibility, and who knows it, assumes responsibility for the constraints of power; he makes them play spontaneously upon himself; he inscribes in himself the power relation in which he simultaneously plays both roles; he becomes the principle of his own subjection. By this very fact, the external power may throw off its physical weight; it tends to the non-corporal; and, the more it approaches this limit, the more constant, profound and permanent are its effects: it is a perpetual victory that avoids any physical confrontation and which is always decided in advance. (Foucault 1995, 200–203)

Matters for Consideration

1. Foucault's allegorical Panopticon, unlike Bentham's actual panopticon, is not a prison, but society itself.
2. To what extent are we, as members of society, inmates of a panopticon?
3. To what extent are we, as members of society, guards in a panopticon?
4. Although we are members of a "free" society, how much freedom do we actually have to express our individuality?
5. What can be done to enhance our freedom to express our individuality?

CHAPTER

15

ELEMENTARY POLICY ANALYSIS: POSITION PAPERS

The "X Memorandum"

On February 22, 1946, George F. Kennan, career foreign service officer serving as minister-counselor in the U.S. Embassy in Moscow, sent a telegram to Secretary of the Navy James Forrestal. The telegram sparked Forrestal's interest. "The result," wrote Kennan, "was that on January 31, 1947, I sent to him, for his private and personal edification, a paper discussing the nature of Soviet Power as a problem in policy for the United States" (1967, 354).

Kennan's paper appeared anonymously as an article in the July 1947 issue of *Foreign Affairs*. The author was listed as "X." The "X Article" became the most famous position paper ever written. In the article, Kennan described the two postwar power centers (Soviet-Communist and Western-Capitalist) and advocated the political "containment" of communism in Eastern Europe within its postwar boundaries, which became the cornerstone of American foreign policy for the remainder of the cold war.

Kennan notes in his memoirs that his statements were misconstrued by Walter Lippmann and others as referring to military as well as political containment. Similar ideas had been discussed by others. The fact remains, however, that Kennan's impressive exposition of the possibilities of American foreign policy remained at the center of the debates that determined the core of American foreign policy for more than three decades. Not all position papers are this influential. They do, however, have a daily, continuing significant effect on the formation of public domestic and foreign policies. Position papers are elementary exercises in policy analysis. As a student of political science you need to understand the techniques necessary for writing effective and influential position papers.

15.1   WHAT IS A POSITION PAPER?

A position paper is advice. It is a document written to provide a decision maker with guidance on how to solve a problem. In a position paper, the author takes a position on how to solve a particular problem. Although position papers are not identical in format or style, all successful examples

- clearly define a specific problem
- evaluate alternative approaches or methods for solving the problem
- recommend a course of action to solve the problem

Hundreds of position papers are written in business and government every day. Business managers and public officials (presidents, governors, mayors, city managers, bureau directors, and others) are constantly faced with problems. They usually ask their staff members for information on the problems and for recommendations on how to solve them. Sometimes subordinates write position papers to provide the requested information in a clear, precise, and persuasive manner. Position papers are particularly effective for making presentations to committees and boards of directors.

The Purpose of Position Papers

Successful political science position papers all share the same general purpose and objective: to persuade a public official to take a specific action to resolve a problem.

Public managers are problem-solvers. Their primary responsibility is to make decisions that solve problems. The person who helps decision makers make decisions is responsible for presenting appropriate and relevant information that they can use. A position paper is therefore an entirely practical exercise. It is neither theoretical nor general in nature. It has a very narrow focus: to solve one specific problem. Theoretical treatises and general subject essays have their place in communication, but not here. The object of the exercise is to persuade a public official to take the course of action that you recommend. You should not recommend an action in which you do not believe, and if you do believe your recommendation is the best way to solve the problem, you need to persuade the decision maker to implement it. Otherwise your work is of no value; it is a waste of time and effort.

15.2   SELECTING TOPICS FOR POSITION PAPERS

General Guidelines

Several considerations govern the selection of topics for position papers for courses in political science. First, the topic should be a problem facing a public or government official. Although position papers are frequently written for managers of private concerns, such as businesses or research institutes, such papers in political science should normally deal with problems and policies of public (government) managers.

A second parameter for selecting position paper topics is that such papers should address current, not historical, problems and issues. When you write a paper on an issue that has yet to be resolved, you are participating in the political and governmental environment. A current issue is more likely to be of interest than one that has already been decided. There is even a possibility that the paper, if actually submitted to the appropriate government manager, may influence public policy. Analyses of problems already solved are best placed within the context of a history course.

A third requirement is that position paper topics should have an appropriate scope. A common mistake is, for students, to choose topics that are too complex or that require special technical knowledge or skills beyond those readily available. A good general rule for your position paper is to work with the lowest level of government possible. Even local governments deal with problems that entail numerous social, economic, and environmental factors. In general, the higher a level of government is on the federal scale, the more varied are the interests served and the more complex are the issues to be settled. In addition, information from local sources is often much more easily and quickly obtained than information from the state capital or Washington. Local government officials are also more likely to be personally available and thus able to provide you with a direct experience with government. However, regardless of the level of government that is being examined, keep the topic narrowly defined.

Here are some examples of topics. Which are sufficiently narrow to be suitable for position papers in courses in American national, state, or local government or policy analysis? Which are too vague or complex?

1. Equipment Failures at Madison North Fire Station
2. Free Speech
3. The Balanced Budget Amendment
4. Discipline Problems at Vandever High School
5. Inadequate Budget Procedures in Washington County
6. Abortion
7. Inadequate Personal Financial Accountability of Missouri State Legislators
8. Ineffective Affirmative Action Procedures of the Ohio Department of Education

On the above list, topics 2, 3, and 6 are too vague or complex.

A fourth guideline for writing position papers is to avoid legal questions. Remember that the point of the paper is to present sufficient information clearly enough to allow a public official to make a decision. You are not trying to argue fundamental principles of law. The moral, ethical, legal, legislative, and historical facets of abortion, for example, are more appropriately presented in the format of a legal brief rather than a position paper. Topics in constitutional law are therefore best reserved for courses in the subject (see Chapter 19). Problems in judicial administration, however, such as court docket procedures or jail overcrowding, are often very interesting position paper topics.

Personal Interest

There are two general approaches to selecting a topic for a position paper. The first is to select a topic tied to your own interest, perhaps one that relates to your future vocation. Government policy affects every vocation in some way and affects most of them directly. You may find a topic by asking yourself: "What are my career goals and interests? In what way does government affect me?" Many college students, for example, are affected by government student loan policies. Or, if you want to be a teacher, for example, you may want to investigate the quality of schools in your home school district or a specific educational policy or problem of state or national government. If you are an aspiring athlete, you may want to study a particular aspect of U.S. Olympic policy, whereas if medical school is in your plans, you may want to look at problems in medical reimbursement.

Once you have decided on a general topic from personal interest, an excellent way to narrow the topic is to contact a public administrator concerned with that subject and have the person identify a related problem currently facing his or her agency. Remember that the purpose of a policy paper is to define a problem and recommend the best way to solve it. One of the best ways to define a valid problem is to have a public official currently involved in working on a particular problem define that problem for you. For example, if you are interested in aviation, a good first step would be to contact an appropriate government employee in the field. You may start by looking in the blue pages of the phone book, which contain entries under the following headings:

Helpful Numbers
Government Offices, City
Government Offices, County
Government Offices, State
Government Offices, United States

You then select an appropriate number and call that office. After identifying yourself, explain that you are writing a paper for a class in political science, and ask for an appointment with the agency's public information officer. If they do not have a person with this title, explain your topic and ask to speak to the person at the agency who knows the most about it. Most public employees will take time to talk to citizens who call to request information. The first official called may refer you to someone else, but continue to follow referrals until you find someone who will give you an interview.

Current Events

If you have no luck finding a topic based on your personal interests, a second approach is to select a subject related to a current event. Newspapers, television, and radio continually present actual problems currently being faced by decision makers at all levels of government. Investigate the problem by contacting government officials and other individuals identified in the article or on the broadcast.

Newspaper Articles

Every day your local newspaper contains viable topics for position paper topics, and Sunday editions usually discuss a variety of issues in more detail. Sometimes newspapers will highlight community problems and activities on a specific day of the week.

15.3 CONDUCTING RESEARCH FOR POSITION PAPERS

Whereas most traditional research projects begin in a library, position paper research starts with a government official. Because position papers investigate topics of current concern to the government, much of the most pertinent information is not available in libraries. Instead, much of it is in the form of technical reports written by consultants, government employees, or citizen groups interested in specific problems. By first contacting an appropriate official, you may find that agency staff members have collected much of the best available information and will provide it to you upon request. By asking questions, you can identify further sources of information. When speaking to the government employee you have contacted, ask for the names of people and organizations that have a direct interest in the matter under investigation. Call some of these sources and ask for more information.

Interviews

You will usually find it essential to interview public officials, representatives of interest groups, and technical experts to get all the information necessary to write a position paper.

Other Sources of Information

Since the purpose of your paper is to help an actual government decision maker make a decision, the information you present must be as reliable as possible. Newspaper and news magazine articles (unless used as incidental illustrations) are often inaccurate and therefore unacceptable as primary sources. Also unacceptable as sources for college-level work are encyclopedia articles. Appropriate sources include government documents and reports, academic journal articles, technical reports of private consultants, and direct interviews. The number of sources, of course, varies with the subject, but in general, undergraduate papers in political science should cite three sources per page of text. (For more on how to find information for position papers, see Chapters 6 and 7.)

15.4 CONTENTS OF POSITION PAPERS

The format of a position paper should follow the directions provided in Chapter 7.

NOTE. The directions for position papers are much more specific than those for other paper assignments because position papers have a much more narrow purpose: to help a busy decision maker arrive at the correct decision as quickly as possible. The format for position papers given in Chapter 7 has proved to be effective in telling decision makers precisely what they need to know to make a decision: (1) the nature and extent of a problem; (2) the relative merits of the options available to solve the problem; and (3) the best solution to the problem. A position paper assignment is not intended primarily as an opportunity for a student to express creativity. It is instead an exercise in precision, in problem-solving, and in clear, concise communication.

The Contents of a Position Paper

Each position paper contains five basic elements:

1. Title page
2. Outline page that summarizes the paper
3. Text, or body, of the paper
4. References to sources of information
5. Appendixes

Title Page

Follow directions for title pages in Chapter 7 of this manual.

The Outline Page

The outline page in a position paper deserves special attention, because the paper's audience is likely to be someone who needs to gain information quickly. A one-page, single-spaced outline immediately follows the title page. An outline page supersedes a table of contents, which is not necessary in a position paper. The outline will be composed of complete sentences that express the central concepts to be more fully explained in the text. It consists of a series of the topic sentences of the first paragraphs of each major section of the text.

The purpose of the outline is to allow the decision maker to understand, in as little time as possible, the major considerations to be discussed in the paper. Each statement must thus be clearly defined and carefully prepared. The decision maker should be able to get a thorough and clear overview of the entire problem, major alternative solutions, and your recommendation by reading nothing but the one-page outline. The content of the outline follows the content of the text of the paper. The outline should thus be written after the text is completed and should utilize the topic statements of the text as the sentences in the outline.

The outline (and the text of the position paper) should always begin with the words "The problem is. . . ." In addition, every position paper outline should use verbatim the italicized words in the sample below. The number of possible solutions, of course, will vary with the particular topic of the paper.

Outline of Contents

I. The problem is that parking, picnic, and restroom facilities at Oak Ridge Community Park have deteriorated and are of inadequate quantity to meet public demand.
   A. The park was established as a public recreation "Class B" facility in 1943. Only one major renovation has occurred, in the summer of 1967,
   B. The Park Department estimates that 10,000 square feet of new parking space, fourteen items of playground equipment, seventeen new picnic tables, and repairs on current facilities would cost about $43,700.

II. Three possible solutions have been given extensive consideration:
   A. One option is to do nothing. Area residents will use the area less as deterioration continues. No immediate outlay of public funds will be necessary.
   B. The first alternative solution is to make all repairs immediately. Area residents will enjoy immediate and increased use of facilities. About $43,700 in funds will be needed. Sources include: (1) Community Development Block Grant funds; (2) raised property taxes; (3) revenue bonds; and (4) general city revenues.
   C. A second alternative is to make repairs according to a priority list over a five-year period, using a combination of general city revenues and a $20,000 first-year bond.

III. The recommendation of this report is that alternative "C" be adopted by the City Council. The benefit/cost analysis demonstrates that residents will be satisfied if basic improvements are made immediately. The City Council should, during its May 15 meeting: (1) adopt a resolution of intent to commit $5,000 of funds per year for five years from the general revenue fund, dedicated to this purpose; and (2) approve for submission to public vote in the November 1995 election a $20,000 bond issue.

The Text

The text, or body, of the paper should follow the outline shown below:

The Text of a Position Paper

  I.   A clear, concise definition of the problem
       A. A statement of the background of the problem
       B. A description of the extent of the problem
 II.   Possible solutions to the problem
       A. The first possible solution is always to take no action
          1. An estimate of the benefits of this alternative
          2. An estimate of the costs of this alternative
       B. The first alternative to taking no action
          1. An estimate of the benefits of this alternative
          2. An estimate of the costs of this alternative
       C. The second alternative to taking no action
          1. An estimate of the benefits of this alternative
          2. An estimate of the costs of this alternative
III.   A precise recommended course of action in two parts:
       A. Policy recommendation
       B. Implementation recommendation

Two general rules govern the amount of information presented in the body of the paper. First, content must be adequate for making a good decision. All the necessary facts must be present. If a critical fact is omitted, a poor decision will likely be made. Never delete important facts simply because they tend to support a recommendation other than your own. Write this paper as if you were a member of the staff of the person to whom you are writing. As a staff member, your role is to inform your superior. The decision is his or her responsibility. It is far better for the decision maker to select an alternative different from your recommendation, based on a review of all the facts, than to make the wrong decision based on inadequate information.

The second guideline for determining the length of a position paper is to omit extraneous material. Include only the information that is helpful in making the particular decision at hand. If the paper addresses the crime rate in Atlanta,

Georgia, for example, national crime statistics are of little use unless some direct application to Atlanta's problem is evident. A theoretical discussion about the causes of crime is of no value at all, unless differences in philosophy in the community are contributing to the city's inability to reduce crime.

References

All sources of information in a position paper must be properly cited, following the directions in Chapter 8.

Appendixes

Appendixes can provide the reader of position papers with information that supplements the important facts presented in the text. For many local development and public works projects, a map and a diagram are often very helpful appendixes. You should attach them to the end of the paper, after the reference page. You should not append entire government reports, journal articles, or other publications, but selected charts, graphs, or other pages. The source of the information should always be evident on the appended pages.

CHAPTER
16

ANALYTICAL PAPERS IN AMERICAN GOVERNMENT AND INTERNATIONAL RELATIONS

16.1 PRELIMINARY CHOICES FOR RESEARCH PAPERS IN POLITICAL SCIENCE

The starting point for any research paper in political science is the process of making three initial choices:

1. the topic of the paper;
2. the purpose of the paper; and
3. the method of research.

Paper Topics in American Government and International Relations

Before proceeding you may find it helpful to review the material on selecting and narrowing paper topics in Chapter 5 of this volume (pages 100–101). If you have not yet found a topic you may want to peruse the following lists for something that appeals to you.

Topics in American Government and Politics

accountability	appointing judges	congressional leadership and rules
affirmative action	campaigns	Constitution of the United States
amending the constitution	cities and towns	
American parties today	citizenship	constitutional convention of 1787
American political culture	Congress and the presidency	constitutional rights
	congressional elections	

counties
crime and law
   enforcement
current problems for
   democracy
definitions of democracy
development of
   democracy
due process of law
economic policy
education policy
elections
equal protection
   of the laws
equal rights
federal administrative
   system
federal judiciary
federalism
fiscal policy
free speech
freedom of assembly
freedom of religion
freedom of the press

governors
health policy
history of American
   political parties
history of the presidency
intergovernmental
   relations
interpretations of the
   U.S. Constitution
job of the legislator
judicial power
judicial review
law enforcement
lobbyists
media and politics
monetary policy
money and politics
parties and democracy
planning
political ideology
political parties in
   the states
power of interest groups
presidential power

privacy
process of legislation
property rights
public opinion
public participation
   in politics
regulation
rights of association
rights of the accused
social policy
social services
state and local elections
state and local
   governments
state constitutions
state courts
state legislatures
structure and powers
   of Congress
structure and powers
   of the presidency
Supreme Court
types of interest groups
voting rights

Topics in American International Relations

alliances
anarchy
arms control
atmosphere
ballistic missiles
binational states
biodiversity
biological weapons
capital formation
capitalism
causes of war
chemical weapons
coalitions
coastal and marine areas
collaboration
collective hegemony
collective security
conventional weapons
cooperation

crises of authority
cultural capabilities
defense
dependency theory
deterrence
diplomatic
   communications
diplomatic immunity
diplomatic missions
disarmament
dual hegemony
economic integration
environment
finance
forests
fresh water
globalists
globalization
hegemonic systems

historic international
   systems
human rights
humanitarian
   intervention
interdependence
international law
international monetary
   regime
international
   organizations
international security
international systems
intervention
Islam
justice
just-war theory
land
law

liberals	noncombatants	religion
mercantilism	nuclear weapons	security
military capabilities	pacifism	social constructionists
multiethnic states	peacekeeping	statecraft
multinational states	pluralists	strategy
national security	political capabilities	technological capabilities
national	political economy	terrorism
self-determination	poverty	trade
nationalism	power	transnational crime
nation–states	realists	weapons proliferation
NGOs	refugees	world government

The Purpose of the Research Paper

Research papers in political science are typically written for one or more of four basic reasons:

1. to explain
2. to evaluate
3. to predict
4. to persuade

After you select a topic you need to decide what your paper is for. Do you want to *explain*

the voting behavior of Kansas Republicans, or
who benefits from the current national budget process, or
why the Supreme Court selects certain cases to decide, and not others?

Or, do you want to *evaluate*

the effectiveness of campaign advertising in Kansas in 2008, or
the effectiveness of current national budget process, or
the fairness of the Supreme Court case selection process?

Or, do you want to *predict*

the effectiveness of campaign advertising in Kansas in 2012, or
the national budget expenditures for defense in 2010, or
when the Supreme Court will revisit *Roe* v. *Wade?*

Or, do you want to *persuade*

the Republican Party to discontinue negative campaign advertising in Kansas in 2012, or
the Congress to increase national budget expenditures for defense in 2010, or
the Supreme Court to revisit *Roe* v. *Wade?*

In any case, be sure to consult with your instructor about an appropriate purpose for your paper.

Political Analysis

In order to achieve any of these purposes, both *description* and *analysis* of some kind are normally necessary. You may want to write a paper that is simply *descriptive*. You could simply review the current literature on, say, for example, the influence of politics on current monetary policy, or the key current issues relating to weapons proliferation, and then describe current state of the discipline with respect to these issues. If you attempt to *explain* the strengths and weaknesses of the current literature, however, you will find yourself conducting at least some *analysis*. Analysis is also necessary in order to evaluate, persuade, or predict. *Most political science research papers are, therefore, analytical.*

Let us start with the basics. Political scientists are most often engaged in three activities. They collect data, analyze it, and interpret it. This sounds simple, and as a linear process, it is. A linear process is one in which the steps simply follow each other, one at a time. The comparative politics process, however, is more complex than that. Each of the three steps is in tension with and constantly affects the other two. For example, as you analyze the data, you find that you do not have enough information, and so you go back and collect more. Again, as you interpret the data you find that your analysis is deficient, so you go back and employ additional statistical techniques, and so on. This complex process is sometimes referred to as being recursive because as opposed to being a simple linear progression from one step to another, it involves complex interactions among the three basic steps in the process. The political science process, then, might be portrayed like this:

collect data

$\downarrow\uparrow$ $\downarrow\uparrow$

interpret data ⬑ analyze data

We may say, then, that political science can be described as a recursive process of data collection, analysis, and interpretation that helps us understand a wide array of political, social, economic, cultural events, practices, and institutions.

16.2   STEPS IN WRITING ANALYTICAL PAPERS

You will find it most helpful to go to your college library and browse some articles in political science journals, before your start your paper. You will find a list of these journals in pages 193–196 of this manual. Writing your cross-sectional study will require completing the following seven steps.

1. Select or identify the variables you wish to study;
2. Conduct a literature review;
3. Formulate a research question and a hypothesis;
4. Construct or adopt a methodology;
5. Data collection;

6. Data analysis; and
7. Compose the narrative (thesis).

Step 1. Select or Identify the Variables You Wish to Study

If, for example, you choose to evaluate the effectiveness of campaign advertising in Kansas in the 2008 presidential election, your independent variable (see Chapter 4 of this manual) may be the number of campaign ads placed for respective candidates, and your dependent variable may be the percentage of votes cast for each candidate.

Step 2. Conduct a Literature Review

Please see Chapter 9 of this manual for some general directions on how to conduct a literature review. Remember that you are not just looking for information about the variables you have selected, and on methodologies that have been employed to study those variables. Among the more promising sources for good articles will be JSTOR and EBSCOHOST.

Step 3. Formulate a Research Question and a Hypothesis

A research question is a clear statement of what you are attempting to find out in your study. Using our example, a research question for our paper might be:

> "How did the number of campaign ads affect the presidential vote in Kansas in 2008?"

An hypothesis is an education guess about what your research will ultimately discover. Making such guesses helps you to focus more clearly on what you want to discover. An hypothesis for our example paper might be:

> "In 2008 the winner of the presidential vote was the person who provided the most campaign ads."

Step 4. Construct or Adopt a Methodology

This may be the most difficult part of your study. You may find a methodology that has been used in a study similar to the one you are conducting. You may want to review the quantitative research methodologies and the approaches to the study of politics that are described in Chapters 3 and 4 of this manual.

Step 5. Data Collection

Next, you will need to identify sources of data. The sources listed in the "Literature Review" section (Step 2) will probably be a good place to start. By concentrating on academic articles and books and government agencies, you will be able to compile information that is relevant to the study you are undertaking. Do not hesitate to ask your instructor about the quality of information you get and the sources of new information. Much of the information that you find can be compiled as charts and tables (see Chapter 7 of this manual), thus placing paragraphs that explain the data in appropriate places before and after the charts and tables.

Step 6. Data Analysis

Your data analysis will be as sophisticated as your knowledge of statistics. You will find it most helpful to find several recent academic studies similar to the one you are conducting, examine the data analysis methods they employ, and adapt the method you find most appropriate.

Step 7. Compose the Narrative (Thesis)

The narrative of your paper will be composed of three elements: (1) findings, (2) interpretation of findings, and (3) areas for further research. In the findings section of your narrative you will explain as clearly as possible, with as little interpretation as possible, exactly what the data tells you and what it does not tell you with respect to the research question you are trying to answer. In this section, state clearly what the data *says*, not what it *means*.

The *interpretation* section of the paper is the most important and the trickiest part of your study. Your paper will be only as valuable as the validity of the conclusions you draw. Be modest. DO NOT draw conclusions that are not warranted by the data. Try to be as precise as you can in stating the conclusions you have drawn from the information you have found.

In your final section, areas for further research, you may be more expansive than in your interpretation section. Here you can speculate on what you might find if you had more or better data. Here you can suggest new research questions and areas of study that may be helpful in understanding your selected subject matter in the future.

CHAPTER

17

COMPARING GOVERNMENTS

17.1   HOW GOVERNMENTS ARE COMPARED

You are off to a good start. You have made a very wise choice: you have opted to study comparative politics, and there are few more challenging, rewarding, and beneficial subjects in any discipline. Comparative politics is the most promising key to answering some of the most pressing questions in the world today. What kind of government is most likely to survive the violence in Iraq? How can the people of Afghanistan, who have had little experience with democracy, come to appreciate it, and apply it to their own benefit, and help it withstand the brutal totalitarian violence of the Taliban? You will grapple with these and many similar vital questions in the course of your studies.

As you are writing a paper for a course in comparative politics your text has already introduced you to what this fascinating subdiscipline is all about, and so this chapter will help you apply what you know so far to making the decisions that will produce a meaningful and beneficial paper.

As mentioned in Chapter 16, let us start with the basics. Most simply, what do comparative political scientists do? Three things. They collect data, analyze it, and interpret it. This sounds simple, and as a linear process, it is. A linear process is one in which the steps simply follow each other, one at a time. The comparative politics process, however, is more complex than that. Each of the three steps is in tension with each other and constantly affects the other two. For example, as you analyze the data you find that you do not have enough information, and so you go back and collect more. Again, as you interpret the data you find that your analysis is deficient, so you go back and employ additional statistical techniques, and so on. This complex process is sometimes referred to as being recursive because as opposed to being a simple linear progression from one step to another, it involves complex interactions among the three basic steps in the process. The comparative political science process, then, might be portrayed like this:

collect data

↓↑   ↓↑

interpret data ⇄ analyze data

We may say, then, that comparative politics can be described as a recursive process of data collection, analysis, and interpretation that helps us understand a wide array of political, social, economic, cultural events, practices, and other phenomena around the world.

To provide some context for the task you are about to undertake, it may be helpful to know that on the professional level, there are two main groups of comparative politics professionals: practitioners and academics. Literally hundreds of people in the United States alone—employees of the Departments of State and Commerce, the intelligence agencies, and the military to name a few—are active practitioners of the profession of comparative politics. They practice their profession in two ways. First, they produce data about elections, parties, movements, and many other phenomena that they and others can analyze. Second, they continually read studies written by other practitioners and academics, looking for information that helps them solve the problems they are working on. They then apply this information in actual situations, such as in negotiating, tracking political movements, or in moderating disputes among other nations.

Academic comparativists are found in universities and research institutes. What is the cutting edge of academic comparative political science? Work in recent decades has become increasingly theoretical and quantitative. In a recent overview of his subdiscipline, Stanford political scientist David D. Laitin describes the recent emergence of a "new consensus" among academic comparativists that embraces a "tripartite methodology," which explains how they collect, analyze, and interpret data.

The first part of the tripartite methodology employs a variety of cross-sectional and diachronic statistical techniques. Cross-sectional studies select certain aspects of politics, such as the structure of nations' political economy, the variety and ideologies of political parties, or the concentrations of power among elites, and then compare how these factors affect political developments from one nation to another. Cross-sectional studies often *compare large numbers of nations.* Diachronic studies examine how things such as methods of building consensus, techniques of conflict resolution, or concentrations of power develop *over specific periods of time.*

The second of the three methods is formalization, which means the development and testing of formal models. In political science, a formal model is not Christie Brinkley in a tuxedo. If that was the case, there would be a lot more political scientists. Formal models are complex statistical methodologies, some borrowed and modified from the study of econometrics, that explain or predict the effects that certain variables (such as substantial immigration, recession, or expansion of the right to vote) have on political systems.

The third component of Laitin's tripartite methodology is narrative. Narratives, most simply, are stories. In comparative political science, however, the word narrative has a more specific meaning. Political science narratives are attempts to explain what the data means, and what conclusions can be drawn from it. Are there anomalies (discrepancies or contradictions) in the statistical results? What can explain them? Does the data support or refute particular current theories about how people interact in specific political situations? These questions and many more are addressed in comparative political narratives.

17.2 ELEMENTS OF COMPARATIVE POLITICS PAPERS

As in other subdisciplines of political science, there is no one formula for comparative politics papers. Your instructor may provide detailed instructions for your assignment that will help you meet her or his particular objectives. *Be sure to ask your instructor if the paper assignments described in this chapter are acceptable for your course.*

In this chapter, you will find directions for how to write an elementary cross-sectional paper. It will be a cross-sectional study because you will select certain aspects of politics, and then compare how these factors affect phenomena in more than one country. It will be elementary because (1) you will not be collecting original data yourself, but you will be using data collected by other people, (2) you will not construct or apply formal models, and (3) the statistics you employ will be relatively simple. The purpose of your paper will be to compare the relationship between two political variables as these two variables interact with each other within the three different countries. The information below will explain how to select appropriate variables and countries for your study.

Before You Begin

You will find it most helpful to go to your college library and browse some articles in comparative politics journals before your start your paper. On pages 193–196 of this manual you will find a list of more than 200 academic journals that publish articles in political science, including journals specifically dedicated to comparative studies, such as *Comparative Political Studies, Comparative Politics, Comparative Strategy,* and *Comparative Studies in Society and History.* You will also find numerous journals that specialize in area studies, such as *Asian Affairs, Atlantic Community Quarterly, East European Quarterly, Modern China,* and *Pacific Affairs.* By browsing recent articles, you will quickly gain a better understanding of what comparative political scientist study is, the methods they use, and what they have learned. You can also find many, if not most, of these journals online through your college library Internet portal.

Steps in Writing an Elementary Cross-sectional Comparative Politics Paper

Writing your cross-sectional study will require completing the following eight steps.

1. Select the variables you wish to study;
2. Select the countries you wish to study;
3. Conduct a literature review;
4. Formulate a research question and a hypothesis;
5. Adopt or construct a methodology;
6. Data collection;
7. Data analysis; and
8. Compose the narrative (thesis).

Step 1. Select the Variables You Wish to Study

You have a wide array of variables to choose from and it is always a good idea to consult with your instructor for assistance in selecting and defining variables in a manner most likely to produce interesting and significant results. Although an exhaustive list would be far more extensive, you may find the Chart of Comparative Political Phenomena (below) to be useful. Here you will find several different categories of variables that comparative political scientists often study and examples of variables within each category that you might find interesting.

Chart of Political Phenomena

CATEGORY	VARIABLE	MEANING OR EFFECT OF VARIABLE
Power	Possession and exclusion	Who wields power, and who is excluded from it?
	Concentration and dispersion	To what extent is power concentrated and dispersed?
	Legitimacy and corruption	To what extent is existing power perceived to be legitimate or corrupt?
Nation States	Nationalism	How strong is national sentiment overall? In what groups is it strongest and weakest?
	Cohesion	To what extent do the political, social, and economic structures and processes result in a strong, cohesive state?
	Environment	How do the state's neighbors, region, and the international system as a whole affect its vitality?
Institutions	Legislative	Who makes the laws, and what are the processes by which the laws are made?
	Executive	Who carries out the laws? How effective is the execution of the laws?
	Judicial	Who interprets the laws? What role does the judiciary play in the politics of the state?

(continued)

CATEGORY	VARIABLE	MEANING OR EFFECT OF VARIABLE
	Bureaucracy	How is the bureaucracy organized and led? How effective and efficient is it? How corrupt is it?
	Military	How large, strong, well-armed, and effective is the military? What political role does it play?
	Mediating	What institutions (such as churches, social clubs, labor and unions) play a mediating role between the government and the people? How effective are they?
Democracy	Constitution and structure	How democratic are the constitution and the legally constituted structures and procedures of government?
	Processes	To what extent do processes designed to provide democracy actually succeed in doing so?
	Values	How much and what kinds of freedom, justice, and equality actually exist in the society?
Participation	Election process	How numerous, frequent, and open are the elections?
	Election participation	How many people participate? What groups participate more than others?
	Political parties	How many political parties exist, and what ideological, ethnic, and economic interests do they represent?
	Interest groups	What are the major influential interest groups, and what interests do they represent?
	Movements	Do any influential social or political movements exist? What effect do they have?
	Dissent	To what extent is dissent tolerated? How much dissent is currently expressed and how is it expressed?
Political Culture	Traditions	What are the society's major politically relevant traditions and customs?
	Ethnicity	What are the major ethnic groups, and what role do they play in politics?
	Religion	What are the major religions, and what role do they play in politics?
	Education	What is the extent and quality of education? How does the educational system affect politics?
Ideology	Liberalism	How are liberals and conservatives defined within this society? How strong is each group?
	Socialism	To what extent does the government own the country's means of production? How influential are socialist parties and groups?
	Authoritarian and totalitarian	To what extent do authoritarian and/or totalitarian ideologies influence power structures and policies?
Economy	Industry	What is the extent, content, and influence of the country's industrial base?
	Commerce	What is the extent, content, and influence of the country's commercial enterprises?

CATEGORY	VARIABLE	MEANING OR EFFECT OF VARIABLE
	Resources	What are the country's major resources? Who controls them?
	Development	What is the overall status of the country's economic development?

From the above list (or select other variables in consultation with your instructor) select two variables that you believe might affect each other. For example, you might be interested in studying the relationship between religion and political cohesion. You may want to determine the extent to which certain religions contribute to or detract from the political cohesion of different societies.

Step 2. Select the Countries You Wish to Study

The second step is to select three countries in which to examine the relationship between the two variables you have selected. For the purposes of this class assignment you will probably find it is a good idea to select three countries that are geographically similar (contiguous if possible) and that are in at least one variable. For example, if the two variables are religion and cohesion, you may want to pick three countries that are all predominantly Muslim, and all in the Middle East. By doing this you will reduce the number of intervening variables that may affect your result.

Step 3. Conduct a Literature Review

See Chapter 9 of this manual for some general directions on how to conduct a literature review. Remember that you are not just looking for information about the countries and variables you are studying, but you are also looking for information on the variables you have selected, and on methodologies that have been employed to study those variables. So, following the example we are using, in this case, you will be particularly interested in finding information on (1) the relationship between religion and social cohesion in general, (2) the relationship between Islam and cohesion in particular, and (3) methodologies that have been used to determine the relationship between religion and cohesion.

Although you may find some good sources using Google or Yahoo, you will find far better quality of information about substantive topics such as methodologies and religions by using the academic databases subscribed to by your university or college. Among the more promising of these will be JSTOR and EBSCOHOST. For a wide variety of information about the countries you will be studying, a good place to start is with the following:

U.S. Department of State—Countries—Background Notes:
   http://www.state.gov/r/pa/ei/bgn/

Central Intelligence Agency—The World Fact Book:
   https://www.cia.gov/cia/publications/factbook/index.html

United Nations—InfoNation:
   http://www.un.org/Pubs/CyberSchoolBus/infonation3/menu/
   advanced.asp

Step 4. Formulate a Research Question and a Hypothesis

Comparative politics text provides you with information about research questions and hypotheses in comparative politics, so we shall not repeat that information here. It is sufficient for our purposes to remember that a research question is a clear statement of what you are attempting to find out in your study. Using our example, a research question for our paper might be:

> "How does the religion of Islam affect the internal political cohesion of Egypt, Libya, and Tunisia?"

A hypothesis is an educated guess about what your research will ultimately discover. Making such guesses helps you focus more clearly on what you want to discover. A hypothesis for our example paper might be:

> "While moderate Muslims contribute to political cohesion, radical Muslims detract from it."

Step 5. Construct or Adopt a Methodology

This may be the most difficult part of your study. First, you will have to identify what you intend to measure. In this case of our example, you will have to define "political cohesion," in such a way that you can identify quantifiable measures of it. One such measure might be "number and extent of incidents of political violence." Another might be "strength and number of separatist movements." You should identify at least three to six measures of each variable.

Step 6. Data Collection

Next, you will need to identify sources of data, as mentioned in Chapter 16. The sources listed in the "Literature Review" section (Step 3) will probably be a good place to start. By concentrating on academic articles and books and government agencies you will be able to compile information that is relevant to the study you are undertaking. Do not hesitate to ask your instructor about the quality of information you are getting and sources of new information. Much of the information that you find can be compiled as charts and tables (see Chapter 7 of this Manual), thus placing paragraphs that explain the data in appropriate places before and after the charts and tables.

Step 7. Data Analysis

Your data analysis will be as sophisticated as your knowledge of statistics. At most, you will be able to compile charts that simply display in visible form comparisons of the countries you are studying. See, for example, the following chart.

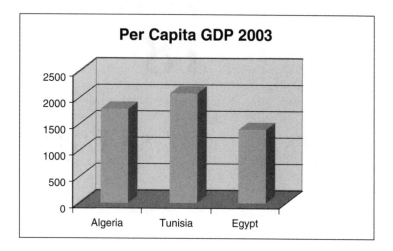

You will find it most helpful to find several recent academic studies similar to the one you are conducting, examine the data analysis methods they employ, and adapt the method you find most appropriate.

Step 8. Compose the Narrative (Thesis)

As mentioned in Chapter 16, the narrative of your paper will be composed of three elements: (1) findings, (2) interpretation of findings, and (3) areas for further research. In the findings section of your narrative, you will explain as clearly as possible, with as little interpretation as possible, exactly what the data tells you and what it does not tell you with respect to the research question you are trying to answer. In this section, state clearly what the data *says*, not what it *means*.

The *interpretation* section of the paper is the most important and the trickiest part of your study. Your paper will be only as valuable as the validity of the conclusions you draw. Be modest. DO NOT draw conclusions that are not warranted by the data. Try to be as precise as you can in stating the conclusions you have drawn from the information you have found.

In your final section, areas for further research you may be more expansive than in your interpretation section. Here you can speculate on what you might find if you had more or better data. Here you can suggest new research questions and areas of study that may be helpful in understanding your selected subject matter in the future.

18

POLICY ANALYSIS PAPERS

18.1 THE BASICS OF POLICY ANALYSIS

What is Policy Analysis?

Policy analysis is the examination of the components of a decision in order to enable one to act according to a set principle or rule in a given set of circumstances (a policy). This analysis is conducted at the local, state, national, and international levels of government. The most publicized reports tend, naturally, to be those of presidential commissions. Presidents create commissions to do policy analysis. This means that the president appoints a group of people to study possible government policies on a certain topic or problem, and report their findings and recommendations.

Policy Analysis in Action: The Brownlow Commission Report (1937)

Numerous presidential commissions have studied a wide range of subjects, including crime, poverty, and violence. One of the most famous, and one that had far-reaching effects, was the President's Committee on Administrative Management of 1937, known as the Brownlow Commission for one of its three primary authors, Louis Brownlow.

President Roosevelt appointed the Brownlow Commission to find ways to make the operation of the bureaucracy more efficient. The commission found "in the American government at the present time that the effectiveness of the chief executive is limited and restricted; . . . that the work of the executive branch is badly organized; that the managerial agencies are weak and out of date." In response to these problems, the commission made the following five recommendations to the president:

1. To deal with the greatly increased duties of executive management falling on the president, the White House staff should be expanded.

2. The managerial agencies of the government, particularly those dealing with the budget, efficiency research, personnel, and planning, should be greatly strengthened and developed as arms of the chief executive.

3. The merit system should be extended upward, outward, and downward to cover all nonpolicy-determining posts; the civil service system should be reorganized; and opportunities established for a career system attractive to the best talent in the nation.

4. The whole executive branch of the government should be overhauled and the present 100 agencies reorganized under a few large departments in which every executive activity would find its place.

5. The fiscal system should be extensively revised in light of the best governmental and private practice, particularly with reference to financial records, audit, and accountability of the executive to Congress. (President's Committee 1937, 4)

18.2 POLICY ANALYSIS RESEARCH PROPOSALS

This chapter includes directions for two types of paper assignments: a policy analysis research *proposal* and a policy analysis research *paper*. The proposal is a description of the research that will be conducted during the writing of the research paper. This assignment is included here because students who hope to become policy analysts will find that, when working in or consulting to government organizations, they will almost always be required to submit a proposal explaining and justifying the research that they expect to do before they are commissioned or funded to conduct the research itself.

The Purpose of Research Proposals

Research proposals are sales jobs. Their purpose is to "sell" the belief that a research study needs to be done. As part of this "selling" process, you will have to submit a policy analysis research proposal designed to accomplish the following seven tasks:

1. Prove that the study is necessary.
2. Describe the objectives of the study.
3. Explain how the study will be done.
4. Describe the resources (time, people, equipment, facilities, etc.) that will be needed to do the job.
5. Construct a schedule that states when the project will begin and end, and gives important dates in between.
6. Prepare a project budget that specifies the financial costs and the amount to be billed (if any) to the government agency.
7. Carefully define what the research project will produce, what kind of study will be conducted, how long it will be, and what it will contain.

The Content of Research Proposals

An Overview

In form, policy analysis research proposals contain the following four parts:

1. Title page (You may follow the format prescribed by your instructor or institution, or use the format shown in Chapter 7.)
2. Outline page (This is very important and must be done correctly. For directions and an example, see Chapter 7.)
3. Text
4. Reference page

An outline of the content of policy analysis proposals appears below:

I. Need for a policy analysis study
   A. An initial description of the current policy problem
      1. A definition of the deficiency in or problem with the current policy
      2. A brief history of the policy problem
      3. The legal framework and institutional setting of the policy problem
      4. The character of the policy problem, including its size, extent, and importance
   B. Policy analysis imperatives
II. Objectives of the proposed policy analysis study
   A. Clarification of the current policy problem
      1. A better problem definition
      2. A better estimate of the quality and quantity of the problem
      3. A more accurate projection of policy problem development
   B. An accurate evaluation of current relevant public policy
      1. An evaluation of the primary current applicable public policy
         a. A clarification of the primary policy
         b. A clarification of the legal foundation of the primary policy
         c. A clarification of the historical development of the policy
         d. A clarification of the environment of the policy
         e. A description of current policy implementation
         f. An evaluation of the effectiveness and efficiency of the policy
      2. An evaluation of secondary applicable public policies
   C. An evaluation of alternatives to present policies
      1. A presentation of possible alternative policies
      2. A comparative evaluation of the expected costs and benefits of the present and alternative policies
III. Methodology of the proposed policy analysis study
   A. Project management methods to be used
   B. Research methods to be used
   C. Data analysis methods to be used
IV. Resources necessary to conduct the study
   A. Material resources
   B. Human resources
   C. Financial resources

18.3 POLICY ANALYSIS PAPERS

Definition: A Policy Analysis Paper

A policy analysis paper evaluates a decision by reviewing current and potential government policies. It is a document written to help decision makers select the best policy for solving a particular problem. In writing a policy analysis paper, you should:

1. Select and clearly define a specific government policy;
2. Carefully define the social, governmental, economic, or other problem which the policy is designed to solve;
3. Describe the economic, social, and political environments in which the problem arose and in which the existing policy for solving the problem was developed;
4. Evaluate the effectiveness of the current policy or lack of policy in dealing with the problem;
5. Identify alternative policies that could be adopted to solve the selected problem, and estimate the economic, social, environmental, and political costs and benefits of each alternative; and
6. Provide a summary comparison of all policies examined.

Policy analysis papers are written every day at all levels of government. Public officials are constantly challenged to initiate new policies or change old ones. If they have a current formal policy at all, they want to know how effective it is. They then want to know what options are available to them, what changes they might make to improve current policy, and what the consequences of those changes will be. Policies are reviewed under a number of circumstances. Policy analyses are sometimes conducted as part of the normal agency budgeting processes. They help decision makers decide what policies should be continued or discontinued. They may be very narrow in scope, such as deciding the hours of operation of facilities at city parks. Or they may be very broad, such as deciding how the nation will provide health care or defense for its citizens.

The Purpose of Policy Analysis Papers

Successful policy analysis papers all share the same general purpose: to inform policymakers about how public policy in a specific area may be improved.

Elected officials are employed full time in the business of making public policy. Legislators at the state and national levels hire staff people who continually investigate public policy issues and seek ways to improve legislated policy. At the national level, the Congressional Research Service continually finds information for representatives and senators. Each committee of Congress employs staff members who help it review current laws and define options for making new ones. State legislatures also employ their own research agencies and committee staff. Legislators and other policymakers are also given policy information by hundreds of public interest groups and research organizations.

A policy analysis paper, like a position paper, is an entirely practical exercise. It is neither theoretical nor general. Its objective is to identify and evaluate the policy options that are available for a specific topic.

The Contents of a Policy Analysis Paper

Summary of the Contents

Policy analysis papers contain six basic elements:

1. Title page
2. Executive summary
3. Table of contents, including a list of tables and illustrations
4. Text (or body)
5. References to sources of information
6. Appendixes

Parameters of the Text

Ask your instructor for the number of pages required for the policy analysis paper assigned for your course. Such papers at the undergraduate level often range from twenty to fifty pages (double-spaced, typed) in length.

Two general rules govern the amount of information presented in the body of the paper. First, content must be adequate to make a good policy evaluation. All the facts necessary to understand the significant strengths and weaknesses of a policy and its alternatives must be included. If your paper omits a fact that is critical to the decision, a poor decision will likely be made.

Never omit important facts merely because they tend to support a perspective other than your own. It is your responsibility to present the facts as clearly as possible, not to bias the evaluation in a particular direction.

The second guideline for determining the length of a policy analysis paper is to omit extraneous material. Include only the information that is helpful in making the particular decision at hand.

The Format of a Policy Analysis Paper

Title Page

The title page for a policy analysis paper should follow the format provided in Chapter 7.

Executive Summary

A one-page, single-spaced executive summary immediately follows the title page. An executive summary is composed of carefully written sentences expressing the central concepts that are more fully explained in the text of the paper. The purpose of the summary is to allow the decision maker to understand, as quickly as possible, the major considerations to be discussed. Each statement must be clearly defined and carefully prepared. The decision maker should be able to get a clear and thorough overview of the entire policy problem and the value and costs of available policy options by reading nothing but the one-page summary.

Table of Contents

The table of contents of a policy analysis paper must follow the organization of the paper's text and should conform to the format shown in Chapter 7.

Text

A policy analysis paper should follow the outline shown below:

I. Description of the policy currently in force
   A. A clear, concise statement of the policy currently in force
   B. A brief history of the policy currently in force
   C. A description of the problem the current policy was aimed at resolving, including an estimate of its extent and importance
II. Environments of the policy currently in force
   A. A description of the social and physical factors affecting the origin, development, and implementation of the current policy
   B. A description of the economic factors affecting the origin, development, and implementation of the current policy
   C. A description of the political factors affecting the origin, development, and implementation of the current policy
III. Effectiveness and efficiency of the current policy
   A. How well the existing policy does what it was designed to do
   B. How well the policy performs in relation to the effort and resources committed to it
IV. Policy alternatives
   A. Possible alterations of the present policy, with the estimated costs and benefits of each
   B. Alternatives to the present policy, with the estimated costs and benefits of each
V. Summary comparison of policy options

Each of the policy analysis components listed in the outline above is described in detail in most public policy analysis text books. Be sure to discuss the outline with your instructor to make ensure that you understand what each entails.

References

All sources of information in a policy analysis paper must be properly cited, following the directions in Chapter 8.

Appendixes

Appendixes can provide the reader of policy analysis papers with information that supplements the important facts contained in the text. For many local development and public works projects, a map and a diagram are often very helpful appendixes. You should attach them to the end of the paper, after the reference page. You should not append entire government reports, journal articles, or other publications, but selected charts, graphs, or other pages may be included. The source of the information should always be evident on the appended pages.

CHAPTER

19

AMICUS CURIAE BRIEFS

19.1   HOW TO WRITE AMICUS CURIAE BRIEFS FOR THE U.S. SUPREME COURT

When people are parties to disputes before the U.S. Supreme Court, the attorneys representing each side prepare written documents called *briefs on the merit*, which explain the nature of the dispute and present an argument for the side the attorney represents. The justices read the briefs, hear oral arguments, hold conferences to discuss the case, and then write opinions to announce both the Court's decision and the views of justices who disagree in whole or in part with that decision. Cases that come before the Supreme Court are usually important to many people who are not actually parties to the specific case being presented because the Court's decisions contain principles and guidelines that all lower courts must follow in deciding similar cases. *Roe v. Wade*, for example, did not become famous because it allowed one person to have an abortion free from the constraints of the laws of Texas, but because it set forth the principle that state law may not restrict abortions in the first three months of pregnancy to protect the fetus.

Because Supreme Court cases are important to people other than those directly involved in the case, sometimes groups and individuals outside the proceedings of a specific case want their views on cases to be heard by the Court before it makes a decision. It is not proper, however, to go to the justices directly and try to influence them to decide a case in a particular way. Influencing government officials directly through visits, phone calls, or letters is called *lobbying*. When people want to influence the way Congress handles a law, they lobby their representatives by writing letters or talking to them personally. The lobbying of Supreme Court justices, however, is considered improper because the Court is supposed to make decisions based on the content of the Constitution and not on the political preferences of one or more groups in society.

There is a way, however, for outsiders to submit their views to the Supreme Court. The Court invites interested parties, most often organizations, to submit briefs of *amicus curiae* (*amicus curiae* means "friend of the court"). A party that submits an amicus curiae brief becomes a friend of the Court by giving it information that it may find helpful in making a decision. As the Court explains, "an amicus curiae brief which brings relevant matter to the attention of the Court that has not already been brought to its attention by the parties is of considerable help to the Court. An amicus brief which does not serve this purpose simply burdens the staff and facilities of the Court and its filing is not favored" (*Rules of the Supreme Court* 1990, 45).

In the summer of 1971, the Supreme Court began its review of *Roe v. Wade*. Roe, who was arrested for violating a Texas law forbidding abortions except to save the mother's life, argued that the Texas law was a governmental violation of the right to privacy guaranteed to her by the Constitution. Many national organizations filed amicus curiae briefs in this case. Acting as attorneys on behalf of the National Legal Program on Health Problems of the Poor, the National Welfare Rights Organization, and the American Public Health Association, Alan F. Charles and Susan Grossman Alexander filed a brief of amici curiae (*amici* is the plural of *amicus*) in support of the right to an abortion. The Summary of Argument that Charles and Alexander included in that brief appears below as an example to assist you in writing your own amicus curiae brief:

Brief of Amici Curiae

Summary of Argument

A woman who seeks an abortion is asserting certain fundamental rights which are protected by the Constitution. Among these are rights to marital and family privacy, to individual and sexual privacy; in sum, the right to choose whether to bear children or not. These rights are abridged by the state's restriction of abortions to saving the mother's life. To justify such an abridgment, the state must demonstrate a compelling interest; no such compelling interest exists to save the Texas abortion law.

The state's interest in protecting the woman's health no longer supports restrictions on abortion. Medical science now performs abortions more safely than it brings a woman through pregnancy and childbirth. Any state interest in discouraging non-marital sexual relationships must be served by laws penalizing these relationships, and not by an indirect, overly broad prohibition on abortion. There is no evidence, in any case, that abortion laws deter such relationships. The state's purported interest in expanding the population lacks any viability today; government policy in every other area is now squarely against it. And any purported interest in permitting all embryos to develop and be born is not supported anywhere in the Constitution or any other body of law.

Because of its restriction, the Texas statute denies to poor and non-white women equal access to legal abortions. It is an undeniable fact that abortion in Texas and in virtually every other state in the United States is far more readily available to the white, paying patient than to the poor and non-white. Studies by physicians, sociologists, public health experts, and lawyers all reach this same conclusion. The reasons for it are not purely economic, i.e., that because abortion is an expensive commodity to obtain on the medical marketplace, it is therefore to be expected that the rich will have greater access to it. It is also because in the facilities which provide health care to the poor, abortion is simply not made available to the poor and non-white on the same conditions as it is to paying patients. As a result, the poor resort to criminal abortion, with its high toll of infection and death, in vastly disproportionate numbers.

Largely to blame are restrictive abortion laws, such as the Texas statute, in which the legislature has made lay judgments about what conditions must exist before abortions can be legally performed, and has delegated the authority to make such decisions to physicians and committees of physicians with the threat of felony punishment if they err on the side of granting an abortion. Unlike more privileged women, poor and non-white women are unable to shop for physicians and hospitals sympathetic to their applications, cannot afford the necessary consultations to establish that their conditions qualify them for treatment, and must largely depend upon public hospitals and physicians with whom they have no personal relationship, and who operate under the government's eye, for the relief they seek. The resulting discrimination is easily demonstrated.

Restricting abortion only to treatment necessary to save the mother's life irrationally excludes those classes of women for whom abortion is necessary for the protection of health, or because they will bear a deformed fetus, or who are pregnant due to sexual assault, or who are financially, socially or emotionally incapable of raising a child or whose families would be seriously disrupted by the birth of another child, and these exclusions bear most heavily on the poor and non-white.

In the absence of any compelling state interest, the harsh discriminatory effect on the poor and the non-white resulting from the operation of the Texas abortion law denies to poor and non-white women the equal protection of the laws in violation of the Equal Protection Clause of the Fourteenth Amendment. (Charles 1971, 5–7)

Scope and Purpose

Your task in this chapter is to write an amicus curiae brief for a case that is being considered by the U.S. Supreme Court. You will write your own brief, making your own argument about how the case should be decided. Of course, you do not have to be entirely original. You will examine the arguments used in others' briefs, add new arguments of your own, and write the entire brief in your own carefully chosen words. In completing this assignment, you will also be meeting five more personal learning objectives:

1. You will become familiar with the source, form, and content of legal documents.
2. You will become acquainted with the procedures of brief preparation.
3. You will become familiar with the details of a selected case currently before the Court. As you follow the news reports on this case, you will eventually learn the Court's decision.

4. You will come to understand a Supreme Court case in sufficient depth to be able to integrate the arguments of actual amicus curiae briefs into your own argument.
5. You will learn how to write a clear, logical, effective, and persuasive argument.

Remember that your goal is to *persuade* the Supreme Court to make a certain decision. Before you begin, reread Part Two of this manual, especially the sections on how to write clearly and persuasively.

General Considerations and Format

Briefs provide the Supreme Court with the facts in a particular case and make arguments about how the case should be decided. The *Rules* of the Court state that "a brief must be compact, logically arranged with proper headings, concise, and free from burdensome, irrelevant, immaterial, and scandalous matter. A brief not complying with this paragraph may be disregarded and stricken by the Court" (1990, 28). The Court also requires those who submit an amicus curiae brief to provide a statement of permission, which may be (1) the evidence that either permission to submit the amicus curiae brief has been granted by both parties to the dispute or the permission of both parties has not been granted and (2) the reason for the denial and the reason that the Court should consider the amicus brief in spite of the absence of permission of the parties.

Of course, as a student writing an amicus brief for a class in political science, you will not actually submit your brief to the Supreme Court, so you need not write a statement of permission. Information on such statements is provided here so that you will understand their purpose when you encounter them in your research.

Ask your instructor about the page limit for your assignment. The Supreme Court's limit for the actual text of amicus curiae briefs (exclusive of the questions-presented page, subject index, table of authorities, and appendix) is thirty pages, single-spaced. Your brief, however, will be double-spaced for the convenience of your instructor and as few as fifteen pages, depending on your instructor's requirements. Because a central purpose of this assignment is for you to understand the arguments to be made in the case, your brief will be shorter than actual amicus briefs submitted to the Court, which require much more detail than you will need to know. As you read actual amicus briefs, use your own judgment to select the material that you believe is most important for the Court to understand, and include this information, in your own words, in your brief.

The proper presentation of briefs is essential. Briefs to the Supreme Court are normally professionally printed, and the *Rules* of the Court include directions for this process. The Court does, however, also accept typed briefs, and your amicus curiae brief will conform to the Court's instructions for typed briefs in most respects, with modifications to allow your instructor sufficient space to write comments. You must therefore prepare your amicus curiae brief according to the following specifications:

• Black type on white paper, 8½ by 11 inches, double-spaced, printed on one side only;

- Text and footnotes in 12-point type;
- A typeface as close as possible to that used in actual briefs;
- Margins of 1½ inches on the left and 1 inch on all other sides;
- A binding that meets your instructor's requirements.

You will submit one copy of your brief to your instructor. It is always wise, when submitting any paper, to retain a copy for yourself in case the original is lost. (The Supreme Court requires that sixty copies of a brief be submitted for a case coming to it directly under its original jurisdiction, and forty copies for a case coming to it under appellate jurisdiction from lower courts.)

19.2 RESOURCES FOR WRITING AN AMICUS CURIAE BRIEF

You will find resources for amicus curiae briefs in the library and on the Internet. When you conduct your research in the library, you will need access to two periodicals that may be found in some college, and in most, if not in all law school libraries:

- *Preview of United States Supreme Court Cases,* a publication of the American Bar Association's Public Education Division;
- *The United States Law Week,* published by The Bureau of National Affairs, Inc. If they are not available in your college library, you may request copies through interlibrary loan, or ask your instructor to request that the department or library order them.

Internet Resources for Writing an Amicus Curiae Brief

Chapter 11 provides an introduction to political science resources on the Internet. If you are not familiar with the Internet or with political science resources on the Internet, you may need to read the directions in Chapter 11 before proceeding. The Internet provides a wealth of material related to constitutional and international law.

To find cases on the Internet that are currently before the Supreme Court, go to Cornell University's Legal Information Institute (LLI) (http://supct.law.cornell.edu/supct/). On this page, you will find a link entitled "Cases Argued This Term." Peruse the links for current cases, selecting the one that most interests you.

Steps in Writing an Amicus Curiae Brief

Select a Case and a Side

Using the most recent issues of *Preview of United States Supreme Court Cases, The United States Law Week,* or the appropriate Internet sites, select a case and decide which side of the argument you support. The case you choose must fulfill the following two requirements:

1. It must be of personal interest to you.
2. It must be a case that has not yet been decided by the Court.

Obtain Copies of the Amicus Briefs

Your next step is to obtain copies of the briefs on the merits of the appellant and the respondent as well as any available amicus briefs on the side of the case that you support and one amicus brief on the opposing side. There are three ways to obtain amicus briefs. You may obtain them by going in person to the Office of the Clerk of the Supreme Court of the United States at the following address, where you will be allowed to photocopy the briefs (the clerk will not send copies of the briefs in the mail):

Office of the Clerk
Supreme Court of the United States
1 First Street, NE
Washington, DC 20543
Telephone: (202) 479-3000

The second way to obtain the briefs is to request them from the attorneys of record for the organizations that are filing the briefs; *Preview of United States Supreme Court Cases* lists their names, addresses, and telephone numbers. *The United States Law Week* provides this information for some cases, but not for all. If this information is not given in either of these publications, you may request it by mail or telephone from the Clerk of the Supreme Court at the above address. Be sure to provide the name and the docket number of the case in which you are interested.

When you contact the attorneys of record, tell them the following:

your name and address;
the college or university you attend;
the nature of your assignment;
the name and docket number of the case in which you are interested;
your interest in obtaining a copy of their amicus brief; and
your appreciation of their assistance.

The third way to obtain the briefs, when they are available, is to print or download them from the appropriate sources on the Internet.

Write an Argument Outline

Read the arguments in the briefs you have collected, and then construct an outline of an argument that makes the points you believe are most important. Your outline should normally have from two to six main points. Follow the directions for constructing outlines that you find in Chapter 5 of this manual, and read Chapter 9 very carefully. Submit your outline to your instructor for advice before continuing.

Write the Argument

Following the outline you have constructed, write your argument. Your writing needs to be clear and sharply focused. Follow the directions for writing in the first part of this manual. The first sentence of each paragraph should state its main point.

The *Rules* of the Court state that the argument of a brief must exhibit "clearly the points of fact and of law being presented and [cite] the authorities and statutes relied upon"; it should also be "as short as possible" (1990, 27). In addition to conforming to page limitations set by your instructor, the length of your argument should be guided by two considerations. First, content must be of adequate length to help the Court make a good decision. All the arguments necessary to making a decision must be present. Write this paper as if you were an officer of the Court. Under no circumstances should you make a false or misleading statement. Be persuasive, but be truthful. You do not need to make the opponents' argument for them, but the facts that you present must be accurate to the best of your knowledge.

The second guideline for determining the length of your argument is to omit extraneous material. Include only the information that will be of help to the Court in making the decision at hand.

The *Rules* of the Court require that an amicus brief include a "conclusion, specifying with particularity the relief which the party seeks" (1990, 27). Read the conclusions of the briefs you collect, and then write your own, retaining the same format but combining the arguments for the groups you are representing, and limiting your conclusion to two pages.

Write the Summary of Argument

After you have written the argument, write the summary, which should be a clearly written series of paragraphs that include all the main points. It should be brief (not more than three double-spaced typed pages). The Summary of Argument written for *Roe* v. *Wade* that is included at the beginning of this chapter provides an example.

According to the *Rules* of the Court, briefs should contain a "summary of the argument, suitably paragraphed, which should be a succinct, but accurate and clear, condensation of the argument actually made in the body of the brief. A mere repetition of the headings under which the argument is arranged is not sufficient" (1990, 27).

The summary of your argument may be easily assembled by taking the topic sentences from each paragraph and forming them into new paragraphs. The topic sentences contain more information than your subject headings. As complete sentences arranged in logical order, they provide an excellent synopsis of the contents of your brief. Your argument summary should not exceed two double-spaced pages.

20

Public Opinion Survey Papers

20.1   THE SCOPE AND PURPOSE
OF A SURVEY PAPER

A poll, most simply, is a device for counting preferences. When we go to the polls on election day, the polling officials count the preferences for candidates (and sometimes laws or other issues) that are produced when people mark their ballots. The officers then transmit these results to local, state, or national officials. A survey is a series of statements or questions that define a set of preferences to be polled. If a poll is conducted on the subject of national welfare programs, for example, a survey will be constructed consisting of a series of questions, such as "Do you think that welfare benefits ought to be increased or reduced?" or "Do you believe there is a lot of fraud in the welfare system?"

Writing your own public opinion survey paper will serve two purposes. First, you will learn how to construct, conduct, and interpret a public opinion poll, the means by which much research is done within the discipline. You will thus begin to learn a skill that you may actually use in your professional life. Large and small public and private organizations often conduct polls on the public's needs and preferences, in order to make their services more effective and desirable. Second, by writing a survey paper, you will understand how to evaluate polls thoughtfully and critically by knowing the strengths and weaknesses of the polling process.

In this chapter, you will learn how to construct and conduct a simple public opinion poll and how to apply some elementary data analysis and evaluation techniques to your poll results. Your instructor may want to add supplemental tasks, such as other statistical procedures, and your text in political science methods will tell you much more about the process of public opinion research. The following set of directions, however, will provide the information needed to create and interpret a public opinion poll.

20.2   STEPS IN WRITING A SURVEY PAPER

Focus on a Specific Topic

The first step in writing a public opinion survey paper is to select a topic that is focused on one specific issue. Although nationally conducted polls sometimes cover a broad variety of topics, confining your inquiry to one narrowly defined issue will allow you to gain an appreciation for even a single topic's complexity and the difficulties inherent in clearly identifying opinions. Precision is **important** in clearly understanding public opinion.

Public opinion surveys are conducted on topics pertaining to local, state, national, or international politics, topics nearly as numerous as the titles of articles in a daily newspaper. You will usually increase the interest of the audience of your paper if you select an issue that is currently widely discussed in the news.

Formulate a Research Question and a Research Hypothesis

Once you have selected a topic, your task is to determine what you want to know about people's opinions concerning that topic. If you choose the environment, for example, you may want to know the extent to which people are concerned about environmental quality. You need to phrase your questions carefully. If you ask simply, "Are you concerned about the quality of the environment?" you will probably receive a positive reply from a substantial majority of your respondents. But what does this actually tell you? Does it reveal the depth and strength of people's concern about the environment? Do you know how the respondents will vote on any particular environmental issue? Do people have different attitudes toward air pollution, water quality, and land use? To find out, you will need to design more specific questions. The following sections of this chapter will help you to do this.

To create these specific questions, however, you will first need to formulate a research question and a research hypothesis. Before continuing, read Chapter 4 on formulating and testing research hypotheses.

A research question asks exactly what the researcher wants to know. Research questions posed by national polls include the following:

- What is the president's current approval rating?
- What types of voters are likely to favor free trade agreements?
- What is the social issue about which Americans are most concerned?

Research questions for papers for political science classes, however, should be more specific and confined to a narrowly defined topic. Consider the following:

- Is the population to be surveyed in favor of universal handgun registration legislation?

- To what extent do the people polled believe that their own personal political actions, such as voting or writing to a representative, will actually make a difference in the political process?
- What are the attitudes of the selected population toward legislation that promotes gay rights?

Select a Sample

Surveys of public opinion are usually conducted to find out what large groups of people, such as American voters, members of labor unions, or religious fundamentalists, think about a particular problem. It is normally unnecessary and too costly to obtain the views of everyone in these groups. Most surveys therefore question a small but representative percentage of the group that is being studied. The elements of surveys are the individual units being studied. Elements might be interest groups, corporations, or church denominations, but they are most often individual voters. The population is the total number of elements covered by the research question. If the research question is, "Are voters in Calaveras County in favor of a 1 percent sales tax to pay for highway improvements?" then the population is the voters of Calaveras County. The sample is the part of the population that is selected to respond to the survey. A representative sample includes numbers of elements in the same proportions as they occur in the general population. In other words, if the population of Calaveras County is 14 percent Hispanic and 52 percent female, a representative sample will also be 14 percent Hispanic and 52 percent female. A nonrepresentative sample does not include numbers of elements in the same proportions as they occur in the general population.

All samples are drawn from a sampling frame, which is the part of the population being surveyed. To represent the population accurately, a sampling frame should include all types of elements (e.g., youth, women, Hispanics) of interest to the research question. If the population is the voters of Calaveras County, a sampling frame might be the parents of children in an elementary school who are registered to vote. Strata are groups of similar elements within a population. Strata of the voters of Calaveras County may include voters under 30, women, labor union members, or Hispanics. Stratified samples include numbers of respondents in different strata that are not in proportion to the general population. For example, a stratified sample of the population of Calaveras County might purposely include only Hispanic women if the purpose of the survey is to determine the views of this group.

A survey research design of the Calaveras County issue would thus be constructed as follows:

Research question: Are voters in Calaveras County in favor of a 1 percent sales tax to pay for highway improvements?
Research hypothesis: Fifty-five percent of the voters in Calaveras County will favor a 1 percent sales tax to pay for highway improvements.
Elements: Individual registered voters
Population: Registered voters in Calaveras County

Sampling frame: Five hundred registered voters in Calaveras County selected at random from voter registration lists

Sample: Of the 500 registered voters in Calaveras County selected at random from voter registration lists, those who answer the survey questions when called on the telephone.

How large must a sample be in order to represent the population accurately? This question is difficult to answer, but two general principles apply. First, a large sample is more likely, simply by chance, to be more representative of a population than a small sample. Second, the goal is to obtain a sample that includes representatives of all of the strata within the whole population.

You will find it most convenient if you use as your sample the class for which you are writing your survey paper. The disadvantage of this sample selection is that your class may not be representative of the college or university in which your survey is conducted. Even if this is the case, however, you will still be learning the procedures for conducting a survey, which is the primary objective of this exercise.

NOTE. Public opinion surveys ask people for their opinions. The people whose opinions are sought are known as human subjects of the research. Most colleges and universities have policies concerning research with human subjects. Sometimes administrative offices known as institutional review boards are established to review research proposals in order to ensure that the rights of human subjects are protected. It may be necessary for you to obtain permission from such a board or from your college to conduct your survey. Be sure to comply with all policies of your university with respect to research with human subjects.

Construct the Survey Questionnaire

Your research question will be your primary guide for constructing your survey questions. As you begin to write your questions, ask yourself what it is that you really want to know about the topic. Suppose that your research question is, "What are the views of political science students regarding the role of the government in regulating abortions?" If you ask, for example, "Are you for abortion?" you may get a negative answer from 70 percent of the respondents. If you then ask, "Are you for making abortion illegal?" you may get a negative answer from 81 percent of your respondents. These answers seem to contradict each other. By asking additional questions you may determine that, whereas a majority of the respondents finds abortion regrettable, only a minority wants to make it illegal. But even this may not be enough information to get a clear picture of people's opinions. The portion of the population that wants to make abortion illegal may be greater or smaller according to the strength of the legal penalty to be applied. In addition, some of the students who want no legal penalty for having an abortion may want strict medical requirements imposed on abortion clinics, while others may not. You will need to design additional specific questions in order to accurately determine respondents' views on these issues.

The number of questions to include in your questionnaire is a matter to be carefully considered. The first general rule, as mentioned earlier, is to ask a sufficient number of questions to find out precisely what it is you want to know. A second principle, however, conflicts with this first rule. This principle, which may not be a problem in your political science class, is that people in general do not like to fill out surveys. Survey information can be very valuable, and pollsters are found on street corners, in airports, and on the telephone. Short surveys with a small number of questions are more likely to be answered completely than long questionnaires. The questionnaire for your paper in survey research methods should normally contain between ten and twenty-five questions.

Surveys consist of two types of questions: closed and open. Closed questions restrict the response of the respondent to a specific set of answers. Many types of closed questions are used in public opinion surveys, but they may be grouped into three categories:

- two-choice questions;
- three-choice questions; and
- multiple-choice questions.

Two-choice questions may ask for a simple preference between candidates, such as if the election were held today, for whom would you vote: John Kerry or George W. Bush?

Issue-centered two-choice questions offer respondents a choice of one of two answers, most often "yes" and "no," or "agree" and "disagree," as shown below:

Is a mandatory five-day waiting period for the purchase of a handgun desirable?

Yes   No

A balanced budget amendment to the Constitution should be passed.

Agree   Disagree

Two-choice questions ask respondents to choose between two statements, neither of which they may entirely support. To find out how many people are ambivalent on these issues, three-choice questions are often asked, giving respondents a third selection, which is most often "undecided," "no opinion," "uncertain," "do not know," "does not apply," or "not sure":

The political party that does the most for Hispanic people is

☐ Republican   ☐ Democratic   ☐ Uncertain

Simple multiple-choice questions are sometimes constructed to provide a wider range of choices, such as in the following:

If the Democratic primary election were held today, for whom would you vote:

☐ Hillary Clinton   ☐ John Edwards
☐ Howard Dean   ☐ John Kerry

Just as often, however, multiple-choice questions are constructed to discriminate more clearly between positions in a range of attitudes. For example,

Likert scale multiple-choice questions are used to distinguish among degrees of agreement on a range of possible views on an issue. A Likert-scale question might be stated like this:

"American military expenditures should be reduced by an additional 10 percent to provide funds for domestic programs." Select one of the following responses to this statement:

☐ Strongly agree   ☐ Agree   ☐ Not sure
☐ Disagree   ☐ Strongly disagree

Guttmann-scale multiple-choice questions allow discrimination among a range of answers by creating a series of statements with which it is increasingly difficult to agree or disagree. A respondent who selects one item on the scale of questions is also likely to agree with the items higher on the scale. Consider this example.

Select the answer with which you agree most completely:

1. Citizen ownership of military weapons such as rocket launchers should be restricted.
2. Citizen ownership of fully automatic weapons such as machine guns should be restricted.
3. Citizen ownership of semiautomatic weapons should be restricted.
4. Citizen ownership of handguns and concealed weapons should be restricted.
5. Citizen ownership of hunting rifles should be restricted.

Closed questions have the advantage of being easy to quantify. A number value can be assigned to each answer, and totals can be made of answers of different types.

By contrast, open questions, or open-ended questions, are not easy to quantify. In open questions, respondents are not provided a fixed list of choices but may answer anything they want. The advantage of using open questions is that your survey may discover ideas or attitudes of which you were unaware. Suppose, for example, that you ask the following question and give space for respondents to write their answers:

What should be done about gun control?

You might, for example, get a response like the following:

All firearms should be restricted to law enforcement agencies in populated areas. Special, privately owned depositories should be established for hunters to store their rifles for use in target practice or during hunting season.

Open questions call for a more active and thoughtful response than do closed questions. The fact that more time and effort are required may be a disadvantage because in general the more time and effort a survey demands, the fewer responses it is likely to get. Despite this disadvantage, open questions are to be preferred to closed questions when you want to expand the range of possible answers in order to find out how much diversity there is among opinions on an issue. For practice working with open questions, you should include at least one in your survey questionnaire.

Perhaps the greatest difficulty with open questions is that of quantifying the results. The researcher must examine each answer and then group the responses according to their content. For example, responses clearly in favor, clearly opposed, and ambivalent to gun control might be differentiated. Open questions are of particular value to researchers who are doing continuing research over time. The responses they obtain help them to create better questions for their next survey.

In addition to the regular open and closed questions on your survey questionnaire, you will want to add identifiers, which ask for personal information about the respondents, such as gender, age, political party, religion, income level, or other items that may be relevant to the particular topic of your survey. If you ask questions about gun control, for example, you may want to know if men respond differently than women, if Democrats respond differently than Republicans, or if young people respond differently than older people.

Once you have written the survey questionnaire, you need to conduct the survey. You will need to distribute it to the class or other group of respondents. Be sure to provide clear directions for filling out the questionnaire on the survey form. If the students are to complete the survey in class, read out the directions loud and ask if there are any questions before they begin.

Collect the Data

If your sample is only the size of a small political science class, you will be able to tabulate the answers to the questions directly from the survey form. If you have a larger sample, however, you may want to use data collection forms such as those from the Scantron Corporation. You may be using such forms (on which respondents use a number 2 pencil to mark answers) when you take multiple-choice tests in some of your classes now. The advantage of Scantron forms is that they are processed through computers that tabulate the results and sometimes provide some statistical measurements. If you use Scantron sheets, you will need access to computers that process the results, and you may need someone to program the computer to provide the specific statistical data that you need.

Analyze the Data

Once you have collected the completed survey forms, you will need to analyze the data that they provide. Statistical procedures are helpful here to perform three tasks:

1. describe the data
2. compare components of the data and
3. evaluate the data

There are many statistical procedures especially designed to carry out each of these tasks. This chapter provides only a few examples of the methods that may be used in each category. Consult your instructor or a survey research methods textbook to learn about other types of statistical measurement tools.

Statistics designed to describe data may be very simple. We will start our discussion with two example questions, both employing the Likert scale:

QUESTION 1

"American military expenditures should be reduced by an additional 10 percent to provide funds for domestic programs." Select one of the following responses to this statement:

    ☐ Strongly agree   ☐ Agree   ☐ Not sure
    ☐ Disagree   ☐ Strongly disagree

QUESTION 2

"Congress should provide the Department of Defense with more funding for research into germ warfare techniques." Select one of the following responses to this statement:

    ☐ Strongly agree   ☐ Agree   ☐ Not sure
    ☐ Disagree   ☐ Strongly disagree

Our objective in describing the data is to see how our hypothetical respondent sample of forty-two students, as a group, answered these questions. The first step is to assign a numerical value to each answer, as follows:

ANSWER	POINTS
Strongly agree	1
Agree	2
Not sure	3
Disagree	4
Strongly disagree	5

Our next step is to count our survey totals to see how many respondents in our hypothetical sample marked each answer to each question:

ANSWER	POINTS	Q1 RESPONSES	Q2 RESPONSES
Strongly agree	1	8	13
Agree	2	16	10
Not sure	3	12	1
Disagree	4	4	12
Strongly disagree	5	2	6

We may now calculate the mean (numerical average) of responses by performing the following operations for each question:

1. Multiply the point value by the number of responses to determine the number of value points.
2. Add the total value points for each answer.
3. Divide the total value points by the number of respondents (forty-two in this case).

To see how this procedure is done, examine the chart below, which analyzes the responses to Question 1. Notice that column 1 contains the answer choices provided to the respondents; column 2 contains the point value assigned to each choice; column 3 contains the number of respondents who selected each answer; and column 4 contains the value points assigned for each answer choice, multiplied by the number of responses.

VALUE POINTS

ANSWER CHOICES	ASSIGNED POINT VALUE	NUMBER OF RESPONSES	POINT VALUE × NUMBER OF RESPONSES
Strongly agree	1	8	8
Agree	2	16	32
Not sure	3	12	36
Disagree	4	4	16
Strongly disagree	5	2	10
Total	42	102	
Mean			2.43

We can see that there are 42 total responses and 102 total value points. Dividing the number of value points (102) by the total number of responses (42), we get a mean of 2.43.

If we conduct the same operation for the responses to Question 2 in our survey, we get the following results:

VALUE POINTS

ANSWER CHOICES	ASSIGNED POINT VALUE	NUMBER OF RESPONSES	POINT VALUE × NUMBER OF RESPONSES
Strongly agree	1	13	13
Agree	2	10	20
Not sure	3	1	3
Disagree	4	12	48
Strongly disagree	5	6	30
Total		42	114
Mean			2.71

We see from the above table that the mean of the responses for Question 2 is 2.71. Comparing the means of the two questions, we find that the mean for Question 1 (2.43) is lower than the mean for Question 2. Because the lowest value (1 point) is assigned to a response of "strongly agree," and the highest value (5 points) is assigned for a response of "strongly disagree," we know that a high mean score indicates that the sample surveyed tends to disagree with the statement made in the survey question. It is possible to conclude, therefore, that there is slightly more agreement with the statement in Question 1 than with the statement in Question 2. Comparing the mean values in this fashion allows us to easily compare the amount of agreement and disagreement on different questions among the people surveyed.

Another frequently used statistical measure is the standard deviation, which provides a single number that indicates how dispersed the responses to the question are. It tells you, in other words, the extent to which the answers are grouped together at the middle ("agree," "not sure," and "disagree") or are dispersed to the extreme answers ("strongly agree" and "strongly disagree"). To calculate the standard deviation (S) for Question 1, we will follow these steps:

Step 1:   Assign a value to each response and the frequency of each response.
Step 2:   Find the mean for the question.
Step 3:   Subtract the value from the mean.
Step 4:   Square the results of Step 3.
Step 5:   Multiply the results of Step 4 by the frequency of each value.
Step 6:   Sum the values in Step 5.
Step 7:   Divide the values in Step 6 by the number of respondents.
Step 8:   Find the square root of the value in Step 7, which is the standard deviation.

Our calculation of the standard deviation of Question 1 therefore looks like this:

STEP 1	STEP 2	STEP 3	STEP 4	STEP 5	STEP 6	STEP 7	STEP 8
VALUE (V) AND FREQUENCY (F)	MEAN	MEAN MINUS VALUE	STEP 3 SQUARED	STEP 4 TIMES THE FREQUENCY	SUM OF VALUES IN STEP 5	STEP 6 DIVIDED BY NO. OF RESPOND-ENTS	SQUARE ROOT OF STEP 7: STANDARD DEVIATION
$V = 1, F = 8$	2.43	1.43	2.04	16.32			
$V = 2, F = 16$	2.43	0.43	0.18	2.88			
$V = 3, F = 12$	2.43	2.57	0.32	3.84			
$V = 4, F = 4$	2.43	21.57	2.46	9.84			
$V = 5, F = 2$	2.43	22.57	6.6	13.2			
					46.08	1.10	1.05

The standard deviation of Question 1 is 1.05. To understand its significance, we need to know that public opinion samples usually correspond to what is known as a normal distribution. In a normal distribution, 68.26 percent of the responses will fall between (1) the mean minus one standard deviation ($2.43 - 1.05$, or 1.38, in Question 1); and (2) the mean plus one standard deviation ($2.43 + 1.05$, or 3.48, in Question 1). In other words, in a normal distribution, about two-thirds of the respondents to Question 1 will express an opinion that is between 1.38 and 3.48 on the scale of assigned point values. Another one-third of the respondents will score less than 1.38 or more than 3.48.

For convenience, we will call the responses "strongly agree" and "strongly disagree" as extreme responses, and we will designate "agree," "not sure," and "disagree" as moderate responses. We see that a score of 1.38 is closest to our first extreme, "strongly agree." A score of 3.48 inclines to "disagree," but is "not sure." We may conclude that a substantial portion of the respondents (about one-third) tend to give extreme answers to Question 1. We may also notice that the score 1.38, which indicates strong agreement, is closer to its absolute extreme (1.38 is only 0.38 away from its absolute extreme of 1.0) than is the score 3.48 (which is 1.52 points from its absolute extreme of 5). This means that the responses are slightly more tightly packed toward the extreme of strong agreement. We may conclude that extreme respondents are more likely to strongly agree than to strongly disagree with the statement in Question 1. We can now see more completely the degree of extremism in the population of respondents. Standard deviations become more helpful as the number of the questions in a survey increases because they allow us to compare quickly and easily the extent of extremism in answers. You will find other measures of dispersion in addition to the standard deviation in your statistical methods textbooks.

After finding the amount of dispersion in responses to a question, you may want to see if different types of respondents answered the question in different ways; that is, you may want to measure relationships in the data. For example, from examining our political party identifier, we find, among our respondents to Question 1, fifteen Democrats, fourteen Republicans, and thirteen independents. To compare their responses, we need to construct a correlation matrix that groups responses by identifier:

ANSWER	DEMOCRAT RESPONSES	REPUBLICAN RESPONSES	INDEPENDENT RESPONSES	TOTAL (FREQUENCY)
Strongly agree	4	2	2	8
Agree	8	4	4	16
Not sure	3	5	4	12
Disagree	0	2	2	4
Strongly disagree	0	1	1	2

Each number of responses in the matrix is found in a location known as a response cell. The numbers in the total (frequency) column are known as response total cells. From this matrix, it appears that Democrats are more likely to agree with the question 1 statement than are either Republicans or independents. If this is true for the sample population, there is a correlation between party affiliation and opinion on the issue.

20.3 ELEMENTS OF A PUBLIC OPINION SURVEY PAPER

A public opinion survey paper is composed of five essential parts:

1. Title page
2. Abstract
3. Text
4. Reference page
5. Appendixes

Title Page

The title page should follow the format directions in Chapter 7. The title of a public opinion survey paper should provide the reader with two types of information: the subject of the survey and the population being polled. Examples of titles for papers based on in-class surveys are "University of South Carolina Student Opinions on Welfare Reform," "Ohio Wesleyan Student Attitudes about Sexual Harassment," and "The 2006 Gubernatorial Election and the Student Vote."

Abstract

Abstracts for a public opinion survey paper should follow the format directions in Chapter 7. In approximately 100 words, the abstract should summarize the subject, methodology, and results of the survey. An abstract for the example used in this chapter might appear something like this:

> A survey of attitudes of college students toward the amount of U.S. military expenditures was undertaken in October 2006 at Western State University. The sample was composed of forty-two students in a political science research methods class. The purpose of the survey was to determine the extent to which students are aware of and concerned about recent defense expenditure reductions, including those directly affecting the Seventh Congressional District, in which the university is located, and to determine student attitudes on related defense questions, such as germ warfare. The results indicate a weak correlation between political party affiliation and attitude toward expenditures, with Democrats favoring reductions more than Republicans.

Text

The text of the paper should include five sections:

1. Introduction
2. Literature review

3. Methodology
4. Results
5. Discussion

Introduction

The introduction should explain the purpose of your paper, define the research question hypothesis, and describe the circumstances under which the research was conducted. Your purpose statement will normally be a paragraph in which you explain your reasons for conducting your research. You may want to say something like the following:

> The purpose of this paper is to define Howard University student attitudes toward federal student aid programs. In particular, this study seeks to understand how students view the criteria for aid eligibility and the efficiency of application procedures. Further, the survey is expected to indicate the amount of knowledge students have about the federal student aid process. The primary reason for conducting this study is that the results will provide a basis for identifying problems in the aid application and disbursement process, and facilitate discussion among administrative officers and students about solutions to problems that are identified.

Next, the introduction should state the research question and the research hypotheses. The research question in the above example might be "Is student knowledge of federal student aid programs related to student attitudes about the effectiveness of the programs?" A hypothesis might be "Student ratings of the effectiveness of federal student aid programs are positively correlated with student knowledge of the programs."

Literature Review

A literature review is written to demonstrate that you are familiar with the professional literature relevant to the survey and to summarize that literature for the reader. Your literature review for a public opinion survey paper should address two types of information: the subject and the methodology of the survey.

The subject of the survey, for example, may be a state's proposed secondary education reforms. In this case, the purpose of the subject section of your literature review would be to briefly inform your readers about (1) the history, content, and political implications of the proposed reforms; and (2) the current status of the proposed reforms. In providing this information, you will cite appropriate documents, such as bills submitted to the legislature.

The purpose of the methodology section of your literature review will be to cite the literature that supports the methodology of your study. If you follow the directions in this manual or your course textbook to write your paper, briefly state the procedures and statistical calculations you use in the study and the source of your information (this manual or your text) about them.

Methodology

The methodology section of your paper describes how you conducted your study. It should first briefly describe the format and content of the questionnaire. For example, how many questions were asked? What kinds of questions (open, closed, Likert scale, Guttmann scale) were used, and why were these formats selected? What identifiers were selected? Why? What topics within the subject matter were given emphasis? Why? Here you should also briefly address the statistical procedures used in data analysis. Why were they selected? What information are they intended to provide?

Results

The results section of your paper should list the findings of your study. Here you report the results of your statistical calculations. You may want to construct a table that summarizes the numbers of responses to each question on the questionnaire. Next, using your statistical results, answer your research question; that is, tell your reader if your research question was answered by your results and, if so, what the answers are.

Discussion

In your discussion section, draw out the implications of your findings. What is the meaning of the results of your study? What conclusions can you draw? What questions remain unanswered? At the end of this section, provide the reader with suggestions for further research that are derived from your research findings.

Reference Page

Your reference page and source citations in the text should be completed according to the directions in Chapter 8.

Appendixes

See Chapter 7 for further directions on placing appendixes at the end of your text. Appendixes for a public opinion survey paper should include the following:

- a copy of the questionnaire used in the study
- tables of survey data not sufficiently important to be included in the text but helpful for reference
- summaries of survey data from national polls on the same subject, if such polls are available and discussed in your text.

NOTE. Students and instructors should note that the applications of the mean and standard deviation suggested in this chapter are controversial because they are applied to ordinal data. In practice, however, such applications are common.

Glossary of Political Science Terms

Affirmative action The correcting of discrimination, usually racial in motivation, through government policy

Amendment A formal action taken by the legislature to change an existing law or bill

Amicus curiae brief A "friend of the court" brief, filed by a third party to a lawsuit who is presenting additional information to the court in the hopes of influencing the court's decision

Anarchism The belief that all political authority is inherently oppressive and that government should be reduced to a minimum

Anarchy Political chaos; as a political movement, the belief that voluntary cooperation among members of a society is better than any form of organized government, because government generally favors one group over others

Antifederalist One who opposed ratification of the United States Constitution in 1787

Antinomianism A belief that faith without adherence to law is sufficient for religious practice

Appeal The process of asking a higher court to consider a verdict rendered by a lower court

Apportionment The system under which seats in the legislative houses are apportioned among the states

Appropriation The act of designating funds in the legislature for particular agencies and programs

APSA American Political Science Association

Aristocracy A system of government in which power is held by a small ruling class whose status is determined by such factors as wealth, social position, and military power

Authoritarianism Rule without popular consent, requiring obedience to law but not necessarily active support for a regime

Authority The power to make, interpret, and enforce laws

Autocratic Having unrestricted power

Autonomous Self-governing; independent

Bandwagon effect The practice of government officials' attaching themselves to a piece of legislation or a political movement because of its popularity

Bicameral legislature A legislature that is divided into two branches or houses

Bourgeoisie For Karl Marx, the capitalist middle class

Brief A compilation of facts, arguments, and points of law concerning a specific law case, prepared by an attorney and submitted to the court.

Bureaucracy Any large, complex administrative system, but used most often to refer to government in general

Calendar The agenda listing the business to be taken up by a legislative body

Capitalism An economic system in which the means of production and distribution are privately owned and operated for profit

Case study A detailed examination of a representative individual or group

Caucus A closed meeting of party officials for the purpose of selecting candidates for government office

Censure A method by which a legislative body may discipline one of its members

Census The counting, every ten years, of the total population of the United States, for such purposes as the apportionment of legislators and the determination of direct taxes

Centralization The concept of focusing power in a national government instead of in state or local governments

Checks and balances A method of government power distribution in which each major branch of the government has some control over the actions of the other major branches

Circuit court A superior court that hears civil and criminal cases, and whose judges serve in courts in several jurisdictions or counties, thus going on the "circuit"

Civil rights The rights of a citizen that guarantee protection against discriminatory behavior by the government or private owners of public facilities

Civil servants Government employees who are not in the military

Claims court A court that hears various kinds of claims brought by citizens against the government

Class stratification The differentiation of classes within a society for political or economic purposes

Closed primary A primary election in which only party members may vote

Cloture (closure) A rule allowing a three-fifths vote of the Senate to end a filibuster

Coattail effect The tendency of a candidate or officeholder to draw votes for other candidates of his or her party

Cognitive dissonance A perceived discrepancy between what is stated to be reality and what is reality in fact

Collectivism An economic system in which the land and the means of production and distribution are owned by the people who operate them

Commerce clause A clause in Article 1, section 8, of the U.S. Constitution, giving Congress the power to regulate trade among the states and with foreign nations

Communism A collectivist social system in which the means of production are owned by the state and in which the products of society are distributed according to need

Communitarian One who advocates communal life, in which possessions are shared by commune members

Concurrent powers Powers shared by state and national governments, including the power to tax and the power to maintain a system of courts

Confederacy A political system characterized by a weak national government that assumes only those powers granted it by strong state governments

Conservatism An ideology normally associated with resistance to changes in culture, and less government intervention in the social and economic life of the nation

Conservatives Citizens who resist major changes in their culture and their society; political conservatives tend to favor less government intervention in the social and economic life of the nation

Constituent An individual who resides in a government official's electoral district

Constitutionalism A belief in a system of government limited and controlled by a constitution, or contract, drawn up and agreed to by its citizens

Contract theory An explanation of the relationship of the government to the governed in terms of contractual obligation by consenting parties

Corporatism An approach to the study of politics focusing on the activities of economic interests

Court of appeals One of twelve national courts in the United States set up to hear appeals from district courts

Cybernetics The study of government that focuses on how information is transmitted and received

Dark horse A candidate for political office who has little chance of winning

Deductive logic Reasoning from a general premise to a specific conclusion

Demagogue A political leader who obtains popularity through emotional appeals to the prejudices and fears of the voters

Democracy A system of government in which the majority governs and in which the rights of minorities are protected

Deregulation The process of reducing government regulatory involvement in private business

Detente The relaxing of tension between nations

Dialectic A process of arriving at the truth in which succeeding propositions transform each other

District court The most basic federal court, where federal cases generally are first heard

Divine right The belief that a ruler maintains power through a mandate from a Supreme Being

Due process The right accorded to American citizens to expect fair and equitable treatment in the processes and procedures of law

Eclectic Combining a variety of approaches or methods

Electoral college Electors who meet in their respective state capitals to elect the president and vice president of the United States

Elite theory The concept that, in any political system, power is always controlled by a small group of people

Empiricism The idea that all knowledge results from sense experience; a scientific method that relies on direct observation

Epistemology The study of what knowledge is

Ethnocentricity A tendency to believe that one's own race is superior to other races; a focus of attention upon one race, to the exclusion of others

Faction A group of people sharing certain beliefs who seek to act together to affect policy

Fascism A totalitarian political system in which power is concentrated in the hands of a dictator who keeps rigid control of society and promotes a belligerent nationalism

Favorite son A presidential candidate, usually with no chance of winning the party nomination, whose name is placed in nomination at the national convention by the person's home state, usually either to honor that individual or to allow the state's delegation to delay committing their votes to a viable candidate

Federal A type of government in which power is shared by state and national governments

Filibuster The Senate process of interrupting meaningful debate on a bill with prolonged, irrelevant speeches aimed at "talking the bill to death"

Flow model A diagram illustrating the relationships among elements of a system

Franking privilege The ability of a member of Congress to substitute his or her facsimile signature for a postage stamp and thereby send mail free of charge

Gag rule A rule limiting the amount of time that can be spent debating a bill or resolution in the legislature

Gaia hypothesis James Lovelock's conservationist concept of the earth as a living entity needing the same sort of nurture that all organisms require

Game theory A method of understanding and predicting sociopolitical attitudes and events through devising mathematical models of social behavior

Gerrymandering Redesigning the boundaries of a legislative district so that the political party controlling the state legislature can maintain control

Grand jury A group of twelve to twenty-three citizens selected to hear evidence against persons accused of a serious crime in order to determine whether or not a formal charge should be issued

Grants-in-aid Funding given to state and local governments for them to achieve goals set by the national government

Green In politics, a name for those policies, politicians, and activists who advocate environmental responsibility in policy decisions

Habeas corpus A court order requiring that an individual in custody be presented in court with the cause of his or her detention

Hard left In Gabriel Almond's methodological approach to the study of politics, the mode that stresses the scientific analysis of quantitative data in the interests of promoting social, economic, and political equality

Hard right The method of studying politics, in Gabriel Almond's research, that stresses the scientific analysis of quantitative data and rational thinking and focuses on the study of power

Humanism The concept that humanity, and not a deity, is and should be the central focus of concern in philosophy, politics, the arts, etc.

Ideology The combined beliefs and doctrines that reveal an individual's or a culture's value system

Impeachment The process by which the lower house of a legislature may accuse a high official, such as the president or a Supreme Court justice, of a crime, after which the official is tried by the upper house

Implied powers Powers held by the federal government that are not specified in the U.S. Constitution but are implied by other, enumerated powers

Incumbent A political official currently in office

Independent A voter not registered as a member of a political party

Indictment A formal accusation, brought by a grand jury, charging a person with a crime

Individualism The belief in the importance of the needs and rights of the individual over those of the group

Inductive logic Reasoning from a series of specific observations to a general principle

Inefficient game   In game theory, a game in which no player completely achieves a desired end

Inherent powers   Powers not specified in the U.S. Constitution that are claimed by the president, especially in foreign relations

Initiative   A process by which individuals or interested groups may draw up proposed legislation and bring it to the attention of the legislature through a petition signed by a certain percentage of registered voters

Interest group   An organization of like-minded individuals seeking to influence the making of government policy, often by sponsoring a political action committee (PAC)

Intrasocietal   The environment existing inside the structure of a given society

Iron curtain   Those countries of Eastern Europe dominated by the Soviet Union

Iron law of oligarchy   The principle stating that all associations eventually become dominated by a minority of their members

Iron triangle   The interrelationship of government agencies, congressional committees, and political action groups as they influence policy

Irrationalist   One who believes that human behavior is determined by factors other than reason

Item veto   The power of governors in most states to veto selected items from a bill and to approve others

Knesset   The legislative body of the Israeli government

Laissez-faire   A "hands-off" policy rejecting government involvement in the economic system of a state

Left wing   An outlook favoring liberal political and economic programs aimed at benefiting the masses

Legitimacy   The quality of being accepted as authentic; in politics, the people's acceptance of a form of government

Libel   A written statement aimed at discrediting an individual's reputation. See also Slander

Liberals   Citizens who favor changes in the system of government to benefit the common people

Libertarians   Advocates of freedom from government action

Literature review   In a research project, the task of canvassing publications, usually professional journals, in order to find information about a specific topic.

Lobbyists   People who seek to influence legislation for the benefit of themselves or their clients—usually interest groups—by applying pressure of various kinds to members of Congress

Logrolling   A process by which two or more legislators agree to support each other's bills, which usually concern public works projects

Majority rule   The concept, common in a democracy, that the majority has the right to govern

Millenarian   Member of any of many religious movements that challenged the church after the year CE 1000

Millennium   A period of 1,000 years

Moderate   Within reasonable limits; in politics, one who is opposed to extremely liberal or conservative views

Monarchy   A political system in which power is held by a hereditary aristocracy, headed by a king or queen

Myth   A story or narrative intended to explain a natural or social phenomenon beyond normal human understanding

Naturalization   The process by which an alien becomes an American citizen

Natural law   The concept, popularized by eighteenth-century philosophers, that human conduct is governed by immutable laws that are similar to the laws of the physical universe and can, like physical laws, be discovered

Nazism   The political movement led in Germany by Adolf Hitler, combining nationalism with anti-Semitism

Negative freedom   Isaiah Berlin's phrase for the freedom from obligation or restraint on one's actions

Neoconservatism   A conservative reaction to liberal and radical movements of the 1960s

Nepotism   The policy of granting political favors, such as government contracts or jobs, to family members

New Left   A liberal political movement begun in the 1960s, largely due to the civil rights movement and the Vietnam War, that brought about widespread reevaluation of political beliefs

Normative theory   Any theory attempting to assign value judgments to its conclusions, as opposed to quantitative theory, which attempts to produce value-free results

Oligarchy   A political system in which power is held by a small group whose membership is determined by wealth or social position

Open primary   A primary election in which voters need not disclose their party affiliation to cast a ballot

Orthodox   "Right belief," holding the basic beliefs of the faith. A model or example

Panopticon   A model prison designed by philosopher Jeremy Bentham and used by philosopher Michel Foucault as a metaphor for freedom in society

Paradigm   A member of the wealthy class or aristocracy

Patrician   The study of the development of human consciousness and how it attempts to assimilate sensory data

Patronage   The power of government officeholders to dole out jobs, contracts, and other favors in return for political support

Phenomenology   In common use, of the common people, as opposed to the aristocracy

Pigeonhole   The action of a congressional committee that, by failing to report a bill out for general consideration, assures its demise

Platform   The set of principles and goals on which a political party or group bases its appeal to the public

Plebeian   Ordering societal relations

Pluralism   The concept that cultural, ethnic, and political diversity plays a major part in the development of government policy

Plurality   The number of votes by which a candidate wins election if that number does not exceed 50 percent of the total votes cast; a plurality need not be a large number of votes, as long as it is a higher number than that claimed by any other candidate

Pocket veto   A method by which the president may kill a bill simply by failing to sign it within ten days following the end of a legislative session

Police power   The power, reserved to legislatures, to establish order and implement government policy

Political action committees (PACs)   Officially registered fund-raising committees that attempt to influence legislation, usually through campaign contributions to members of Congress

Political correctness   A measure of how closely speech, attitude, or policy conforms to certain affirmative action standards. The term is pejorative when used by conservatives warning of liberal attempts at controlling the public's modes of expression and thought processes

Political machine   A political party organization so well established as to wield considerable power

Political party   An organization of officeholders, political candidates, and workers, all of whom share a particular set of beliefs and work together to gain political power through the electoral process

Politics polity   For Aristotle, government by the many in the interests of all

Poll   A survey undertaken to ascertain the opinions of a section of the public

Poll sample   A selection, usually random, of the larger population of individuals polled

Populism   A political philosophy that aims at representing the needs of the rural and poor populations in the United States rather than the interests of the upper classes and big business

Pork barrel legislation   A congressional bill passed to benefit one specific congressional district, with the aim of promoting the reelection of representatives from that district

Positive freedom   Isaiah Berlin's phrase for the freedom to do what one wills.

Pragmatism   The notion that ideas and concepts should be judged by their practical consequences instead of their correspondence to abstract or ideal criteria

Precedent   A court decision that sets a standard for handling later, similar cases

Primary election   An election, held prior to the general election, in which voters nominate party candidates for office

Progressivism   Any doctrine calling for changes within a system, to be made in light of recent findings or achievements

Proletariat   The urban, industrial working class

Quantification   Determining or measuring quantity or amount

Quorum   The minimum number of members of a legislative body that must be present to conduct business

Radical   One calling for substantial change in institutions, society, political systems, etc.

Ratification   The process by which state legislatures approve or reject proposed agreements between states and proposed amendments to the U.S. Constitution

Rational actor theory   In public policy analysis, the theory that people and institutions tend to act in ways which they perceive to be in their own best interests.

Rationalism   The belief that reasoned observation is the proper foundation for problem solving

Reactionary   One who opposes liberal change, favoring instead a return to policies of the past

Recall   A process by which an elected official can be turned out of office through a popular vote

Recidivism   A tendency for criminal offenders to return to criminal habits

Referendum   Method by which voters in certain states can register their approval or dissatisfaction with a bill proposed in their state legislature

Republic   A government that derives its power from the consent of the people, who control policy by electing government officeholders

Reserved powers   Powers of the U.S. Constitution reserved to the state governments

Right wing   An outlook favoring conservative or reactionary political and economic programs

Sample plan   An essential step in setting up a survey; the task of establishing which elements of the general population are to be asked to participate in the survey

Sampling frame   That specific part of a population from which a sample is drawn for a survey

Separation of powers   A method of stabilizing a government by dividing its power among different branches or levels of government

Short ballot   A ballot listing candidates for only a few offices, as opposed to a long ballot, which lists candidates for a great number of offices

Single-issue group   A lobby group attempting to influence legislation concerning only one cause or issue, such as gun control or funding for education

Single-member district   An electoral district from which voters elect only a single representative

Slander   An oral statement intended to damage an individual's reputation. See also Libel

Social contract   The agreement, either formally stated or implied, among members of a society that allows for the establishment and continuance of the social structure and the government

Socialism   An economic system in which the state owns the means of production

Soft left   In Gabriel Almond's terms, a methodological approach to the study of politics which favors philosophical and descriptive analysis of political in the interests of social, economic, or political equality

Soft right   The analytical mode described by Gabriel Almond that takes a philosophical or descriptive rather than a quantitative approach to the study of power and rational thinking in politics

Sovereignty   The concept that the state is self-governing and free from external control

Soviet Bloc   Those Eastern European countries dominated by Soviet communism from 1945 to 1990

Split ticket   A situation in which a voter casts ballots for candidates from different political parties

Spoils system   The practice of rewarding supporters and friends with government jobs

Stalking horse   A candidate whose primary function is to set up a constituency and a campaign base for another candidate, deemed stronger by the party, who will be announced later

Statute   A law passed by Congress or a state legislature

Straight ticket   The practice of voting for all candidates on a ballot solely on the basis of their party affiliation

Structural-functionalism   A method of studying political systems introduced by Gabriel Almond in which various elements of a political system are analyzed according to the types of tasks they perform

Subjectivism   A theory of knowledge in which truth is individually determined by each person's preferences or perceptions

Theocracy   A political system whose leaders assume that their power to govern comes from a Supreme Being who guides the actions of the government

Third party   A political party different from the two traditional parties and typically formed to protest their ineffectualness

Totalitarianism   A type of authoritarian government in which the state demands active support of its policies

Typology   A classification of phenomena according to differing characteristics

Unicameralism   A legislature with only one house or chamber

Unitary   Referring to a political system in which all power resides in the national government, which in turn delegates limited power to local governments

Utopia   An ideal social environment

Validity   In statistics, the characteristic that a measuring instrument, such as a survey, has when it actually measures what it purports to measure

Variables   The elements of an equation, experiment, or formula that are under study and subject to change in accordance with changes in their environment

Veil of Ignorance   A hypothetical state, proposed by philosopher John Rawls, in which people, before beginning their lives, are unaware of what characteristics, advantages, and disadvantages they will have in life

Veto   The process by which the president may send a bill back to Congress instead of signing it into law

Welfare state   A state in which the government is characterized by governmental redistribution of income

Bibliography

Adorno, T. W. et al. 1950. *The Authoritarian Personality*. New York: W.W. Norton.

Agassiz, Louis. 1958. *A Scientist of Two Worlds: Louis Agassiz*. Ed. Catherine Owens Pearce. Philadelphia: Lippincott.

Allison, Graham. 1971. *Essence of Decision, Explaining the Cuban Missile Crisis*. Boston: Little, Brown.

Almond, Gabriel. 1990. *A Discipline Divided, Schools and Sects in Political Science*. Newbury Park, Calif.: Sage Publications.

Bartels, Larry M., and Henry E. Brady. 1993. "The State of Quantitative Political Methodology." In *Political Science: The State of the Discipline II*. Ed. Ada W. Finifter. Washington, DC: American Political Science Association.

Bary, William Theodore de, Wing-tsit Chan, and Burton Wilson, comps. 1966. *Sources of Chinese Tradition*. New York: Columbia University Press.

Brundage, D., R. Keane, and R. Mackneson. 1993. "Application of Learning Theory to the Instruction of Adults." In *The Craft of Teaching Adults*. Ed. Thelma Barer-Stein and James A. Draper, 131–44. Toronto: Culture Concepts.

Buchanan James. 1972a. "Toward Analysis of Closed Behavioral Systems." In *Theory of Public Choice*. Ed. James M. Buchanan and Robert D. Tollison. Ann Arbor: University of Michigan Press.

Buchanan, James. 1972b. "The Inconsistencies of the National Health Service." In *Theory of Public Choice*. Ed. James M. Buchanan and Robert D. Tollison. Ann Arbor: University of Michigan Press.

Charles, Alan F. 1971. *Motion for Leave to File Brief Amici Curiae in Support of Appellants and Briefs Amici Curiae. Roe v. Wade*. U.S. 70–18, 5–7.

Coole, Diana. 1990. "Feminism and Politics." In *New Developments in Political Science: An International Review of Achievements and Prospects*. Ed. Adrian Leftwich. Brookfield, Ver.: Edward Elgar Publishing.

Crick, Bernard. 1960. *The American Science of Politics Its Origins and Conditions*. Berkeley: University of California Press.

Dacey, John S. 1989. *Fundamentals of Creative Thinking*. Lexington, Mass.: Lexington Books.

Dahl, Robert A. 1961. "The Behavioral Approach in Political Science: Epitaph for a Monument to a Successful Protest." *American Political Science Review* 55:763–72.

Deutsch, Karl. 1963. *The Nerves of Government: Models of Human Communication and Control*. New York: Free Press.

Easton David. 1966. "Categories for the Systems Analysis of Politics." In *Varieties of Political Theory*. Ed. David Easton. Englewood Cliffs, NJ: Prentice Hall.

Easton, David 1993. "Political Science in the United States: Past and Present." In *Discipline and History Political Science in the United States: Part 4*. Ed. James Farr and Raymond Seidelman. Ann Arbor: University of Michigan Press.

Easton, David, John G. Gunnell, and Luigi Graziano, eds. 1991. *The Development of Political Science: A Comparative Survey*. London and New York: Routledge.

Easton, David. 1991. *Political Science in the United States Past and Present*. London and New York: Routledge.

Eliade, Mircea. 1971. *Myth of the Eternal Return or Cosmos and History*. Princeton: Princeton University Press.

Esposito, John L., ed. 1997. *Political Islam: Revolution, Radicalism, or Reform?* Boulder, CO: Lynne Rienner Publishers.

Farr, James, and Raymond Seidelman. 1993. "Introduction." In *Discipline and History: Political Science in the United States: Part II*. Ed. James Farr and Raymond Seidelman. Ann Arbor: University of Michigan Press.

Foucault, Michel. 1995. *Discipline and Punish: The Birth of the Prison*. New York: Vintage Books.

Fromm, Erich. 1960. *Escape from Freedom*. New York: Holt, Rinehart, and Winston.

Goodspeed, Edgar J., Trans. 1950. "The Martrydom of Polycarp." In *The Apostolic Fathers: An American Translation*. New York: Harper & Brothers.

Haddow, Anna. 1969. "Early American Political Science." In *Political Science in American Colleges and Universities 1636–1900*. Ed. William Anderson. New York: Octagon Books.

Hartwell, Patrick. 1985. "Grammar, Grammars, and the Teaching of Grammar." *College English* 47:105–27.

Holub, Robert. 1991. *Jurgen Habermas: Critic in the Public Sphere*. London: Routledge.

Kahn, Kim Fridkin. 1994. "Does Gender Make a Difference? An Experimental Examination of Sex Stereotypes and Press Patterns in Statewide Campaigns." *American Journal of Political Science* 38:162–95.

Laitin, David D. 2002. "Comparative Politics: The State of the Subdiscipline." In *Political Science: The State of the Discipline*. Eds. Ira Katznelson and Helen V. Milner. New York: W.W. Nelson.

Kennan, George F. 1967. *Memoirs*. Boston: Little, Brown.

Kennedy, John F. 1963. "John F. Kennedy's Inaugural Address." In *Documents of American History Since 1898*. Vol. 2 of *Documents of American History*. 7th ed. Ed. Henry Steele Commager, 688–89. New York: Appleton-Century-Crofts.

Lieber, Francis. 1881. "An Inaugural Address Delivered on the 17th of February, 1858, on Assuming the Chair of History and Political Science, in Columbia College, New York." In *Miscellaneous Writings*. Vol. 1. Philadelphia: J.B. Lippincott.

Lijphart, Arend. 1997. "Unequal Participation: Democracy's Unresolved Dilemma." *American Political Science Review* 91:1–14.

Lincoln, Abraham. 1946. *Abraham Lincoln: His Speeches and Writings*. Ed. Roy Basler. Cleveland, OH: World.

Lippincott, Benjamin E. 1993 "The Bias of American Political Science." In *Discipline and History Political Science in the United States*. Ed. James Farr and Raymond Seidelman. Ann Arbor: University of Michigan Press.

Lowi, Theodore J. 1993. *The State in Political Science: How We Become What We Study*. Ann Arbor: University of Michigan Press.

Lunsford, Andrea, and Robert Connors. 1992. *The St. Martin's Handbook*. 2nd ed. Annotated instructor's ed. New York: St. Martin's.

Machiavelli, Niccolo. 1979. *The Prince.* In *The Portable Machiavelli.* Trans. Peter Bondanella and Mark Musa. New York: Viking Press.

Macridis, Roy C. 1955. *The Study of Comparative Politics.* New York: Random House.

Madison, James, Alexander Hamilton, and John Jay. 1961. *The Federalist Papers.* New York: New American Library/Mentor.

May, Rollo. 1975. *The Courage to Create.* New York: Norton.

Merriam, Charles E. 1993. "Recent Advances in Political Methods." In *Discipline and History: Political Science in the United States : Part 2,* Ed. James Farr and Raymond Seidelman. Ann Arbor: University of Michigan Press.

Ordeshook, Peter C. 1993. "The Development of Contemporary Political Theory." In *Political Economy: Institutions, Competition, and Representation.* Ed. William A. Barnett, Melvin J. Hinich, and Norman J. Schofield. Cambridge: Cambridge University Press.

Park, Andrus. 1994 "Ethnicity and Independence: The Case of Estonia in Comparative Perspective." *Europe-Asia Studies* 46:69–87.

President's Committee on Administrative Management. 1937. *Administrative Management in the Government of the United States, January 8, 1937.* Washington, DC: Government Printing Office.

Rawls, John. 1971. *A Theory of Justice.* Belknap Press.

Roosevelt, Franklin D. 1963. "F. D. Roosevelt's First Inaugural Address." In *Documents of American History Since 1898.* Vol. 2. 7th ed. Ed. Henry Steele Commager, 239–42. New York: Appleton-Century-Crofts.

Rules of the Supreme Court of the United States. 1990. Washington, DC: Government Printing Office.

Scott, Gregory M. 1998. Review of *Political Islam: Revolution, Radicalism, or Reform?* Ed. John L. Esposito. *Southeastern Political Review* 26(2): 512–14.

Stone, I. F. 1988. *The Trial of Socrates.* Boston: Little, Brown.

Strauss, Leo Strauss. 1959. *What Is Political Philosophy.* New York: Free Press.

The Chicago Manual of Style. 1993. 14th ed. Chicago: Univ. of Chicago Press.

Thucydides. 1986. *History of the Peloponnesian War.* Trans. Rex Warner. Harmondsworth: Penguin.

Tocqueville, Alexis de. 1990. *Democracy in America.* New York: Vintage Books.

Voegelin, Eric. 1952. *The New Science of Politics.* Chicago: University of Chicago Press.

Walzer, Michael. 1985. *Exodus and Revolution.* New York: Basic Books.

Washington, George. 1991. *Washington's Farewell Address to the People of the United States.* 102d Cong., 1st sess. S. Doc. 3.

Weale, Albert. 1990. "Rational Choice and Political Analysis." In *New Developments in Political Science: An International Review of Achievements and Prospects.* Ed. Adrian Leftwich. Brookfield, VT.: Edward Elgar Publishing.

Willoughby, W. W. 1993. "The American Political Science Association." In *Discipline and History Political Science in the United States: Part 1.* Ed. James Farr and Raymond Seidelman. Ann Arbor: University of Michigan Press.

Index